Slow

Cranberry Sauce

A traditional favorite with roast turkey.

To serve eight, you will need:
1⅓ cups fresh cranberries; grated zest and juice of 1 orange; 4 tbsp. marmalade; heaped ½ cup light brown sugar; 4 tbsp. port wine.

1 Put the cranberries into a pan. Add the orange zest and juice, marmalade, sugar, and port wine, and mix well.
2 Bring to a boil, then reduce the heat and simmer for 5–10 minutes, stirring occasionally, until the cranberries burst and the sauce is thick.

SAVE TIME

To make ahead and freeze, complete the recipe, then tip into a freezer container and cool. Label and freeze for up to one month. To use, thaw and serve warm or cold. To serve warm, put into a pan and simmer over medium heat for 2–3 minutes until heated through.

Originally published in 1992 by Schocken Books Inc., New York, N.Y.

Published in the 2010 paperback edition by Quid Pro Books.

QUID PRO, LLC
5860 Citrus Blvd.
New Orleans, Louisiana 70123
www.quidprobooks.com

Publisher's Cataloging-in-Publication

Neiman, Susan.

Slow fire: Jewish notes from Berlin / by Susan Neiman.

p. cm.

ISBN: 1610270312
ISBN-13 9781610270311

Series: *Journeys & Memoirs*

1. Jews—Germany—Berlin. 2. Holocaust, Jewish (1939–1945)—Germany—Berlin—Influence. 3. Neiman, Susan—Journeys—Germany—Berlin. 4. Berlin (Germany)—Social life and customs. 5. Berlin (Germany)—Ethnic relations. I. Title. II. Series.

DS135.G4B47 2010
943.1'55004924-dc20 2010-52699

Also available in multiple digital and ebook formats.

Contents

"Every time I see you I think of Dachau . . . baby."

The words echoed, pain-filled, across the empty April night of a rain-drenched *Biergarten.* I thought, for a moment, of Theodor Adorno: if poetry after Auschwitz could be barbarism, would taste after Auschwitz be atrocity? But then I think Adorno is wrong, very wrong, as I have argued passionately on other evenings, in many a Berlin café.

This is the record of a foreigner observing a foreign city. Does the fact that the city was Berlin, forty years after the war, and the fact that the observer was an American Jew, make this record something other than a personal one? In the Berlin of those years every personal question threatened to plunge into the world-historical. And this was both monstrous and moving, giving the most ordinary experience a depth you'd never dreamed, making room for obscenity on a scale you couldn't measure.

"You want to write a book about *what?*" asked Claudio.

"It was said to me once. The 'baby' was implied. By a German man I was having an affair with. He wanted to talk about our relationship."

"But that's normal. Like the time I was with a Jewish woman who couldn't decide whether or not she wanted to sleep with me. So she stayed up all night telling me about her father's experiences in the concentration camps."

"That's what I want to write about."

"You should hear people talk about their torture scars in Chile."

"Don't you think it's different here? Anyway *more?*"

Claudio thought not. Besides, he found my thesis on the nature of human reason interesting. It ought to be rewritten in a less academic form, obviously, but that's what I should concentrate on. It's always dangerous when philosophers start trying to write literature.

"But I don't want to write literature," I said. "I just want to tell some stories. The way they happened."

I lived in Berlin throughout most of the eighties. The stories told here began in a city whose division seemed inevitable. They end, where they must, with the collapse of the Wall. The Berlin of the future will look rather different. Yet nothing could be more essential to Berlin than the present pandemonium, beginning fresh from nothing; and the stubborn presence of past in the very attempt to escape it.

Slow Fire

Looking Backward

I was born in the Diaspora.

My parents moved from Chicago to Atlanta two months before my birth. It was a far cry from home, but part of the New World nonetheless. The Klan bombed the synagogue in 1957, but they didn't go further than that. By the time I was old enough to attend it, everything had been magnificently rebuilt. The ark of the covenant was painted gold, and opened automatically when the rabbi pressed a hidden button.

My brother's first crisis of faith occurred when he discovered that the eternal lamp was electric, but I was not a particularly religious child. Once a week I learned a little about Jewish history and ethics at the Reform Sunday School, and I sang at Shabbos services with the junior choir. This had more to do with music than with Judaism: I was happy singing almost anything. Christmas carols in school were a yearly quandary which I resolved by refraining from singing certain lines. With all the casuistic facility available to an eight-year-old, I determined that it was alright, for example, to sing *Adeste Fideles*, up to the words "Christ the Lord." "Born the king of angels" might have presented a problem, but since Jewish theology seemed unclear about the existence of angels anyway, Jesus might, for all I cared, be the king of them.

Generations ago, in the old country, my family had produced talmudic scholars, but nothing of the kind survived the emigration to America. According to my mother, Judaism consisted of two tenets: a belief in the value of a good education, and a liberal solidarity with the struggles of other oppressed peoples. And we believed, in a general way, in God. I prayed alone, every night. There were air-raid drills in the elementary school; after the Cuban Missile Crisis most of the families we knew built bomb shelters. I was mystified by my parents' smiling response to my pleas that we build one too. Their refusal left me no recourse but prayer. At the age of seven I lay in bed and prayed that God would start a war between the Chinese and the Russians which would result in their mutual annihilation. I suspected this might have been sinful, but I kept praying: we lived near an air-force base, and I knew we were particularly vulnerable. That year the sound of an airplane in the night was enough to wake me in terror. Still my nightmares were peopled less by atomic wastelands than by snarling Nazis. I don't know how they got there.

Yet it was hardly an unhappy childhood. Most days I played with my brother in the woods behind our house. We built tree houses, caught crawfish, constructed secret codes and tried to learn how to walk like the Indians. When the schools were finally integrated, we were occasionally cursed as we sat next to one or the other of the twelve new silent black children on the school bus. We did, like most children, what our parents had told us to do. In the other children's invective I heard the "nigger-lovin' " and not the "Jews"; violence in the South of the early sixties was mostly directed toward black people. Once my brother was beat up by a gang yelling "Jew-boy," but boys always have fistfights and besides, Adam had a perfectly innocent way of provoking outrage.

My mother had arranged to visit every classroom of our overwhelmingly Episcopalian school each December. She lit a menorah, told the story of Judah Maccabee, sang a couple of songs and distributed shiny pennies. This is the way we celebrate our holiday while you celebrate yours. When Adam was six, he was thought old enough to help her. Remember that this was December: the classrooms crammed with Christmas decorations, papier-mâché angels hung from the ceiling. My brother began to tell the Hanukkah story: the Maccabees had refused to bow down to idols. "You kids probably don't know what an idol is," said Adam.

"No, we don't," said the five-year-olds.

"Then I'll show you," he said, drawing a plastic sword from its sheath on his belt. "That's an idol!" With this he proceeded to shatter one of the Christmas angels.

It was the last of my mother's ecumenical visits.

Still I never connected the sense that we were outsiders with the fact that we were Jewish. The popular girls were blond and Christian, but they were also slim, athletic, and wore no glasses. I read novels and dreamed of leaving Atlanta for New York City, or a European capital. Any inclination I might have developed to seek refuge in the small Jewish community was thoroughly extinguished by the reaction of my contemporaries to the death of Martin Luther King. Atlanta was turned upside down, and the Sunday School teacher requested a moment of silence. As the students said something about too much fuss being made over a goddamned nigger, I left the room; it was years before I entered the premises of a synagogue again. The incident scuttled my faith in the righteousness of particular Jews but not in the correctness of my mother's version of the fundamental tenets of Judaism, a faith I managed to cling to through the dissolution of the Jewish-black alliance of the sixties and the rise of racism in Israel. The other tenet came to fruition in college where I met really educated Jews for the first time. Something about them felt deeply familiar: a tonefall remembered, the kind of jokes in my ear. A faraway ear: my grandparents had rushed to assimilate, none of them even had a classically Yiddish sense of humor. One professor compared philosophy to doing midrash; I laughed and went to occasional High Holiday services. By the time I was twenty-seven and ready to leave Cambridge, I was no longer surprised that something about me was recognizably Jewish. Nor was I particularly proud of it. If any book about Jewish identity seemed written for me, it was Isaac Deutscher's *The Non-Jewish Jew.*

Why did I go to Berlin?

It's a question I got tired of answering, though it was easier to answer than the one which preceded it. After a few sentences they noted the accent: "You're not German, are you? Where do you come from?" There was a period when I made them guess. Hardly anybody ever got it right, but I grew tired of their surprise, tired of being told I don't look like a typical American, tired of asking how a typical American looks. Once in a while I was able to say, with forced confidence, "From the land of unlimited possibilities," let them wonder whether Americans understand anything about irony. For a time I learned to say "USA"; the alternative was imperialist, wasn't it, but even the Latinos I know say "America." It's no use. Myths have names, names have histories. I came from America.

There the questioning stopped and the telling began. If they'd been to America, they told me about their trip: New York was exciting, so many bright lights and black people; the Rocky Mountains were beautiful; the people were friendly and not as dumb as one thought, really, just different. If they hadn't been to America, they usually told me that they never wanted to go. Once a schoolteacher told me that he'd never gone to Spain as long as Franco was alive and he'd never go to America as long as... His sentence had no ending. Because we were at a gallery opening where there was, for once, enough champagne, or because he'd told me the same thing the first time I'd met him, I smiled nicely and said, "I understand how you feel—so many Americans still refuse to come to Germany."

And you thought I was digressing.

Why did I go to Berlin? Perhaps it had to do with all the questions I'd stopped wanting to answer in America. The question as to my profession, for example; there were times when it was easiest to lie. In the land of *Dicker* and *Denker* nobody's eyes fill up with that remarkable mixture of contempt and discomfort when they hear that you study or teach philosophy. Not at first, anyway, and when they ask you why, they don't mean to be asking: why didn't you go to law school? Then there was the question about where I had studied and practiced this profession for which America had no use. It was always asked, and if I told the truth about that one, I could forget about talking easily to anyone who hadn't been to Harvard himself. (Or just possibly Yale.) While I was working at the Pussy Cat Lounge in Boston's Combat Zone, a customer once told me he had gone to college. When he hesitated after I asked him which one, I answered for him. "How did you guess that?" he wondered. "Only people who went to Harvard hesitate before saying where they went to college." "You're very smart," he said smiling. "No," I'd said, "I just go to Harvard."

Digressing again? I went to Berlin because I wanted to sit in bars like that again, and the Combat Zone has changed, I couldn't work there anymore. *Nostalgie de la boue*, they call it? Maybe. There wasn't enough air in Cambridge, and I thought there would be even less at any other university where I might teach. Every American intellectual thinks, in his heart, that only Europeans have the real thing. This isn't simply a matter of knowledge; they're freer with what they know. How did I imagine the real thing in America? For years my favorite movie was Bertolucci's *The Conformist*, and not just because it's the only movie I know containing a long recitation from Plato's *Republic*. Its lighthanded combination of sex and politics and philosophy and permanent uncertainty about the nature of betrayal was very foreign—not foreign enough, anymore, to be an object of longing. So the real thing looked like that. The real thing was a sentence in Simone de Beauvoir's autobiography: "One afternoon in May, when I was at the Flore with Sartre and Camus, Genet came over to our table." The real thing was in the sound of the names: I'll never believe that the words "a trip to New York" can produce the dizziness of the sounds "a weekend in Paris," "a winter in Rome," "the train to Vienna." The real thing was not having to worry that the real thing might be on some other continent. Europeans wonder if any thing is real at all, but the whole debris of two millennia is theirs, to play with or to contemn or to honor, the way that grown-up natural children have the luxury of treating their parents. Are Americans orphans, or bastards? Our inheritance is always in question.

* * *

The promise of philosophy was to learn to see from a vast number of perspectives, never getting mired in a single one, becoming critical of every particular point from which the world can be viewed. From that hope one was led to a search for generality, to a point so abstract that it cannot *conflict* with any particular perspective. The fantasy of a way into every form of life became a realm too empty to offend any living thing. But how could such an error arise?

* * *

"Kantstrasse," I exclaimed as the taxi turned right. "I'm going to live near the Kantstrasse."

It was late. The journey from Freiburg to the city I'd never seen had lasted ten hours, and I strained to look. I had been warned: Berlin is an ugly city, everybody says so. Still nothing could prepare me for the arrival at Bahnhof Zoo, less ugly than ridiculous, this train station with two tracks.

"And Leibnizstrasse. Look, Kantstrasse intersects Leibnizstrasse."

Could I say why this thrilled me? If I thought about it at all that night, it was to waver between finding the German comic, wonderfully comic, and finding my own wonder naive. (It would indeed be only a few months before I found it perfectly normal to say, "It's on the Leibnizstrasse between Kant and Goethe.") What were the streets I had known before? For five years I lived on Trowbridge Street. One day, looking at a map of England, I saw a town called Trowbridge, and was satisfied. Before that I lived on Mass. Ave., which only the tourists call Massachusetts Avenue. That was easy, it was in Massachusetts, and so was Cambridge Street, it was in Cambridge. Harvard Street led straight to, or away from, Harvard. And the others? Brattle Street was named for William Brattle, a general in the Continental Army, who owned the tavern that is now a Viennese bakery. Quincy Street was named for a cousin or a nephew or a grandfather of the second president of the United States. Prescott Street comes next, then Ellery, Dana, Hancock, and Lee. Names whose sound means nothing to me, or rather too much. What part of me had hoped, back then, to believe New England mine?

Would it have been different if there were a Chayes Street in Boston? Or Torchinsky, after my other great-grandfather, before he came to America and became Abram Torch? How do they name streets in America? Boston has no Emerson Street, no Longfellow Street, no Thoreau Street, no James Street—William or Henry—though it was they, for a start, who made her the Athens of America. American streets are named for something easy, like trees: Oak Street, Elm Street, Peachtree Drive. Or numbers: New York is not the only place where you can walk down Second Avenue and turn right on Eighty-first Street. Or names, sometimes, but names which are there to be neutral, names like Prescott, Ellery, Hancock, and Lee.

There's no Chayes Street in Berlin either, needless to say, but I heard about the battle over the naming of Karl-Marx-Strasse a few days after arriving there. Was I looking for a city where people had argued about whether Kantstrasse should intersect with Leibnizstrasse, whether Goethestrasse and Schillerstrasse should run parallel?

* * *

Nobody would pay me to study in Paris or Rome, I sometimes answered, just to beg the question completely; for it was reading Nietzsche at seventeen which had led me to study at all. When I was told somewhat later that my relation to darkness was distinctly German, I learned all the words to *The Threepenny Opera*, looking at the lights over San Francisco Bay. Arriving at Bahnhof Zoo, I knew little more about the city where I meant to stay a year. I knew that everybody would look at me oddly, not quite hostile, all the months before I left, and the ones who didn't know me would ask uncertainly, "But—you're Jewish, aren't you?"

Of course I had to come to Berlin.

A Brief Theoretical Introduction

Let me introduce a few concepts. Most basic is the Wall. The spies and wrenching dramas surrounding it were fairly shortlived; by the seventies the Wall was much the province of the tourists, who came in droves to the wooden observation platforms placed at strategic points by the West German government. They climbed sixteen steps, looked out to the soldiers guarding empty space with machine guns, and shook their heads, clucking, glad to be living in the free West. Sometimes they expressed disappointment: after all the ballyhoo it was only a wall, 12 feet high, 2 feet thick, 128 miles long. Yet some called it the most important fact about Berlin. Because of the Wall, West Berlin was an island, virtually cut off from everywhere else. At the same time, they'd claim, the Wall had turned the city into the central point of the political world, the outpost of democracy, the showplace of capitalism. When the cold war threatened to erupt into violence, opinions were divided. Some argued that the Wall made Berlin the safest haven, apart from New Zealand, if the bombs started falling; others swore it would be the first to go.

Berliners themselves referred to it rarely, as if the Wall were less *painful* to notice than gauche. Access from the East was limited by bright lights over minefields. Westerners approached their side to spray occasional graffiti. Parts of the Wall were covered with full-scale paintings as well as messages ranging from I LOVE ANDREAS and ABOLISH BOTH GERMAN GOVERNMENTS to JOHN WAYNE WAS BETTER, AND MOREOVER, HE'S ALREADY DEAD, written during Reagan's first visit to the city. West Berliners couldn't deny a sense of finality, driving down the narrow strip of East German highway which connected them to the rest of the world, but once back home they would tend to forget. Punk songs like "Come let's get shot / At the Wall / Hand in hand" were not attacks on the Wall itself but on the world that lay outside it, which never knew the whirl of life lived on the edge.

Sunbathers strolled alongside it, feeding the swans; the Wall only obtruded at points its construction had turned into fringes of town. Still it conditioned lives on both sides of the city. The Wall prevented East Berliners from enjoying the fruits, technology and bright lights of the West, and West Berliners from escaping all the razzle-dazzle to quiet weekends in the country. It was easy for visitors to imagine the options it limited, but only Berliners could tell you how many it increased. There was no denying the Wall's economic importance. Fearing a ghost town after its construction, both sides began pumping massive subsidies into the city to induce people to stay. East Berlin became the most comfortable city in Eastern Europe, displaying few of the pitfalls, and most of the advantages, of state-imposed socialism. West Berlin, even wealthier, was less

They read:

Auschwitz
Stutthof
Maidanek
Treblinka
Theresienstadt
Buchenwald
Dachau
Sachsenhausen
Ravensbrück
Bergen-Belsen

The shield at the top, a little larger than the others, says: PLACES OF HORROR, WHICH WE NEVER DARE FORGET. That's what you see coming out of the subway on your way to get photocopies or lobsters or new shoes.

Some people think it would be a sign of vergangenheitsverarbeitung if the city took down this ridiculous signpost and put up a real monument to the victims. Others say that vergangenheitsverarbeitung must take place in the schools. The West German government never agreed upon a national plan for teaching children about the Nazis, so that many people grew up with the impression that history simply stopped between 1933 and 1945. Even worse, local governments often block individual teachers' initiatives to fill this gap: West Berlin forbade former members of the resistance to lecture at public schools, on the grounds that most of them had been Communists. Vergangenheitsverarbeitung could also mean prosecuting the many war criminals who remain unpunished, finishing their lives on large federal pensions. Like the SS officer in Frankfurt who hanged twenty children used in the medical experiments at Auschwitz. His trial was suspended on the grounds that their deaths were not particularly cruel.

People sometimes argue that vergangenheitsverarbeitung means something completely different. What is past cannot, by definition, be overcome. The history must be learned, the victims remembered, but justice takes place in the present. In an article called "What Does Vergangenheitsverarbeitung Mean?" Adorno wrote: "The past would be finally overcome if the causes of the past were eliminated. The power of the past remains unbroken only because the causes still persist." Everybody on the left would agree with him; the arguments begin when they try to determine what it is that persists. Most of the civil servants who were as diligent in serving the early Federal Republic as they were the Third Reich are dying off. Big industries retain the profits they gained from the "Aryanization" of Jewish businesses and the goods produced by millions of slave laborers worked to death under the Nazis, but nobody's planning to expropriate Siemens or Krupp. A thoroughgoing vergangenheitsverarbeitung, some say, would require a revolution. They cite Max Horkheimer, who wrote that "anybody who doesn't want to talk about capitalism shouldn't bother to talk about fascism." But revolutions are long-term projects. Meanwhile, people agree that vergangenheitsverarbeitung means maintaining vigilance toward everything in the present which shows signs of repeating the past.

Take the Turks. There are other overworked and underprivileged groups of foreigners in Germany, but the Turks are the largest. Berlin, goes the saying, is now the third-largest city in Turkey. Some quarters of Berlin are full of dark-eyed children, silent women wearing veils, shops selling olives and grape leaves and pistachios, music that is utterly foreign. Turks are the victims of discriminatory laws, random violence, and the thoroughgoing contempt of the rest of the population. You will hear that the Turks are to the Federal Republic what the Jews were to the early Third Reich. This is an oversimplification. Still, the words TURKS GET OUT are scrawled on the same walls where JEWS GET OUT was seen fifty years ago. Often people come along later, cross out the word TURKS and substitute NAZIS. That's vergangenheitsverarbeitung. So was the plea to invite a foreign refugee to dinner made by the actors in an antifascist play called *It Wasn't Me, Hitler Did It.* Or the posters saying PROTECT OUR TURKISH FELLOW CITIZENS FROM A POGROM which went up after a right-wing group announced plans to distribute leaflets in Turkish neighborhoods telling the Turks to go home.

For all the confusion surrounding the notion, vergangenheitsverarbeitung was the point at which East-West rivalry grew fiercest. Each side claimed the other lacked the genuine article. East Germans pointed proudly to their trials of war criminals and their elementary-school curricula with antifascist exercises. West Germany vaunted its reparation payments to the State of Israel. East Berlin touted the honor guard watching over an eternal flame at the Memorial to the Victims of Fascism and Militarism, a little marble temple in the center of town. Westerners noted that plaques at concentration camp sites on East German territory seldom mentioned the word "Jew."

Arriving in Berlin in 1982, I was stunned by the array of discussion. "How can you say there's been no vergangenheitsverarbeitung? People talk about it all the time. You turn on the radio and hear rock stars singing 'It's still just Kristallnacht.' There are television programs about it every other night. You can hardly go to an art exhibit without seeing some reference to it."

"Oh, that's a minority. Even in Berlin. And the rest of Germany is worse. There are still neo-Nazi papers that say the gas chambers were nothing but Allied war propaganda. Most people have repressed the past. They don't want to hear another word. A few intellectuals talk about the Nazis. Artists. It isn't enough."

I persisted. "It's a lot more than we have in America. People have stopped talking about Viet Nam. You don't turn on the television and see documentaries about Hiroshima. There's no body of literary work about the exploitation of Latin America. Make allowances for the fact that our worst crimes were committed in distant places. Make allowances for the fact that our fathers were seldom the people who carried the guns. There's still no comparison. People are trying to come to terms with their history here. They're engaged."

"Wait and see," they told me. "Wait and see."

In Medias Res

When I rang the doorbell, it was nearly midnight. Thomas and Ingrid were expecting me: a friend had arranged for me to sublet their apartment while they spent the year in Indonesia. They had planned to leave for Indonesia in September, but plans change.

Ingrid had straight brown hair, a thin nose, and a Peruvian sweater. She was a schoolteacher, she said, of biology and sport; next year she expected to get a position. Thomas was tall and stoop-shouldered, an unemployed architect who had taken to painting. The largest canvas on the living-room wall, he said, was his magnum opus. I got up to look at it. Enormous insects, drawn with precision in blues and browns, stood before an open coffin. Ingrid brought red wine from the kitchen. Tell us about England, they said, tell us about where you come from.

"But I don't come from England. I come from America."

There was a silence.

"But Charley, who arranged for you to take the apartment, Charley is English."

"Yes, Charley is English, and I am American."

There was another silence.

"I've never met an American I liked," said Ingrid.

* * *

I asked what they planned to do in Indonesia. They wanted to experience another culture, a really foreign one. Ingrid had traveled in South America once, she'd liked that. "But why Indonesia?" I asked. "I don't know anything about Indonesia."

"Neither do we," said Ingrid. "We'll find out when we get there."

I didn't know how common it was to head off for a time to Indonesia or Mexico or Sudan: anything, anything, to get away from this Deutschland. They would be leaving in a week or two, meanwhile we could get to know each other; there were, after all, two and a half rooms.

And what rooms. It took me days to notice anything else in the world, because of those rooms. The house, like most houses in Berlin, led you to expect nothing: its flat red front presented only a chunky utility to the world. But facades are the first things to go when the bombs come. Inside, as in most houses in Berlin, was all the useless luxury of the last century. Enormous high ceilings, with moldings shaped as cherubs and vines. Parquet floors, Art Nouveau doorknobs made of brass. Tall French windows looking out to the iron lanterns on the street below, now lit by electricity, but casting the kind of glow that gas lanterns must once have cast in the shadows. Neither Thomas's paintings nor Ingrid's South American chatchkas could spoil the effect. In the corner of each room stood a cast-iron oven, reaching to the ceiling, covered with gilt-edged porcelain tiles.

"We heat with coal in Berlin," said Ingrid. "I expect that will be difficult for you, coming from America, but it's much more economical. And healthier. And better for the environment."

* * *

Several days later I sat fighting tears in the sinking light of the Prussian plain. Leaves surrounded the regal café with the sad brown rotting smell of autumn afternoons. The city was immense, nothing else. The streets seemed enormous, too wide and too long, and I was too small, the same size as the people who were bombed in their cellars, or taken away in cattle cars, or swept off by the Huns, or whatever else happens to people in that Eastern vastness. The picturesque in the melancholy was hard to take in. I stared from windows for hours, watching old people, young people, putting on coats, turning the same color, wrapped in slow gloom. Lives I couldn't imagine.

* * *

I didn't laugh the first time I saw the poster: LESBIANS ATE AN AMERICAN; WILL A BERLINER BE NEXT?

* * *

German pedestrians always stop at red lights. Doesn't matter if there's not a car in sight, all the way down the boulevard. They stay on the corner, looking at the little stoplight. Though you rarely see anyone doing otherwise, there was a publicity campaign to encourage this, with pictures of a child and the words "Set an example: go with green, stop with red." In German it rhymes.

Ute said this is fascist. You're exaggerating, I told her. No, she insisted, it was just this kind of behavior which led to fascism. Not thinking for oneself. Doing what one is told. You're exaggerating, I answered, it's not threatening but ridiculous, these clumps of people on every corner, eyes staring straight over empty streets.

They don't just stand there either. If you cross against the light they stare at you, full of envy and fear. Sometimes they speak up: "It's red for you too!" Later I learned to think of replies to this, but still there were days when I stood with the others, too tired to face all those eyes.

* * *

of humor, why did you come here and when will you go? When you run out of words you can stand simply waiting, not thinking, not thinking at all.

* * *

Thomas and Ingrid delayed their trip to Indonesia. Ingrid had forgotten that her passport was about to expire. She had to travel to Hamburg before they could apply for a visa, it would be a few weeks longer. Ingrid liked to stay at home, but sometimes she went to the movies. One night we went together to see Costa-Gavras's *Missing*. I was struck by how neatly the film was made for American consumption: the daughter corn-fed and unsuspecting, the father decisive and incorruptible. Good for making political points in the right places, but a little provincial in the end. Before I was able to say this, Ingrid interrupted. "That woman was a very untypical American. Much more typically German or French." Sissy Spacek. Who do they think we are?

* * *

One Sunday afternoon, a *Kaffee-und-Kuchen* was held in the *Hinterhöf*, the back courtyards around which Berlin apartments were built. A table was set where we sat with thin smiles, commenting on the little cakes which each of the neighbors brought. Nobody introduced himself; they don't, in Berlin. The young liberal lawyer seated next to me made fun of my accent.

Mocking Americans is perfectly civil in circles where people would bite their tongues before they'd ridicule a Turkish accent. Were my stumblings through the languages less deserving of sympathy? But I faltered, blushed, and said nothing: my vocabulary was too small to express the thought, and I was slow to anger, those days. Afterward, though, I talked to Ingrid.

"I can't take it," I said. "This constant aggression. And America is hardly the only country that ever committed a crime. Suppose I started introducing myself as Jewish, instead of American?" I was new in town.

"I wouldn't do that if I were you," said Ingrid. "People here don't think much of Israel either."

* * *

Here and there you meet an old man speaking fondly of CARE packages gone by. But the pro-American attitude of the right is tempered by resentment: better to have been conquered by the Americans than by the Russians, but wouldn't the very best be never to have been conquered at all? On the left, only the Communists displayed no hostility to Americans. This was partly the result of certain kinds of reporting. If you wanted to hear about the American peace movement, or campaigns against racism or unemployment, you tuned into East and not West German television. Knowing that this was just the other side of the American press's confining its reports on the Soviet Union to stories about jailed dissidents and failing agricultural yields didn't prevent me from feeling a certain gratitude. At least they knew there was opposition in America. Indeed, they tended to touching exaggerations of its importance.

"Did you belong to any political party in America?" Walther was soft-spoken. I'd met him with two other students after a lecture.

"There are no real left-wing parties in America anymore. Political activism takes place at a local level. People organize around specific issues: housing, or disarmament, or the environment."

"Ummm—there is one political party in America which cares about all those things." He hesitated a moment, trying to read me. "Have you ever heard of Gus Hall? Angela Davis?"

"Oh." I smiled. "But the Communist Party in America has absolutely no influence on anything whatsoever."

"I'm not so sure about that. I heard Angela Davis speak here once."

"Angela Davis is the only thing they've got going for them at all. She's a courageous woman and a marvelous speaker. Nevertheless."

"Isn't the Communist Party illegal in the United States?" asked Hans.

"They don't have to outlaw things in the United States," I answered. "They have other ways."

"Are you a Communist, Walther?" Ute interrupted.

"Yes," he answered, with what was meant to be a proud quiet nod.

"I don't see how anybody living in Berlin can become a Communist. How do you defend the Wall?"

"Look," said Walther calmly, "you have to ask what freedom means. For me, freedom means possibilities. It's impossible for most people in East Germany to take a vacation on the Mediterranean. But it's equally impossible for most people in this country. They don't have the money."

There was more than a grain of truth in the party line. Genuine freedom of movement, in the West, is the privilege of the wealthy: the cheap charter flights leaving Düsseldorf for the Canary Islands every weekend didn't quite refute him. This was still no excuse for the span of concrete which divided the city, but I let it go. It was hard to know how to argue with someone who told me he was studying philosophy in order to discover the objective laws of history.

* * *

I had thought it was America that was obsessed with the Old World. Even our towns have no names of their own. There are rivers named for the Indians who no longer tend their banks. But what do you find next to Rome, Georgia, and Moscow, Idaho? Usually nothing better than a Pleasantville.

What surprised me was their obsession with us. American news is on every front page. They get things wrong, of course, but they talk about us all the time. Not only in Berlin, which was an occupied city. It was in Amsterdam that someone told me, "Bell Telephone owns most of Belgium, and the king owns the rest." That was December, and we were sitting in a bar where the Christmas tree was covered with the same kind of plastic and tinsel you might see in a Baltimore shopping center.

But let's not talk politics. Most amazing was the music. I couldn't escape it. Not only the present, but the past. I'd be sitting in a seedy bar in Charlottenburg and the jukebox would suddenly play "If You Go to San Francisco, Be Sure to Wear Some Flowers in Your Hair." I'd be looking at the paintings in the East German capitol building, and piping through the ceiling was quite unmistakably Dylan singing "Knockin' on Heaven's Door." My friends found my wonder amusing. They grew up with the songs I grew up with, they had the same words in their head as I did. Of course Helena and I would sing Janis Joplin in unison when we stepped, a little loaded, into a waiting Mercedes-Benz. Of course when a Pole or a Chilean or a German brought out a guitar after dinner and wanted to play something that everybody knew, it would be Bob Dylan or the Beatles. Sometimes there would be exchanges where I got to hear Dominican ballads or Yugoslavian resistance songs. But even this could misfire. Once I went to a party where everyone was to bring music from his native country. When the nuclear physicist from Peking got around to playing his tape, we heard a woman singing something to the tune of "Red River Valley." In Chinese.

Werner told me there can be no genuine German music. Not anymore. You couldn't draw on old tradition without echoing the Nazis.

Dieter said the current renaissance in German painting is due to the postwar preoccupation with the Nazi era. A conflict between fathers and sons which can only be resolved through Art.

* * *

***R**ainy gray days, the first of very many. I learned to throw on a scarf, to light the coal fire. I liked handling the black bricks which made me warm, watching them turn orange on the ashes of last night's fire, slowly, slowly, every movement was slow. I liked going to the cellar and turning the heavy key in the door, gathering bricks all stacked in a row. Moments running together, calling themselves a life.

* * *

***"D**o they have WG's in America?" asked Ingrid in the kitchen one morning. WG is the abbreviation for *Wohngemeinschaften.* That's the German word for "sharing an apartment with someone."

"Yes of course."

"Oh," she said, "I thought they might not have them there."

* * *

***T**he occupied-house movement led to riots, barricades and several deaths. In the early eighties it was West Berlin's fiercest political struggle. The scenario was simple. Groups of homeless young people would move into the huge empty buildings which had been left to rot by their owners, who were waiting to tear them down and build something more profitable. Then the police would throw them out, sometimes after a couple of hours, sometimes after a couple of years. Some of the houses were just houses, others were collectively organized cultural centers, where you could climb four flights of stairs to watch actors or musicians play an unheated room. You could always tell which houses were occupied: the facades were painted with large flowers or men holding machine guns, and banners hung from the windows, WHETHER ITS LEGAL OR ILLEGAL IS BULLSHIT TO ME. RESISTANCE IN THE FOURTH REICH.

The American press mentioned these people occasionally, calling them squatters, but squatters are not house occupiers, at least in Berlin. The movement began in Amsterdam, where it proceeded with relative civility despite the larger number of houses which were occupied. But history has been kinder to the Dutch, or the Dutch to history. Berliners printed a poster with a photograph of marching Wehrmacht soldiers and the slogan: BETTER TO OCCUPY EMPTY HOUSES THAN FOREIGN COUNTRIES.

After a house was cleared out, there were big demonstrations. Prominent leftists showed their support. Ute told me she lived in one last summer.

"Actually, I had an apartment," she said, "but I moved in out of solidarity."

"What was it like?" I asked.

"Oh, like any other WG. Endless discussions about washing the dishes. Respecting other people's space. Except there was more pressure. You never knew when the police might come. And the worst part was the vigilantes."

"Vigilantes?"

"Groups of people would come around in the night, throw rocks through the windows, write messages."

"What kinds of messages?"

"Oh, you should all be sent to concentration camps and gassed. That sort of thing."

* * *

*T*homas took to staying in his room when he heard me in the kitchen. This was not what they expected. Why aren't you more comfortable in the apartment, why don't you bring your friends home? But that's just it, I said, I'm not comfortable here. We bring our friends home, said Ingrid.

"But it's your apartment. You've lived here for years."

Ingrid said I had a hierarchical and elitist way of thinking.

* * *

*T*he gray became tangible, turning into fog, giving the impression that the city was permanently wrapped in depression. The organ grinder in the Wilmers-dorferstrasse wore a Santa Claus suit. On the next corner a man holding a llama by a leash collected coins in a small tin cup. I wanted to ask him why, but making words was much too hard.

I reread the novels of Jean Rhys, one after the other. It could be worse. Lots worse. You could be nineteen and pregnant and abandoned. Or ageing and penniless and alcoholic. Lots of women have been lost in foreign cities before.

* * *

For there were other moments, at twilight, when the night was about to begin and the possibilities were uncountable. Running from a seminar to catch the subway to cross the border for the production of *The Marriage of Figaro* which was said to be better in the East than in the West, I laughed, breathless. Hearing *Figaro* would have been excitement enough, not so very long ago, but crossing from the Western bloc to the Eastern bloc to hear *Figaro* of an evening ... After a year or two in Berlin one didn't do it anymore, but in the way one doesn't get around to driving in from Queens to go to the Met. It would be a long time before I saw that this city could be taken for granted. Nor did I know that references to the powers of Berliner air, one of the world's most polluted, were mostly ironic. There were days when every breath I drew intoxicated.

* * *

When Ingrid and Thomas started packing, we were just barely on speaking terms.

"At least I've learned something from this experience," said Ingrid. "One should never try to live with foreigners. They're just too ... different from other people."

"Foreigners?" I said. "One should never try to live with people who want to be living alone. You were supposed to be in Indonesia."

"That's true," said Ingrid.

* * *

The Reggae Cellar was a kneipe in a basement in Kreuzberg. Outside, the neon colors: green for the jungles of Africa, red for the blood of the martyrs, yellow for the tropical sun, or is it gold? Inside was nothing but fake wood walls, a table or two, a tiny dance floor. Some Berliner kneipen boast green and gold and potted palms. Here there were no windows, nothing shone but the live reggae from Africa, playing slowly for the pale young Germans who stood shyly, seeking something foreign. The other half of the clientele were African men. Two of them asked us to dance, the night I went with an American friend. We danced for a long time, eyes closed. When I opened them I saw that none of the Germans were moving.

"I buy you beer," said the man I had danced with.

"Oh no, I'll get my own." From his shoes it was clear that he had no money.

"Please."

The music followed us to the table in the corner. Hard to hear, hard to think. He was a refugee from Ghana, and he was twenty-two years old. Something happened there five months before. He spoke no German and his English was terrible. How much did one need to understand? Something happened in Ghana and he had to flee.

"My name is Bismarck," said Bismarck.

"Bismarck?" I repeated.

It wasn't really Bismarck, it was something else that meant Friend-to-the-King, for his father had been Friend-to-the-King in Ghana, that was his name there, and when he came to Berlin he'd been told to call himself Bismarck. For short.

"You come home with me?" asked Bismarck, but I didn't want to come home with him, though he told me it was five months since he'd seen a woman smile. I'm sorry, I said, that's not enough of a reason. Yes I had smiled. Dancing I smile, sometimes, and then sometimes I don't.

"Why they don't smile at me here?" asked Bismarck. He really wanted to know, he wasn't just playing for sympathy. "They come to Africa, everybody smile. So why they don't smile at me here?" When Ellen's husband arrived, the two of them joined us. Dan tried to ask Bismarck about the political situation in Ghana.

"Why you no come home with me?" asked Bismarck.

"No," I said.

"I call you later?"

"I don't have a telephone," I lied. "And I'm married besides."

When I returned from the toilet, Dan was giving Bismarck his telephone number. "Only a man would have done that," said Ellen later, smiling. "He didn't want Dan's sympathy. He wanted a way to find you." "Bismarck called again," she would tell me, for a long time afterward. "And what did he say?" I asked. "Well, he can't say much, you know. 'Here is Bismarck. Where is she?' "

* * *

Not living for anything anymore. The point was simply that the days went by.

It was not the foreign language which made me speechless. I had, quite simply, nothing to say.

When I had to meet someone official, I put on my credentials as if I were wearing stolen goods. Here is a name you've probably heard of, and here is a tide to go with it. Or would you prefer a real introduction? How do you do! I don't remember the past, I have no plans for the future, but I'm ... interested in things.

There were days when I thought of an African proverb: He who comes to a foreign land should open his eyes and not his mouth. But mostly I failed to justify my helplessness. In a notebook I wrote: my ego is dissolving.

* * *

Helena took me into confidence quickly: she was, when I met her, undecided between three admirers. With surly graceful Stefan we went to the annual music festival "Berliner Atonal." We missed the first group, "Collapsing Modern Building." But how can you think about nihilism if you haven't seen punk in Kreuzberg, I repeated silently, when the smoke in the room became sickening and I thought I was turning ashen, like all the other people in the aggressively bare hall. Do the punks dye their hair neon because there are no colors anymore but fake ones, just this black and dirty gray?

The next group was called "Didactic Unity." Two men wearing tattered white loincloths, one in black hat and a monk's robe, the others all leather and nails. The loincloths bowed up and down, smearing themselves with mud from a bucket. Convinced they were going to throw the rest of the mud at the audience, I thought of my broken hot-water heater. But they put the bucket down. The drummer beat without rhythm, the guitarist's notes had no tone. A new number began: the lead singer (but he didn't sing, and nobody seemed to be leading) threw himself repeatedly onto the audience gathered at the foot of the stage. People fell, moving back. A few were smiling, others shouted. A woman sitting on stage tossed a lazy cigarette butt over her shoulder. Someone in the audience threw an empty beer can at the stage. Mad this time, she threw it back hard. Meanwhile, the group started another number: a second singer shouted slowly, over and over: "We want—to humanize—the earth!"

Cold air outside.

"Wotan," said Helena.

"Yes, they're searching for a new form," said Stefan. "Here Christianity is really a very thin imposition on a foreign culture."

"What's it like to live in a country without castles?" Helena asked me.

* * *

West Berlin had next to nothing in the way of public monuments: except for the Reichstag, every building of note fell into the Russian sector. Postcards sent from West Berlin depict the Wall, or occasionally the Kaiser Wilhelm Memorial Church, built in 1897. All but one tower was destroyed by Allied bombers. This was left to stand jagged in the middle of the Kurfürstendamm, called the Kudamm, the main street in town. When it shows signs of further deterioration, teams of construction workers are sent to ensure that it remains in just the state of ruin in which it was left at the end of the war. A bronze plaque beside it reads: A REMINDER OF THE JUDGMENT OF GOD. I'd become used to living in a city whose unofficial symbol is a bombed-out neo-Gothic cathedral, only to be stunned by the carnival which suddenly surrounds it every Christmas. Planted around the ruins are carousels with blinking lights, stalls where couples win stuffed pandas and pounds of coffee, barkers selling taffy apples and popcorn. For Berliners strolling arm in arm through the crowd, the scene hardly merits a shrug of the shoulder. I tried to see the carnival in the ruin as they do: not a preposterous tribute to Berliner insouciance but the source of a possible traffic jam. Or: the unavoidable annual concession to an eager child ("Just *one* more ride"). Might it come to seem just as familiar as the small Christmas tree erected at the Wall?

Practicing indifference I stepped into the Café Möhring, whose yellow lamps glow golden against streaky mirrors and old molding. In the corner stood a large but elegant Christmas tree bearing white satin balls. The yappy Pekinese belonging to the woman at the next table jumped into my lap. Smiling unsteadily, I gave it a pat.

"Are you unfaithful to me, dolly?" said the woman to her puppy. And then to me: "When the husband dies, one gets a dog."

Outside that bastion of Old World Berlin the bombed-out cathedral competed with a wild horde of lanterns strung on all the Kudamm trees to light up the Christmas consumption. I looked at the artfully displayed objects—

perfume, clothing, porcelain—with anthropological interest, wondering why I'd stopped wanting to own things.

* * *

*I*f you're lucky when you move to a foreign city, the people you knew before give you the names of the people they know there. I came to Berlin with seven names and seven telephone numbers, and it was months before I called a single one. Next week, I would tell myself, next week I will do it. My German will be better, even on the telephone I'll be able to say something that sounds witty not pathetic. We'll get together. The world will be the way it was before. On New Year's Eve in a Kreuzberg kneipe I resolved to put an end to this. I would call them tomorrow, one after the other, and I'd begin with the most interesting-sounding of them all. I had the name of a successful painter who was smack-dab, I'd been told, in the middle of the Berlin scene. I would call him tomorrow. Well, the next day. You can't call anyone on New Year's Day.

A cognac to go with the cigarette, if you really think you must. For God's sake, what has happened to you? I rehearsed the German sentences for the tenth time. Hello, is that Peter Becker? I'm an acquaintance of Robert Hahn and I've just moved to Berlin. I picked up the telephone. Then put it down again. Mensch, you've got to have something more to say than that! What if he says nothing in reply? You have to suggest something concrete, he's not the one who's calling you, after all. Suppose you say: would you like to come by for a glass of wine, say Friday, around nine?

I lit another cigarette. I don't know anything about this man, and I don't know anything about this country. If a strange woman calls and invites you for a glass of wine some evening, does that mean she wants to sleep with you? Of course I might want to sleep with him, but then again I might not. Better invite him for coffee, in the afternoon. That's definitely unambiguous.

I poured another cognac. But I hate this *Kaffee-und-Kuchen* ritual. I'd already been invited to a number of them, and though I'd been to awkward social gatherings before, I'd never experienced anything approaching the stiffness and discomfort of a German *Kaffee-und-Kuchen.* Not even high tea in England with the Oxford dons. Besides, I'll be nervous and wanting a drink. As my very first German teacher said, you always speak a foreign language better when you've had a glass of wine. Language problems are mostly inhibitions, she told us. Nothing more.

Another cigarette, then a happy thought. I could call Helena, the woman from Amsterdam I'd met a few weeks before. Like me, she was a graduate student in philosophy who had come to Berlin on a government fellowship. Unlike me, she was thoroughly European, thus effortlessly worldly, radiating all the sassy blasé gaiety I wanted to learn. Helena, surely, would know.

"What kind of a man?" asked Helena.

"I don't know. A painter."

"Is he married?"

"No idea."

"Married is better. It's less complicated."

I stammered. "But I don't know anything about the guy. I don't know if I want to get involved with him or not. I just wanted to meet some more people here—"

"See what he's like."

"Right, but I wanted to ask you: I hate inviting people over for coffee, but if I invite a man I've never seen to my apartment for a glass of wine, will he take that as a come-on, or not?"

Helena laughed for a long time. "My Lord," she said. "It's true what they say. Americans really are puritanical. First invite him over and then ask him what he wants to drink when he gets there."

A little mortified, I persisted. "Does it make a difference if I invite him in the afternoon or in the evening?"

She laughed again. "And I used to think the stories about Americans were exaggerated! Go ahead. Invite him over."

The conversation with Helena had only increased my sense of helplessness. Nevertheless, I dialed the number. There was, of course, no answer.

But when I called the next day, he answered the phone. I was so surprised that I nearly forgot the sentences.

"Hello, is that Peter Becker? I'm an acquaintance of Robert Hahn, he gave me your telephone number because I've just moved to Berlin."

Peter Becker found nothing unusual in this. "Where do you come from?" he asked.

"Umm, from the USA."

"And you're here for a while, or just passing through?"

"I'm here for a while."

"I'm just working in my atelier, why don't you come by?"

"Now?"

"If you're not doing anything else."

Nervousness gave way to astonishment. When strangers call you in America, you meet them for lunch next Wednesday. Even friends are parceled out carefully, drinks with one at six-thirty before dinner with the next at eight. He's in the middle of working and I should come around now, at three o'clock on a Tuesday afternoon? Wasn't this man supposed to be a serious painter?

Nothing to do but to buy a bottle of wine, less so as not to come empty-handed than to make sure there would be something in the atelier to drink. Had I known Berlin a little better, I wouldn't have worried. A bottle of Metaxa stood on the floor next to a half-empty bottle of red wine.

It was the first time I had been inside one of the many Berliner Hinterhöfe, bare and gray, which were filled with ateliers and galleries that had been factories in the time when there was industry in the center of Berlin. Peter Becker's paintings hung on every wall. I thought I liked them better the longer I looked at them, but I wasn't certain. A set of drums stood in the middle of the floor. A cassette recorder played music too foreign to recognize. The light that came through the spattered windows was melancholy. I was dazzled.

Peter Becker folded an easel in the corner to make a table. He brought cold cuts and bread and asked me what I thought of his paintings. Later I would learn that people here always ask you what you think of their paintings, and that it's wrong just to say you find them interesting, but perfectly alright to say you find them awful. I didn't know what to say about Peter Becker's paintings. He was very friendly, and told me about living in Rio and Khartoum. Another painter came in with photographs of his latest work. We finished the wine and started on the Metaxa. Peter Becker made no motions to get back to work, but seemed perfectly prepared to let his interrupted afternoon turn into evening. I tried to answer their questions. Peter Becker had been in America once. In Houston.

"In Houston?" I said. "Why in the world did you go to Houston?"

"The people were friendly. Lots of money. Good place to have a show." He smiled.

"I suppose," I said.

"Tell me," he continued. "I've often wondered whether Americans understand irony."

"Whether they what?" I asked.

"Whether they understand irony. You know, children don't understand irony, they're simply not capable of it. And there are tribes in the Amazon that don't understand irony either. So I've often wondered, maybe Americans are like that too."

"No," I said, "Americans understand irony, sometimes."

The conversation turned to the subject of philosophy. Do tell us what you think.

I hemmed and hawed. "Don't you see, I can't just say what I think the meaning of life is!" That's what I wanted to say, but I stopped. Why can't I just say what I think the meaning of life is? If I were to answer: because it's all much more complicated than that, I would be patronizing. These men were not stupid. They knew these questions are not easy, and they nevertheless had something to say about them. It's only ten years of studying philosophy which took the words out of my mouth. For the hundredth time that year, I cursed my education.

That's not the whole story either, I wanted to explain. Before I came to Berlin I knew what I thought about everything. Now I am taking things in, learning to know nothing. Time enough to form views later.

I didn't say that either. We talked about death and art, the day was over, the light was gone.

"You come from a Jewish family, don't you?" asked Peter Becker.

"Yes," I said.

"It doesn't matter," said the other painter. Doesn't matter? To whom?

"That's the first time anybody here has noticed," I said, trying to make my smile very light.

"I'm a painter," said Peter Becker.

"So what did you see?" I asked.

"You look a little exotic," said Peter Becker.

It doesn't matter? A little exotic? The words were jarring, but I strained to listen, intent on hearing their stories, not on telling mine.

We talked a little longer, the other painter was leaving and Peter Becker had to go. He told me to come by whenever I liked. I did, six weeks later, but then things got busier and we never saw each other again, the way that often happens.

* * *

Tumble-down open, those first months in Berlin. Anything was better than conclusions. Living with an agenda seemed so insolently American: I hadn't come to Europe to confirm what I knew.

On a first brief trip to Germany two years earlier, I had visited Dachau, alone. Shed tears at the bone-white field outside the museum. I knew, or thought I knew, the victims' side of the story.

I spent the summer before my departure memorizing *Faust*, part one—a fact which would bring German friends to incredulous laughter. Nor did I think much of Americans who traveled through Germany seeking concentration-camp sites, restored empty synagogues, and the echo of anti-Semitism behind every hearty "Jawohl!" There was defiance, and not a little arrogance in my stance, but also the sense, the moment I landed, that something more murky than we ever dreamed was at work here. More than anything else I wanted to know.

* * *

"But the stars in the windows are all Stars of David!"

"I guess that's true. Six-pointed."

"How can they do that? Especially here?"

"What kind of stars do Americans use for Christmas decorations?"

"Five-pointed. Six-pointed stars are Jewish symbols."

"That wouldn't do here. Five-pointed stars are communist symbols."

* * *

The rockets start a few days after Christmas. The first time I heard them, I jumped.

"Warming up for New Year's."

"But it sounds like bombs."

"But it's only firecrackers. In a couple of days they really get going."

"Isn't it hard on the old people who lived through the bombing?"

"Who knows?"

Devil's Mountain was made from the ruins of old Berlin. After everything was over, there was the wreckage, tons to be cleared and carted away. Few men were left in the gutted city; cleaning up the devastation was women's work. They stood, drawn, on shattered ground, passing buckets of rubble hand to hand, to a final pile on the edge of the Grunewald. From the top of this monumental dump one can still see the rubble easily: bricks, blocks and broken glass covered only by the thinnest layer of dirt. For days after New Year's, the grayish hill is scattered with thousands of champagne corks. It's the highest point in the city, and people trek up Devil's Mountain to watch the fireworks in the streets below.

Climbing Devil's Mountain on a winter afternoon you may think there is romance to be made from facts like these.

* * *

"The myth of Berlin ... so you came here to see if *la vie Bohéme* was still livable."

"Something like that."

"Susan is Jewish," said Helena, "and masochistic. Only a masochist would be American and Jewish and live in Berlin."

She had introduced me to Dieter, who was perfectly built and fashionably dressed. His small blue eyes nourished disquiet I didn't notice at first, for he glided through Berlin with an ease which I envied. He was a painter, Helena told me, who earned his living teaching art.

"Surely," he asked, "being a Turkish Jew in Berlin would be the worst of all?"

"Perhaps," I said lightly. "Though you wouldn't get it from all sides."

"Berliners," snorted Helena. "Did I tell you what happened this morning? I crossed a street where seven upstanding Germans were waiting for the light to change. One of them shouted: 'What are your eyes for?' So I answered: 'To see whether any cars are coming. Or did you think they're just good for looking at stoplights?' Should have heard them swearing. Cheeky Ausländer." She laughed and I joined her: Helena reveled in abandoned chutzpah I could never quite attain.

"You can laugh," said Dieter very sharply. "You can leave when you want to. It's not your country. I grew up with those people. They're still a part of me."

He had shamed us successfully. Even Helena fell silent and listened. Waiting for stoplights was following orders: nothing had changed since the war. How could it be otherwise? The "Economic Miracle" was a monumental act of repression, directing every bit of energy to economic recovery so there'd be no room to think about what had happened. "I saw it in my parents," finished Dieter. "They had to repress. Otherwise they'd have to acknowledge how attractive they'd found the Nazis. Yes, I mean *sexy*. And they couldn't live with that."

He gazed past us to the bar, thick with standing people dressed in dull colors. The blackboard above read TRINK COCA-COLA.

"So how do you manage? I mean"—I was fumbling—"what does one do?"

"What one does?" Dieter looked at me gravely. "Try to deal with the contradictions in oneself. Art is a medium. Politics is very limited. Though East Germany is different."

"Really?"

"People who risked their lives resisting the Nazis were hardly ready to integrate them quietly into the government when the war was over. Here it's the resistance heroes who've no place to go."

Willy Brandt lost the 1960 election because he'd left the country under the Nazis. Franz-Joseph Strauss led the campaign against him with the slogan: "What was Herr Brandt doing abroad for twelve years? We know what we were doing in Germany." Ten years later, when Brandt was chancellor, Strauss and the Springer Press continued to hound him. "Too soft on the Communists" was code for "too hard on the Nazis."

"And Brandt was only a Social Democrat," said Dieter. "You should see what they do to the Communists."

I stared at the round rubber circles in the linoleum floor. Ronald Reagan, I knew, had just praised Franz-Joseph Strauss effusively: they were, both touted, two of a kind. And long before Reagan, in those first crucial years following the war, American policy put all but the most prominent of Nazi criminals in all but the most prominent of government positions.

"Another Riesling?" asked Dieter, his eyes on my glass. Something like complicity hovered in the space between us.

I shook my head. "Is it really different in the East?" I asked him.

"My uncle in East Berlin was in the resistance. He's treated like a hero." Dieter looked at me casually. "We could visit him together, if you'd like."

"Oh yes." I was more excited than I wanted to show.

"Sometime soon."

I smiled and stood to pay for my wine. Dieter, and then Helena, kissed me on both cheeks.

* * *

Just when I was least expecting it, something always happened to make me wonder about the meaning of the words "cold war." I noticed that the yellow road signs before bridges posted separate weight limits for cars, trucks and tanks. I went out early one day to find my way blocked by a stray American tank rumbling down a major boulevard. I'd be distracted from the paintings by a glance from the window of the splendid exhibit hall whose front entrance was blocked by the Wall. The large gray building on the opposite side housed the East German security service; if the windows were open, one could count the files. The surrounding half-wasteland was once the busiest intersection in Europe. All this made up the city's weird but genuine claim to being *in medias res.*

The U.S. Army radio broadcast mediocre but continuous rock and roll throughout Berlin. I was spellbound one morning by an announcement. "Never use the telephone when discussing sensitive subjects," said the DJ, his voice twangy with amplified enthusiasm. "Telephones are monitored by hostile forces. Don't put your faith in amateur codes, which can be easily broken by the enemy. Remember," he breathed, "one word to the spies is enough." The music continued as suddenly as it had stopped.

Icarus in Kreuzberg

*T*he postcard from Bali showed throngs of people wearing warm-colored robes in boats. On the other side was written: "Hello Susan! Indonesia is not what we thought it would be. We've seen some interesting things. But it's certainly very different. And our money hasn't lasted as long as we thought it would. So we're returning to Berlin. If the mail functions properly, we should arrive about two weeks after you receive this. Greetings. Ingrid and Thomas."

I raged. "The apartment which was to have been mine for a year had been empty for just two months. I hadn't begun to feel at home there, but I had begun to imagine what feeling at home here might be like. But rage was beside the point. I had to find a place to live.

Looking for an apartment in Berlin is like looking for an apartment anywhere. You ask everyone you meet if they know someone who's moving. You stand in line on Saturday night to get the Sunday paper and race to the telephone to call the numbers listed there. You hurry from building to building, street to street, to find three people waiting before you to view dank murky rooms. If the winter is blowing a cold rain all day and you're not at all sure that you understood what was said to you last, then it's all part of living in a foreign city. If you want to be classic about it. That's what I told myself, anyway, at the time.

About half of the ads in the newspapers are prefaced by the words "No Foreigners" or "Germans Only." Some of this is due to private initiative, and some of it is required by law. In the seventies the government got worried that there were too many Turks and Yugoslavians in certain neighborhoods and passed a law called the *Zuzugsperre*, which prohibits other Turks and Yugoslavians from moving into the neighborhoods in question. "It's for their own good too," said the liberals. "They wouldn't want the neighborhoods to turn into ghettos." So some of the ads saying "No Foreigners" mean that the apartment falls under the Zuzugsperre and can't be rented to Turks or Yugoslavians. And some of them mean that the landlord wants only Germans in his building.

For fifty marks I joined an organization which claimed to help its members find housing. I approached the bearded man at the desk where new apartments were listed. "I'm interested in this apartment, but it says 'No Foreigners.' Can you tell me if that's a reference to the Zuzugsperre, or—"

"Where do you come from?" he interrupted.

"I come from the USA."

"You're not a foreigner. You're part of the Occupation." He didn't slam the door. Not quite.

I made up a version of the little signs I had seen posted on tree trunks and lampposts: 100 MARKS REWARD FOR THE RENTAL OF A ONE- OR TWO-ROOM APARTMENT WITH KITCHEN, TOILET AND BATH. I bought Scotch tape and thumbtacks and took the subway to Mehringdamm. A mixture of sleet and rain was turning the day dark, though it was hardly three o'clock in the afternoon. As I fumbled with a thumbtack by the tree at the crossing, I heard an old woman shouting. I didn't realize she was shouting at me until I turned and saw her waving a small white paper. It was one of the signs I had put up a few minutes before.

"This is forbidden!" she shouted. "Forbidden!"

I was too stunned to say anything for a moment. My hands were freezing.

"It is against the law to place unauthorized private notices on public streets! It is forbidden by the police!"

"I didn't know it was forbidden," I replied slowly. "There are signs like this all over Berlin."

"It is nonetheless forbidden. You are required to have known it."

I began walking, too astonished to think of an answer, too intimidated to put up another sign. The woman screamed hoarsely; I could no longer hear what she said.

I drank a coffee at the Turkish *Imbiss*, a cross between a snack-shop and a hot-dog stand, on the corner. After I was warm again, I entered the tobacco and newspaper shop next door. Someone had given advice: tobacco shop owners hear the neighborhood gossip, they will know if someone's moving.

The man behind the counter was about fifty and short. His dark brown hair was combed back with grease where it was beginning to grow thin.

"A pack of Reynos, please." He smiled at me. Though soaking wet, I was wearing my most respectable clothes, and my face bore the vaguely timid, importuning look which pleases certain people in young women who need something. "I'm looking for an apartment in the neighborhood," I said. "Would you happen to know of anything coming vacant?"

"There's nothing vacant. The housing situation is terrible."

"It's pretty bad," I agreed.

"There are no apartments anymore. Do you want to know why?" His voice began to rise. "There are no apartments because this society is *kaputt."*

I nodded vaguely, looking at the pink plastic pig which served as a Scotch tape holder.

"Totally *kaputt.* It's unbearable. Young people wearing one orange stocking and one green one. Not two of the same color. One orange, one green. Don't tell me that's fashion. That has nothing to do with fashion. That's provocation!" His finger began to shake. "This society is *kaputt!* Do you want to know why? There's too much freedom here."

He leaned forward and lowered his voice.

"What we need," he said, "is a man of iron. Someone who will restore order."

I stood frozen. "Someone who will get rid of the foreigners and the punks and the bums. Someone who can make this land what it used to be. A man of iron," he repeated, "like Margaret Thatcher."

The anticlimax brought no relief.

Crossing the street, I saw that the notice I'd put up a few minutes before was gone. I retraced the path I had taken. Not a single sign remained. Fucking Nazis, I swore softly, they're—

I caught myself sharply. The man in the tobacco shop was on his way to fascism, but Margaret Thatcher, and the old woman on the street? What could I know? Only that the history of this country makes it impossible not to look for the past in the present; but everything depends upon learning to see. What could be learned from graffiti which says "USA = SS/SA"?

When do equations become thoughts?

A new poster, printed in red and black, was all over town:

THE 1983 CHANGE OF GOVERNMENT WAS NOT THE 1933 CHANGE OF GOVERNMENT.
1983 UNEMPLOYMENT IS NOT 1933 UNEMPLOYMENT.
THE TURKS ARE NOT THE JEWS.
NATO HAS NOT YET BEGUN ITS WORLD WAR.

* * *

Barbara might know of a vacant apartment. In the empty Italian restaurant we exchanged telephone numbers and ordered spaghetti.

"What kind of a place do you have?" I asked her, tired of talking about my search.

"Three rooms," she answered, "with central heating and hot water. But I don't live alone."

"With friends?"

"I'm married. To a Persian. He's studying engineering."

I waited, not knowing what she wanted to tell me. We'd only met once before.

"He's significantly younger than I am. He's twenty-five. I'm thirty-four." Her blue eyes were uneasy, suppressing intensity.

"Have you been married long?" It was the most harmless question I could think of.

"More than two years."

"*Bon appétit!*" said the waiter, setting down our plates with failed flourish. Barbara waited till he retreated before telling her story. Her marriage had been an arranged one; her husband needed a visa. He was tortured for opposing Khomeini, but German authorities rejected his plea for asylum. Had he been sent back to Iran, he would have been shot.

"So you're officially married but not really?"

"No," said Barbara, pushing spaghetti. "That's why we got married. Having done so, I decided to make the marriage work." She spoke in cool, deliberate tones which betrayed neither piety nor pity. She said she was lucky: her parents didn't mind him. Most of their generation hated foreigners, especially from the East.

"The Nazi years have been repressed," said Barbara, "but not worked through. There's still a lot of anti-Semitism in Germany." Bending over the table, her voice acquired authority. "Perhaps you don't know that anti-Semitism has a long history. The church was anti-Semitic."

"Uh-huh?" I succeeded in suppressing a smile. I couldn't bring myself to tell her that I knew something about the history of anti-Semitism, or that Jews are the sort of people who might turn out to be sitting across the table eating spaghetti. It wouldn't occur to her if we sat there all night: "Jew," for Barbara, was an abstract concept, coupled forever with "six million" and "gas." She couldn't see it, I didn't say it. For the first time, without reasons, I kept my mouth shut.

* * *

After barely three weeks it seemed to have lasted forever. I tried to see the bright side: looking for a place to live had swept me through the city. I'd learned a hundred street names, seen corners and hinterhöfe, rattails and grandeur.

I'd learned to use the telephone, a process which had filled me with such dread that I'd walk for miles, or let things slide, to avoid picking up a receiver. Talking to people in person can be gauged and filled out: not just a disembodied accented voice (unsure of itself, becoming too high) speaking wrong words, making endless mistakes. Looking for an apartment left me no choice but to go to the phone and dial, ten times a day.

"Braun's Management."

"Good morning. I'm looking for one or two rooms with kitchen and bath, for under four hundred marks."

"Four hundred marks? If you want an apartment that cheap you should go back to wherever you came from."

This was the time to be wry, to remark that I didn't come from Turkey or Pakistan but the USA, where four hundred marks wouldn't rent you a hole in the wall. But wryness and retorts were beyond me, part of a time and a place where I could think fast, talk right, and besides, I was loath to claim the status of a privileged foreigner. Looking for housing destroys scruples. It didn't really matter. The secretary at Braun's Management had already hung up the phone.

Then one day it happened. The apartment wasn't ideal: one long thin room with a narrow window cut askew, a second room just large enough for a desk and some shelves. The place had been newly renovated, a modern toilet and shower and tiny kitchen installed. The old coal stove was removed, central heating put in its place. I knew this allowed the landlord to charge three times as much rent as before. But the building itself was a wonder, lumbering and palatial, its elaborate facade painted green like mint. It lay on the most beautiful street I had ever seen. I had wanted to live in Kreuzberg, center of the city's resistance. But I hadn't even dreamed of living here in its heart, on the bank of the Landwehr Canal, heavy wooden barge on the water, thick winter trees lining the curve, cafés in the gardens facing the sky.

"*Ach*, American," said Frau Schultze, the concierge. She was a very short woman, and she moved very slowly. Gray hair curled tightly around her face; she might have been wearing a wig. "Well, you're the first person to see the apartment. That is, there was a young man here, but I sent him away. He was no good."

I stood up straighter, wishing I knew what she was looking for.

"The manager is Herr Wolf," she said after a pause. "Here is his address. If you want the apartment, you should see him today."

So I'd passed review. Holding the scrap of paper she'd given me folded tightly, I thanked her. Three times.

"Go today," she called behind me. "In your place I wouldn't lose any time."

As I swung open the wrought-iron door to the street, light met me. The muddy canal offered water and space. On the bridge an old woman threw crumbs in the air, surrounded by birds.

* * *

"Herr Wolf isn't in today," said one of the secretaries in the long corridor to the office. "Would you care to leave a message?"

"No thank you. Can you tell me when he'll be in?"

"He should be here tomorrow. Wouldn't you like to leave a message?"

"Thank you. I'll come back tomorrow."

* * *

"Ach, it's you. Herr Wolf is not here."

I stood in the doorway, staring at the office. It was hard to believe that people came to work every morning as dental assistants or real-estate agents in rooms which seemed made, at the least, for exquisite salons. Extravagant ceilings, flowery corners.

"What do you wish to discuss with Herr Wolf?"

"I'm interested in renting the apartment on Planufer."

"Then you can fill out an application and I will give it to him when he comes in." She led me to a desk and gave me a form. I filled it out, considering. The other secretary stood next to me arranging papers to be photocopied. She was young, with lightly polished nails. If I filled out the application and left it in this office, I would never hear from them again. I stood up.

"Actually, I would like to give this to Herr Wolf myself."

"But it isn't done that way. I will give him your application when he returns."

Careful now, I smiled, seeking the right combination: just a little aggressiveness, then a bit of helplessness and no more. "But do you expect him this afternoon? You see I really want to rent the apartment."

She softened slightly, smiling back. "I'll give him the application as soon as he returns."

The fourth time I returned to the office in Dahlem, Herr Wolf was in. Both secretaries smiled benignly, as if to a crackpot, while they told me to wait. It is not, in fact, done that way here: if you are told to fill out a form and go away, you fill out a form and go away.

"Come in," said Herr Wolf, briskly professional. "What can I do for you?"

"I would like to rent the apartment on Planufer."

"Have you filled out an application?" I had been right. One corner of the desk was stacked with forms, and mine was somewhere near the bottom. He searched for a while before extracting it.

"Neiman, Susan. American."

Smile. I was wearing a light black jacket with a black skirt, almost a suit. I had been wearing it for the past four days, but there was no way Herr Wolf could know that. I crossed my legs.

"And you're at the university?"

"I'm doing research there." Everyone had said it would be fatal to call myself a student, and I wasn't, in their sense, which includes only undergraduates. No point in insisting that one never stops being a student, in philosophy, till one learns like Socrates that one knows nothing. There's no word for "humble" in the German language.

"How long is your research contract?"

"Two years. But I expect it will be extended." This was a lie, and I was taking a risk. My fellowship would expire in July, and I hoped it could be extended another year. But if I committed myself to staying, I would find a way to live.

"That's not very long."

"It's only two years for certain. I'm planning to stay longer." In the tension of the pause I tried to make a joke. "If I have a wonderful apartment like this one, it will be one more reason to stay."

Herr Wolf didn't smile. Had I been too lighthearted? I took out the documents stuffed into my bag. Fellowship letters in English and German, passport, birth certificate, printed letters of recommendation designating me as a notable member of the university. Herr Wolf looked at the papers with the mildest of interest.

"Normally, you see, we rent neither to foreigners nor academics."

What in the world could I say to that? I tried to meet his eyes. Please give me the apartment, mister, for I can't take it much longer, not another night on the floor of somebody's unheated room, not another day on those wide cold streets, trying not to hate the city which won't give me a home.—But don't look forlorn; landlords want solidity. Sit up a little straighter. I know what you mean about foreigners and academics but you don't know me, the ideal tenant. Give me this apartment and you'll never hear from me again. The rent will be paid on the first of the month, the neighbors will never complain about noises coming from my window, and the roof will fall in before I call to protest about the state of the building. I could try getting tough. I am sitting in your office so you can't throw away my application like you were going to do, without having to look me in the face. Suppose I sat in the corridor when you throw me from the office, waited in the hallway when they clear the corridor? I don't have, at the moment, a better place to go.

Herr Wolf placed his hands together and weighed things. I don't know how long the silence lasted.

"Alright," he said, with a swing of his desk chair, "we'll give it a try."

The secretary photocopied all the documents I had brought. I left the office with two fat keys in my pocket.

* * *

Hitler became chancellor of Germany on January 30, 1933. Though the Nazis referred to this event as the "Power Seizure," they were elected by normal parliamentary procedures. Within six months all other political parties were outlawed, their offices plundered, their leaders in jail.

The Berlin Senate spent months debating how to handle the fiftieth anniversary of this date. Left-wing parties protested when one million marks of city funds were allocated for commemorative projects: far more, they objected, had just been spent on a massive Prussian exhibit devoted to more savory aspects of Berlin's history. The right-wing parties had pleaded for a much lower budget, and profile. In Munich, where they dominate, an afternoon of tepid speeches was all that marked the anniversary. Berlin's diversity of initiative was astounding, with events that filled the entire year. Among the exhibits: "Women in the Third Reich," "Resistance in Neukölln," "The Church Struggle in Spandau," "Gays and Fascism," "Concentration Camps in the Berlin Area." There was theater (Brecht in German and Turkish) and music: performances of pieces banned by the Nazis, concerts and discussion of popular Nazi music, a project devoted to women composers in the Third Reich. There were weekly public lectures. The art academy offered a workshop on making films about the Third Reich.

Kicking off the ceremonies was an evening entitled "We Want to Remember!" It was held in the auditorium of the Technical University, not far from the Reichstag where power changed hands fifty years before, to the day. The large room was filled with people born after the war. I arrived in time to hear a speaker shouting "Collective guilt? No! Collective responsibility? Yes!" The audience eagerly applauded the motley program put together by an organization called "Sign of Atonement." There was a Russian writer wishing the peace movement success, a cabaret troupe presenting skits which showed the continuity between the Nazis and the Federal Republic. A Pole who'd been a prisoner at Auschwitz was full of praise for contemporary Germans: "Fantastic young people!" he said. "But why were they denied opportunity to learn what they wanted to know?" For those listening, his question was rhetorical. Mere presence in this hall could feel like liberation: from the silent present powers bent on burying the past.

The program concluded with a folk trio singing passable Yiddish. "Our last song," announced the female guitarist, "was written in the Wilnauer Ghetto in 1942. We dedicate it as a prayer for the Palestinian people, and to freedom in general." Her words were absent of irony, born in conviction of easy Enlightenment. Yesterday the Jews in Poland, today the Palestinians in Israel. The enemy was oppression; the dedication was to lend just the right touch of universalism to the struggle.

* * *

When you rent an apartment in Berlin you rent four walls and a ceiling, so I needed everything else. I enjoyed sifting through small murky *Trödel* shops, which sell objects lying on the border between secondhand junk and antique. Elated I had bought a giant creaking wardrobe whose beveled mirrors suggested Art Nouveau. It was while looking for coffee cups that I saw the sign on the door in the Grossbeerenstrasse: NO SALES TO TURKS. The sign was printed, in orange and black, the mass production suggesting that the sentiment was marketable. I walked away furious; there was no question of my buying anything there. Halfway down the block I stopped: wouldn't it be better to tell them so? Not because I hoped to bring the owners, whoever they were, to reason; it just seemed cowardly to leave them in the brazen complacence which allowed them to buy and display that sign. I turned back, formulating reproaches. On the window of the store was a handwritten sign I hadn't noticed the first time: WE COLLECT DONATIONS FOR THE PEOPLE OF POLAND. YOUR OLD CLOTHES AND APPLIANCES ARE URGENTLY NEEDED. PLEASE GIVE GENEROUSLY TO THOSE SUFFERING UNDER THE COMMUNIST YOKE. Did those signs make up a contradiction? Worrying about the welfare of the country next door and being so beastly to the neighbors? Only within the logic of liberalism. The twelve-year-old part of me wanted to rush in and ask "how *can* you?" But then I've been noticing, since I got older, how often racism and anticommunism go together. It's not a necessary connection. But does that make it accidental?

I paced the sidewalk in front of the shop and then walked away ashamed, for beside all of the reasons not to enter there was a fear I didn't understand.

* * *

The K.O.B., in the Potsdamerstrasse, was one of the largest of the occupied houses. Silhouettes of falling figures were painted on its facade, together with a long poem about the Liberation. Inside the house was a poorly ventilated kneipe. Beer was served in large, thick bottles; the prices, very cheap, were scrawled on a blackboard over the makeshift bar. Two paintings hung on the main wall. On one dark canvas whose only distinguishable feature was a small red spot stood the title *Final Solution.*

Perhaps a hundred people filled this room on the fiftieth anniversary of the Nazis' public burning of many of Germany's greatest books. Some were outright punks, with dyed green or orange hair, spike bracelets, torn fake leopard skin. Most of the rest wore the usual black leather jacket, single earring and tight pants which made up the working clothes of the Berliner Szene. Their faces were pale; these were people who were slow to smile. Leaning silently against the walls or sitting on the few broken chairs, they turned to the raised platform where a mild-looking middle-aged man in a blue cardigan sat behind a microphone.

Bernt Engelmann is the best-selling author who was president of the German chapter of P.E.N., meeting that weekend to commemorate the Nazi book burning. To the people waiting in the K.O.B., Engelmann offered hope. There was silence when he finished reading from his latest book, a description of everyday life in the Third Reich. Slowly, shy and testing, they began to ask questions.

"How could you talk to people who were such cowards under the Nazis?"

"I have also interviewed the Gestapo. I'm a reporter. We need this information."

"Is it hard to publish books like this?"

"Yes."

"Will it get harder under the new government?"

"There is increasing pressure on the publishing industry."

"What proportion of the people were Nazis?"

"Ten percent."

"What's your definition of 'Nazi'?"

"Ten percent were active party members. About thirty percent were strongly opposed to the Nazis, and the rest wanted nothing to do with politics at all."

"How did *you* manage to resist?"

"I was lucky," said Engelmann, who was imprisoned at Dachau. "I came from an antifascist family. My grandfather always told me, 'Left-wing is the only decent thing to be.' " He thereby touched, while seeking to assuage, the wound which brought many to hear him.

But most of the questions concerned the present: How many former Nazis hold positions of power? How dangerous are the indications of a new kind of fascism? What can be done to prevent it?

"Do you think writers make any difference?" asked a woman in a leather tunic.

Engelmann's answer was both modest and confident. Was it an accident that the Nazis burned books? He read a statement just drafted by P.E.N.: Germany's most prominent writers had resolved to blockade the proposed Pershing missile sites should the Geneva talks fail. "Words are no longer enough," he said. "If Heinrich Böll is arrested, it will have an impact." There was loud applause.

Engelmann had to go, he said, but the questions were coming faster. It was hope he had offered. Could popular resistance affect the government? The audience was casual, trying not to show how desperately they wanted to believe what this adult had to tell them. Yet they wouldn't let him go. The writer finally stood, saying he hoped to continue the discussion in the near future, in the same place. His listeners applauded wildly in the illegally occupied building on what had been the most elegant street in Berlin.

The bartender turned on the music; the beer, he said, was gone. I watched a crowd follow Engelmann onto the street, still plying him with questions. Pleased and hurried, he disentangled himself politely and got into an old station wagon. In a shabby kneipe across the street tired Turkish men sat playing cards. Behind a window under the English words GIRLS GIRLS GIRLS, middle-aged whores smoking cigarettes awaited the beginning of their night.

* * *

"Dieter you've met," said Helena. "He lives with a couple of people. One's an architect I've never seen. He had a fight with the rest of them and spends most of his time at his girlfriend's place. Then there's Anja. A farmer's daughter from Bavaria who's studying sociology. A quiet sort. Lesbian. Gunther is very funny, when he's not too drunk. He's nearing fifty. He was an actor before he became an alcoholic. Dieter keeps him on out of pity. Maybe he owes him something too, I'm not sure. He doesn't pay any rent. Lives in the little attic which used to be the servant's room."

The large door of the building swung open easily. The landing hadn't been painted for decades; some of the banister was missing.

"Rudi Dutschke used to live here. And before that, Alfred Döblin."

"That will never do," said Dieter with a small smile.

"What will never do?" Helena tossed her hair.

"Your clothes. Absolute petit bourgeois. I can't take you out on the town looking like that." He laughed, as if to show he didn't really mean what he said.

"But I'm wearing black, aren't I?" I tried to joke about what I didn't understand. I had dressed carefully for the evening.

"Yes, but that jacket ... C'mon, you provincial mice. I'll find you something to wear."

"You are American, I think?" The pale heavy man, leaning toward fat, had bright brown eyes. "Come in, come in. Delighted to meet you." He mimicked an American accent extremely well. It seemed cheerful, not threatening. "Tell me," he continued, "I've been wanting to know. If we lined up all the Amis in Berlin on the autobahn—face down, mind you, head to toe—would they reach to the West German border? One lane or two?"

"Hey, Gunther, remember," said Dieter, "she's a guest here."

The apartment was enormous, and fine. The elegance of the cherubim on the twenty-foot ceilings was counterbalanced by light blue neon sculpture, hung delicately askew. A nude classical torso stood next to a triangular complex of mirrors. Bright raw canvases were hung over steel benches. Alright, I thought, these people know about style. So I didn't say that the black and yellow jacket Dieter gave me, three sizes too large, seemed far uglier than the plain one I'd been wearing.

"It'll do," said Dieter, scrutinizing me with care. "But leave your coat here."

"Leave my coat here? It's *cold.* It's February."

He shrugged his shoulders. I took my coat, and we left the house.

"You wanted to see Berliner decadence?" I blinked, peering through the smoke. A muscular balding man wearing a leather bracelet looked us over at the kneipe door. Under a feeble strobe light a small dance floor was packed with couples. They all seemed to be men, but sometimes it was hard to tell. The walls were covered with fake wood paneling, hung with what seemed to be Christmas tree lights. Helena and I danced together and talked about metaphysics. Dieter danced alone.

"That's decadence?" I demanded. Dieter had promised a tour of the Szene. Women wearing spangled fishnet and leather, men with faces painted blue. Risk, Grotesque, Fiasco, Modern Times. Those were the kneipen we went to that night. Big stormy paintings, mirrors cut on the walls. Cassette recorders behind the bar blasted tuneless rhythms of the New Wave group German-American Friendship. "Sex under water," said one song. "Waste your youth," said another.

These are no rooms for conversation; one talks, at most, to people one knows. The casual stares are neutral but there's never a smile. Black leather license, admiring the neon. I did not even know if we were waiting for something to happen.

Walk on, into morning, eating dry pastry and pistachios in a bare and glaring Turkish café.

"Good graffiti in the bathroom," said Helena. "DUST IS MODERN."

"I like the graffiti next to my house," I said. "KREUZBERGER NIGHTS ARE WONDERFUL."

"That comes from a song," said Dieter.

Kreuzberger Nächte sind schön
Sie fängen ganz langsam an
Aber dann ... aber dann ...

"The force is in the *aber dann.*" Looking at me with teasing eyes lowered, he sang very well.

* * *

The nights I always wanted. And sometimes the mornings, walking the streets of Kreuzberg like a drunk. There were days when I loved the tiny shop which sold fresh eggs and heaps of potatoes scooped off the floor, the Turkish store full of silver pots which make the syrup-strong coffee I never drank. I loved every kneipe on every corner, and the signs saying FRISCHE BOULETTEN, and the little bakeries with their sticky cakes and sour bread. I loved every bit of Berliner dialect I heard, and couldn't stop saying "mensch," not quite sure how I intended it: the Yiddish word means virtually the opposite of the Berliner. I loved my street on the canal above all: the one side curving to show chestnut trees branching over water, high wrought-iron lanterns and all the elegance I'd ever wanted from the Old World; the other side displaying a bombed-out lot, three occupied houses, a Turkish imbiss, and a green and white building which was once the left side of a synagogue. I loved the pairs of geese which sometimes flew overhead, and the television tower rising from the heart of East Berlin, looming large on my corner. Just a hop skip and a jump away. People take all that in with the words "Berliner contradictions."

* * *

"It's called *Icarus in Kreuzberg,*" said Dieter. "I painted it yesterday. I thought it would fit your apartment."

The painting he gave me was done in many light colors. Through the quick, uneven brushstrokes one could make out a man standing by a river. From his back rose the suggestion of orange wings.

"It's terrific," I said, holding the painting to a spot on the wall.

"Lower down," said Dieter. "No, like that."

"Why *Icarus in Kreuzberg*?" I asked.

"It's the first piece in a new series. The Kreuzberg part is clear. It's the place where all the contradictions are made apparent, today."

"And Icarus?"

"Do you know the myth?"

"Yes," I nodded.

"You never know, with Americans. Icarus is the possibility of flying above all that, breaking free."

"But he *crashes* in the end."

Dieter looked a little startled, and shrugged his shoulders. "The important thing is that he flies. That he creates the wings to rise above his situation. What happens after that is secondary."

"But wasn't it Daedalus who made the wings?"

"Hmmm?"

"Daedalus. His father."

"It doesn't matter who made the wings. That's not the point. I thought it was appropriate for your new life in Kreuzberg."

"I'm delighted." I really was. "But...are you suggesting that I'm going to fall?"

He laughed. "I'm just the painter. You do the interpreting." We had dinner in a kneipe called Ritz, glowing red with mirrors, painted pigs fucking on the walls. "Ritualized apocalyptic," said Dieter. We left after finishing the lasagne. In front of my door he kissed me three times. On the mouth, before saying good night.

* * *

I painted bright colors on all the available surfaces in my apartment, and exchanged the flouncy Viennese curtain I'd bought earlier for a plain white windowshade. Building bookshelves, I cursed myself, my past, my preoccupations. A carton of books which I'd packed six months before to accompany me on a planned Italian vacation stood mocking. There was Livy, there was Cicero, there was Plutarch, Gibbon and Burckhardt and Vasari and more. Just one thing was missing: anything having to do with contemporary Italy. What was worse was that, except for a couple of guidebooks listing places to eat and sleep, it hadn't occurred to me to bring any such thing. The last thing I'd expected to confront in Europe was the present; it turned out to be all that mattered. American friends returning from Paris conferences wrote wistfully of European respect for old things and old people, and yearned for the tradition they saw in the stones. Again and again, I was struck by its opposite, the searing playful testing to which every tradition is subject. Oh, people read old books, if they're good ones, but without reverence or surprise. The theater producing Shakespeare and Robert Wilson on successive evenings does so in the matter-of-course way that a self-respecting restaurant offers more than one dish. The veneration which educated Americans display toward old culture is met with incomprehension, even suspicion. Here conservative means conservative: relics of the *ancien régime* are glorified only by those who would like to restore it. Gunther Anders's remarks upon arriving in Los Angeles help to explain all this:

> Americans have a fully different emotional stance towards old things. For many, the day before yesterday is suspicious, as the day after tomorrow is suspicious for our peasants. Americans view the young "intellectuals" who hang Giotto reproductions

> over their couches as not merely not conservative but as avant-garde, even traitors. Traitors, namely, to the good old pioneering spirit which only acknowledges the future. As we know, love of the past, or the ostensible past, was unequivocally cultivated in Europe by politically right-wing circles. Here that isn't so. On the contrary. Someone who buys records of pre-Bach music is too "continental," "esoteric," "undemocratic," a questionable American—to cut it short, "pink," that means: communist inspired.... *Interest in the past reveals a desire for subversion.* And whoever doesn't understand this paradox will not grasp the specific character of anti-intellectualism here.

But it would be a while before I discovered Gunther Anders. My look backward seemed a personal failing, and I struggled with shame.

* * *

As spring came to Kreuzberg, I took long lone walks down the canal every morning, watching flat barges swaying, birds bursting into sunny sky. Sometimes I followed till it emptied into the river at Schlesisches Tor. WARNING! MORTAL DANGER! THE WATERWAY BELONGS TO EAST BERLIN! The sign was printed in German and Turkish. A row of anglers leaned patiently below it. I supposed they were unemployed: what they might catch in the filthy Spree could hardly be worth the wait. The East German patrol boat hovered on the opposite bank of the river; every once in a while one could see its telescope turn.

One sector for each of the Allies: postwar Berlin was divided four ways. Some borders were unmarked, but there were often signboards. YOU ARE LEAVING THE AMERICAN SECTOR stood posted in English, Russian, French and German at spots before the Wall. There were days when the notice seemed euphoric. Nor was I the only one to think so. The signposts formed the basis of a New Wave discotheque, and a wild rock hit. "You-Are-Leaving-the-American-Sector!" Radio blasting, promise unknown.

* * *

Berlin, Berlin, hier lebt der Mensch gefährlich
Und wenn er sturzt, da dreht sick keiner um
Dock halt er hin, dann ist der Beifall ehrlich
Berlin, Berlin, du bist mein Publikum.

Berlin, Berlin, a person lives dangerously here
And if he stumbles, nobody gives a damn
But if he holds out, the applause is wholehearted
Berlin, Berlin, you're my public.

Was there a catch in her voice when she recorded that number for an album of old Berlin songs? Marlene Dietrich left Berlin when the Nazis came, and sang for Allied troops during the war. Most emigrés were Jews or political activists; Dietrich simply found the Nazis loathsome. Her departure was voluntary, fervid, and much the exception: its price was the permanent loss of a home. Protesters greeted her as a traitor when she returned in the sixties. Now she lives in Paris, and gives no interviews. Perhaps she sang nonchalantly, proverbial Berliner insouciance at her native command.

For Berliners' sentimentality is never without sting. Take another old ballad, "Lieber Leierkastenmann," about the organ-grinders who used to come into the *Hinterhöfe* and play for the pennies people threw from kitchen windows. The few of them left nowadays mostly play for the tourists on the Kudamm. The tune is as schmaltzy as could be, and the chorus fits the tune: "Dear Mr. Organ-grinder, play them again from the start, your old Berliner melodies, my heart turns light again, our city Berlin is still so beautiful!"

But the verses are a celebration of native ways: the poor girl with the sign around her neck saying COMPLETELY BLIND, picking up coins she sees perfectly; the young man whose lame leg stops him from working, till the night takes him dancing: "He's not a Berliner, after all, for nothing." Dietrich gives a little laugh, each time, before sinking into the kitschy chorus.

Was there always something a little risky about a love for this city? Before the war and the Wall and the things which explain?

Frau Schultze

Avoiding Frau Schultze was never easy. As the superintendent of the building, she lived on the ground floor. Taking in sewing for a living left her plenty of time to stand at the window, guarding the courtyard.

"This is a good building," she told me when I moved in. "You've been lucky. It's very quiet, and there are no foreigners."

I blinked. What, then, was I? Later I learned that "foreigner" often means simply "Turk."

"It's a lovely building," I said weakly. "And it's the most beautiful street in the city. All the old facades have been preserved."

"*Ach*," said Frau Schultze. "This is nothing. You should have seen it before the war. It was a beautiful neighborhood then. Most of the houses are gone today. First came the bombs. And so many buildings were torn down after the war. The foreigners have ruined everything."

"Surely it wasn't the foreigners who tore down the old houses?"

"No," she conceded. "That was the contractors. A lovely place to live, this was."

"I like it the way it is."

"It was much nicer then."

It wasn't only her racism that was hard to take. Frau Schultze spoke in a whine, and she ended every conversation the same way.

"And nobody pushes their garbage down in the cans. They just drop it in and go away. See that?" She would point to a tool in the corner, something like a crowbar, leaning next to the garbage cans in the courtyard. "That's for pushing down the garbage. Do you think anybody uses it? No. And they wonder why the cans are always overflowing. Everything's going to ruin."

Once I suggested that four garbage cans weren't enough for a building of this size. Frau Schultze was decisive: if everyone really pushed, using the crowbar in the corner, four cans would be plenty. "Really push!" she shouted from her window, when I failed to evade her while emptying my trash. Her words sound encouraging rather than threatening; still she didn't have the nerve to shout at anyone else.

* * *

The courtyard of the building was full of pigeons. Mornings I found them, cooing and content, ruffled fat on the windowsill. They burst up, startled, when the heavy door slammed, and rested on the wall till the courtyard had been crossed. Then, a little wary, they returned to the paving.

Often I saw Frau Schultze preparing bread crumbs. The birds waited patiently, like trained dogs. It was a ritual they knew.

"They come from the bridge at the canal," she said. "That's why they're so many. Somebody's got to feed them. They are very clean animals, that one must know." She paused to sprinkle a batch of crumbs on the stone. "The pigeons can't help living," she told me. "It's not their fault. And think of all the filth that human beings make!"

* * *

From the doorway of her apartment one could see that Frau Schultze had lived alone for many years: there was no place for other life amid the spotless clutter which filled the space. Her sewing machine and its attachments took up most of the small front room, her bed was hidden behind a heavy flowered curtain. Behind the glass of the polished mail-order walnut cabinet stood framed photos of the husband and son who were killed in the war. Next to the cabinet was the large color television where Frau Schultze would watch "Dallas," and its German imitations, every evening.

Frau Schultze's apartment helped me understand the tobacco seller's wrath: current young Berlin style is not fashion but provocation, born of rage against the coy, cold vulgarity of the petite bourgeoisie. In the bathrooms of northern German villages housewives cover toilet-paper rolls with stiff colored hats hand-knit for that purpose. Their children move to Berlin, don orange and green socks like rockets which might splatter all the careful heaps of junk their mothers had tended. The colors of the rooms they despise clash too, but not deliberately: at Frau Schultze's it was clearly a garish failing, not affected disregard, which accounted for the relentless tackiness of every presence.

Like so many others, Frau Schultze failed to enter the class whose values she guarded like a wary sentinel. For working as concierge Frau Schultze inhabited the smallest, darkest, dampest apartment in that glorious building. On the brightest of summer middays she had to switch on a light to show me the photographs of her husband and son. Hers was the only apartment which hadn't been refurbished with central heating; I suppose the owner will renovate the place when she dies. Each winter morning she limped to the coal bin, brushing up the coal dust when she finished stoking the little brown oven which warmed her dusky room.

* * *

One day the building smelled fearfully; in the courtyard I recognized the boyfriend of the woman who lived above me. Our interaction had been restricted to polite nodding on the stairs. As Frau Schultze had told me, it was a quiet building; I never even saw the other neighbors. The boyfriend, who came from Tunisia, had tidily taken apart his bicycle to clean the pieces in the courtyard. The oil he was using was the source of the smell. Nodding hello I nearly collided with Frau Schultze.

"What filth," she barked, leaving completely unclear whether her referent was the man or the bicycle parts. "I'd like to know who's going to clean that up."

"It's not so bad," I replied, equally ambiguous, before hurrying up the stairs. She retained a certain power of intimidation, for my status as an acceptable foreigner seemed to lie in her hands. But what could I offer Frau Schultze if I were more resolute, more patient? A discourse on connections between racism and anal fixation? A potent allusion to Lady Macbeth?

* * *

Pity and fear are the worst sort of reasons to turn your back on someone, but both, I am sure, fed my determination to shy clear of Frau Schultze. Pity and fear and a good dose of helplessness. Though she surely muttered the same hateful contradictions about Jews, forty years ago, which she mutters about foreigners today, it was hard to take Frau Schultze as an object of moral outrage. Her life was bounded by petty repetition: of phrases blasted by the illustrated dailies, of slender routine without joy or surprise. She accepted the death of her family the way she accepted a change in the weather, the way she accepted everything else. Those deaths cannot be in the nature of punishment for her support of a war which caused millions of others: there wasn't that much room for meaning in Frau Schultze's world. Nor do I really think there ought to be: what sense could there be in Frau Schultze's suffering when thousands of real Nazis escaped unscathed? I don't suppose it was sense she was seeking in those brief certain years before the war but, for a moment, it must have felt like transcendence.

Her life didn't move me any more than it outraged me: its proportions were really too shallow for either. Yet for all my attempts at distant understanding, I avoided Frau Schultze out of fear she might say something which would leave me unable to continue to say good morning.

* * *

"Frau Neiman!"

I whispered a curse. I'd taken to tiptoeing when taking out the garbage, emptying the small bags slowly to mute the sound. Though Frau Schultze spoke in the scrappy tones of the partially deaf, she managed to intercept me often enough.

"Did you remember to push it down tight?"

Forcing a smile, I pushed at the garbage with the remains of the plastic bag.

"Really push! With the crowbar!"

There was no help for it. In the time it took me to go to the corner and return to the garbage can with the crowbar, Frau Schultze had closed her window and descended the three steps to the *Hinterhof.*

"Did you hear the sirens last night? So many demonstrations these days. You wouldn't know it, but this used to be a quiet neighborhood. Excepting Saturdays, that is, when we went dancing. Before the accident." One of Frau Schultze's legs is shorter than the other. Her mouth formed a silent giggle.

"Now, you see, I couldn't dance a bit. Even if the old dance house were still standing. It's a blessing that Hermann died before all that happened. He wouldn't have been able to bear it, just looking at the neighborhood go to pieces—"

"Frau Schultze," I interrupted, "good day now."

Unoffended, stopping only to take a breath, she accompanied me to the door. "Klaus fell in April. His papa—that's my Hermann—he'd been gone for more than a year. The war was already over, really, when they called up the boys. Of course you couldn't say that out loud; that was called defeatism, and they were hanging people for it right and left. At least we thought the war was over. The radio called it a victorious retreat, but the refugees kept coming, and they said the Russians had taken Posen already, and I don't know how much more. 'Course, Klaus wasn't sorry to go; he'd had his fill of the bombings. Night after night, hearing the sirens, running down to the cellar—oh, it was frightful."

"Frau Schultze—"

"Right there on the corner—you know, where they put the Bilka store? Used to be a beautiful building. Forty-three people, killed just like that. The bomb fell right on the cellar, you know. Klaus was sixteen, and he was ready to give the Russians something back for all those nights we'd sat shaking in the cellar."

"Frau Schultze," I asked, "wasn't it the British and the Americans who dropped the bombs?"

"The Americans weren't so bad," said Frau Schultze. "They had chewing gum. And CARE packages, later, when the Russians made the blockade. Those were times, I tell you. It was right here, the cellar"—she pointed to a wooden door with a heavy lock on one side of the courtyard—"where we used to keep the coal. No coal nowadays. Since Herr Wolf has taken over the management, it's become quite a building. Central heating in every apartment, and hot water too. And none of those banners in the windows, like you see in *some* houses on the street. If people would only keep it tidy. I scrub the stairs every morning. But what can I do if nobody thinks to push down the garbage? I can't be after them all day."

* * *

***"Y**ou must double-lock your door if you're going away." Frau Schultze's concern was mysterious. Apartment houses are locked promptly at 8 P.M. It's an old tradition, maintained even in new buildings, where electric doorbells make the custom superfluous. By day, it seems inconceivable that even the stealthiest of intruders could evade Frau Schultze's watch.

Frau Schultze left her native Berlin twice: before the war, on a government ship that took families to vacations on the Baltic; after the war, for a state-sponsored cure in Bad Isenheim. She didn't ask where I was headed; young people travel all over these days. Christmas Day she would spend with her sister-in-law. "Lord knows I don't care for her building, but she came to me Easter, and fair is fair." Frau Schultze rubbed her hands together, twice. "Such a hinterhof, you'd hardly believe it was just around the corner."

There are *Hinterhöfe* with gardens in them, or sandboxes; a few of the larger ones keep chickens or goats. But mostly they look as if light never reached them, trash cans and bicycles adorning broken concrete. Before the war, the hinterhöfe were filled with proletarian children.

"Last time I was there," continued Frau Schultze, "the hinterhof was nothing but a mass of garbage. The neighbors had been drinking, you can bet on that. It seems he said he was leaving. So she told him to go ahead, but quickly, and threw his hat out the window. He got mad, and threw out her teapot. Well, and what do you think? Down came the dishes, and the washstand, and finally the mattress! The icebox was too heavy, or they'd have thrown that too. And do you suppose he left after all that? Not at all! They patched it up again, the very next day; forty years they've been going on that way. Nothing like that in our house, you know!" Frau Schultze stuck out her bosom with satisfaction, but the note of longing in her voice was definite. Besides the four garbage cans and the crowbar, our *Hinterhof* contained nothing but a small patch of grass. The row of bent tulips once planted there only underlined its arid silence.

"It's a mystery to me why she lives there at all. It's not as if you can't find a decent apartment these days. But *tja*"—Frau Schultze leaned toward me—"she came over from *Drüben*, you know, and there's no telling what people will do. When they've lived so long under a dictatorship, why—"

"Frau Schultze," I said, "Merry Christmas."

"And a merry Christmas to you. When you get back, I'll take in that dress you're wearing. Looks a bit ridiculous, like you've got it now, but I'll fix it up right."

"That's very—"

"Now don't you worry, I won't charge you for it. It'll only take a minute."

"Thank you, but I couldn't possibly—

"Don't mention it. You'll come and see me. It looks positively comical, the way that it's hanging."

Night Thoughts

"Neiman."
"Is that a German name?"
"No."
"But it sounds German."
"Yes."

"Neiman."
"Ah, Neumann."
"No. Neiman."
"But that must be a German name. An Americanized version of Neumann. Did your ancestors come to America from Germany?"
"No."
"Are you certain?"
"Yes."

"Neiman."
"Why, that's a German name."
"No, it's not."
"Where did your ancestors come from?"
"Russia. Poland."
"*Ach so.*"

"Neiman."
"Isn't that a German name?"
"No. It's a Yiddish one."
"Oh! So you're ... you know, there was a festival of Yiddish films last year at the Arsenal. Did you go to it?"
"No."
"I saw one of the films. I liked it very much. And once I went to a lecture at the Jewish community center."
"Really."

"Neiman."
"You mean Neumann."
"I mean Neiman. N-e-i-m-a-n."
"Neimann. But that's certainly a German name."
"No, it's not."

"But it sounds German. Perhaps your ancestors were German and you don't even know it. You Americans have no sense of history."
"My ancestors were not German."
"What were they, then? Where did they come from?"
"I don't know exactly."
"You see? You don't know."
"But I know they weren't German."

* * *

Never in my life had I drunk so much champagne.

It was cheap in Berlin, so we drank it everywhere: bottle by little bottle in the gleaming white kneipen on Savignyplatz, passed around more crudely, mouth to mouth, when it got late and we were left standing, pressed tightly into the raunchy Café Central. In the Tiergarten, with picnics, when the weather got warm. In paper cups held in discotheques where it didn't matter if you blinked and stumbled. In bed, all the time: coming home at four in the morning there was nearly always another bottle in the refrigerator, waking lazy and late I would drink in his arms.

I bought a red jacket.

The nights were long, the mornings full of brightness and silence. Waking in Dieter's room I watched the sun filling the window to light up the paintings, enormous wild nudes, which hung on every wall. He brought me breakfast in bed and told stories of his past. Traveling in the East for a year, dancing at Moslem weddings and brothels. Editing a socialist paper. Writing a book about color, producing art with friends. A marriage, old love affairs, with women and men. "I want everything," he said, putting a Beethoven piano concerto on the stereo. Afternoons I would leave early enough for Dieter to paint while it was still light. Down at the Nollendorfplatz I waited for the subway between two tall punks.

Champagne notwithstanding, it felt very strange. It's love, he told me, and nothing but promise: springtime he would bring me, the sun, a full moon. In the language of Goethe and Wagner those words seemed still sayable. Or was I out to prove the wildest of claims about American naiveté?

Sweet fearful confusion. For I'd never seen people or places like these. (It's only style, only style.) Had I thought I would ever wear stars in my hair? So what was left to trust?

My old friend Fred said to trust myself; this new uncertainty worried him. In a hinterhof around the corner he was writing a history of eighteenth-century philosophy, and often dropped by to bring a chapter of his manuscript or to fix the electrical wiring in my apartment. "You haven't changed," he puzzled, "and your German is good enough to make distinctions now. Why let yourself be dazzled by a couple of Krauts?" At sea and uncertain, I tried hard to believe him.

* * *

Summer and winter, you can buy nearly everything you need for the rest of the week on Friday afternoon at the outdoor markets where forty or fifty entrepreneurs stand behind tables laden with broadcloth and cheese, vegetables and meat, sponges and buttons. Every neighborhood has one; Kreuzberg's is known as the Turkish market. Perhaps half of the sellers, and half of the buyers, are Turkish. Toward evening the narrow sidewalk on the canal becomes so crowded that it takes an hour to get from one end of the market to the other; mothers pushing baby carriages like small tanks try to form a wedge in the crowd. The vegetable stand I took to frequenting is owned by two German brothers. One is tall, handsome and foul-tempered. If the other were a little shorter, he could double as a cobbler in a fairy tale. Everything about him seemed four-cornered, even the lines in his face. Besides their dark blue aprons, the only thing the brothers had in common was a disposition to violate every expectation about how customers are to be treated. Where the first refused to give the woman before me the bunch of grapes she wanted, instead of the plainly half-rotten one he proffered, the second would advise against buying too many of the apparently perfect peaches beaming on the shelf.

"They won't keep," he warned. "Take a pound instead. Day after tomorrow even a dog wouldn't eat them."

"I'm taking them to a party," she said. "They'll all get eaten tonight."

"A party, that's different," he answered. "Take two pounds. Take three. How about some tomatoes?"

"Tomatoes taste like cardboard this time of year."

"Here," he replied, offering a tomato. "Go ahead, take a bite. You see? That's what a tomato should be. German tomatoes, the best in the world."

Their fruit was not the cheapest at the market, nor even the best. I came because I liked to watch the brothers. The first spoke only when it was unavoidable, in a way that made you think he could murder if forced to utter one word over an uncertain but definite limit. The second was quick, positively reveling in chatter.

"Going on vacation soon?" asked the wavy blond with the miniature dog in her basket.

"I don't need a vacation, when you're in my neighborhood," he answered, winking lewdly. Other times he would curse: the rudeness of a hurried customer leading straight to the certain decline of the last remnants of civilization as we know it. Often he was conspiratorial, playing off husband and wife. "The old man was making the rounds last night, eh?" he hailed a young woman. "Well, you'd have to be blind not to see *that*. And he leaves you at home with the baby. Ah, it's a curse, the bottle. I never touch a drop myself."

He winked to the unshaven husband. "Got to hand it to the women, they'll drive you into the kneipe every time. Don't suppose they can help it. What is it you wanted today?"

He liked to talk, the little brother, as much and more than he liked selling fruit. I don't know what another age would have made of him: perhaps simply a fruit and vegetable seller. Chance and curiosity kept me here the first few times. After a while I developed a sense of loyalty which was fully absurd. It would have been easy to buy at the next stand, where the young Turkish boy with the missing tooth counted out change gaily and exactly, but I returned to the brothers every week.

* * *

*I*n-the-Ruins was the worst kneipe in town. At least that's how it wanted to be seen. The small room with jagged walls was all that the bombs left of a large building. The former garden looking out to the Winterfeldplatz was full of rubble. People sat there, nevertheless, on hot nights. The punk leaning in the doorway had scratched the words DESTROY EVERYTHING THAT GETS IN MY WAY onto the back of his black leather jacket. As I walked by, he turned and spit at my feet. A man and a woman were fucking clumsily on a bench in the corner. The wooden walls were without decoration. You had to be very drunk to stay there.

"It used to be an SS kneipe," said Dieter.

"What?" I asked him. It was hard to hear over the noise.

"This used to be an SS kneipe."

The door opened. Gunther, shirt unbuttoned to the bottom of his belly, entered the room playing a trumpet. At the table where we were standing he kissed my hand with a flourish, bowing low to the ground, and blew the first bars of "Oh, Susanna!"

"Leave us alone," said Dieter. "We just got here."

"Begging your pardon, m'sieur, may I ask your young lady if she objects to my joining you?"

"What are you drinking, Gunther?" I replied.

"Oh, but allow me. Waiter, waiter, tequilas all around. Take away the beer. I am, as of tomorrow, part of the work force. The wine will flow, there will be caviar for breakfast every morning. And"—he turned to Dieter with a different voice—"I'll be able to pay you the rent for the use of your magnificent apartment."

"Don't worry about it," said Dieter.

"Worry? I *have* no worries anymore." Gunther winked at me and began to play "Oh, Susanna!" I sang along.

"Watch out, you lump of clay!" Gunther roared at the boy, staggering with drink, who had stumbled into him. The boy shook his fist unconvincingly. "No feeling for music, this clientele. My friends"—Gunther's dark eyebrows arched wide over his forehead—"perhaps we should begin to spend our evenings in a more *cul*tivated environment? Waiter! Another round of tequilas, quickly. This woman is dying of thirst. If she doesn't get a drink at once there may be international consequences."

Dieter displayed an irritated half smile. Gunther always made me laugh.

"Hey, I've been meaning to ask somebody. Will you sing me the words to 'Lili Marleen'?"

Gunther started at my question, suddenly almost sober. "I won't sing it," he said.

"Why not? I thought it was written during the First World War."

"I don't know when it was written," said Dieter. "It's a Nazi song."

"So just tell me what the lyrics are. I've never heard them. I want to know."

"I've repressed them," said Dieter. "I don't know them anymore."

"C'mon," I insisted, reckless with tequila. "I know how it starts: '*Vor der Kaserne, vor dem grossen Tor ...*' "

Their faces were blank. I gave it up.

The only time I ever sang "Lili Marleen" in Berlin was years later, roaring drunk on the Savignyplatz at three o'clock in the morning, strolling arm and arm with a Chilean painter and a German Jew.

* * *

Werner was quick, going right to the bone, with a face that hinted vulnerability, if not gentleness, behind the lines. The perpetual undeclared war he inhabited was not his own, but he didn't resent it. He'd abandoned a career as a concert pianist to write on politics and literature for local magazines. His girlfriend Ute gave piano lessons and rocked him to the ground, dragging him off to her beloved Toscana when Berlin beat too hard. They'd return brown, dreamy and bitter on the edges: the Italians are so *warm*, if one could only live that way always.

Shortly after one of those returns I found myself in their living room determined to press. I had asked a casual question about their families; Werner replied with a chill thud.

"But you visit them sometimes?" I persisted.

"If I happen to be near Düsseldorf. And in the mood."

"And that happens...?"

"Every couple of years. I don't know."

"Do they call you?"

"Why should they call me? We have nothing to say to each other."

It passed for reason and came out merely cold: I had heard that tone before. People seldom speak of their families here; Werner's answers were meant to stay further questions, but for once I didn't care.

"Do you have siblings?"

"An older sister. A younger brother." He squeezed unwilling words like dirty water from a sponge.

"And what do they do?"

"My sister is married and has two kids. My brother is a teacher in a little town near Essen. We're very different. Why should I keep in touch with them? Because we happen to have the same parents?"

It was a failure of understanding as well as belief. Werner held family ties to be obsolete and sentimental relics of repressive bourgeois culture. I saw his denial as a raging howl.

"A lot of people," I ventured more gently, "talk like you here."

"Ask Ute," he shrugged. "She sees her mother sometimes."

"My mother had a terrible time during the war," said Ute. Her father fell early, on the Eastern Front. "She had two babies. The Russian soldiers raped her. We were hungry all the time. There was no coal to heat the ovens. I don't know how she got us through." Ute blew cigarette smoke through strands of brown hair.

"I don't really know what my parents did during the war," said Werner. But that was what everything turned on. When he was fourteen, he had asked. "Leave your father in peace, he's suffered enough!" said his mother. It was the tobacco seller on the corner, an old Social Democrat, who finally told him. They hadn't been *big* Nazis, but it was a while before his father found work after the war, and he never really recovered. Werner went home and called his father a Nazi swine. His father hit him and told him not to speak disrespectfully. Werner was big enough to hit him back.

"And after that?"

"After that?" Werner's voice was flat and casual. "My mother wrote me a letter when I was at the university. She was afraid I'd become a Communist. That was the last time we talked about politics. Or anything else, for that matter. My father stays in front of the television if I come to visit. My mother serves cake and complains about the weather. Fortunately, it's usually raining, so that's good for a couple of hours. I don't stay any longer than that."

"What's it like with your family?" asked Ute.

"It's complicated." I strained to remember what it was I took for granted. "Well, look. It's sort of like the Italians. I mean, compared to families here. It's not always easy to visit. We have fights sometimes. People shouting, swearing never to see each other again. But we're connected, all of us, at this very deep point."

"*Tja*," said Werner. "Like the Italians."

* * *

"Synagogues in Berlin: Destroyed Architecture" was an exhibit at the Berlin Museum in connection with the fiftieth anniversary of Hitler's assumption of power. One room was filled with blown-up photographs and architectural plans. On November 9, 1938, there were eighty-two synagogues in Berlin. Three of the four that are now in use survived Kristallnacht because they were small and unassuming, tucked away in the *Hinterhöfe.* The fourth is merely the remaining wing of a much larger building which was burned.

A glass case in a corridor of the museum contained deportation orders, a yellow star. At the bottom was a postcard written in 1942 by a young Berliner to his brother, safe in Shanghai. "Dear Gerhard," it said, "We are leaving tomorrow for an unknown destination in the East. I don't know when I'll be able to write again. Don't worry about me. Anna and I have become engaged. You remember Anna Stern? We are so in love, more than I'd ever hoped for. Thank God, we've managed to arrange to be deported together. I embrace you. Franz." In the corner had been squeezed another line: "Many warm greetings to my future brother-in-law. Anna." A note in the glass case explained that this was the last word ever heard from the senders.

Tears filled my eyes and ran down my face.

Leaving the museum I passed a cabinet full of the few pieces saved from the former Berlin Jewish Museum. An old tallit, a silver menorah, a fine Haggadah, three Kiddush cups.

For the first time in nine months I felt my fists clenching in rage.

* * *

"The guy on our left—no, the one at the table—just published a book called *Last Night in Dschungel.* Good poems too."

Close to midnight on Sundays was the time of the week when people who were or wanted to be fashionable turned up at the unprepossessing club on a sidestreet in the middle of town. This fact said worlds about West Berlin. A spiral staircase encircling a fountain studded with broken blue glass lead to a balcony packed with plain white tables; the drinks were the most expensive in town. Downstairs stood a large fish tank and a small dance floor. "The main attraction of Dschungel was the uncertainty as to whether or not you'd be let in. There was no sign or clue on the building's exterior; you had to know where it was, ring the bell and wait. The doorkeeper looked you over on the sidewalk. If you didn't fit the scene he shook his head and turned around. It all happened very quickly.

Seated safely inside, I tried to guess his criteria. "Transvestites, Rastas and people wearing black leather get in automatically. With the others it's harder to say."

"Most people tonight are regulars," said Dieter. "The tourists come on Fridays and Saturdays."

His voice was so strained when I called him that I'd wondered whether I ought to visit at all; when Dieter was uneasy, he was very far away. Walking arm in arm down the Kudamm we talked about German sexuality, and whether or not the Germans really have a *Dasein,* and whether or not the Germans are too theoretical. By the time we reached Dschungel all the tables were taken; we sat at the bar.

"I threw Gunther out the day before yesterday," said Dieter. "I couldn't take anymore."

"What happened?"

"Thursday was the last straw. I found him at four o'clock in the morning, drunk as always, stark naked in front of the kitchen stove. Then I looked into the pot he was stirring. It was full of old socks."

"And?"

"He was cooking his socks!"

I lit a cigarette. "Where's he living now?"

"No idea." Dieter looked toward the floor where an unsteady strobe light played over tumbling heads. "Do you feel like dancing?"

"I can't dance to this music. Not sober, anyway."

"Then I'll dance alone for a bit."

My glass was empty when Dieter returned. "Do you want another wine?" he asked.

"No," I said. "Let's go somewhere else. I'm almost out of cigarettes. I need to find a machine that sells Salems."

"Salems?"

"Sorry, I mean Reynos. Salem is the American name for Reynos. I don't know why it's different here. All of the other imported cigarettes keep their old names. It's the same cigarette, though, and the same packaging. In America I always smoked Salems. Here I smoke Reynos."

"How's it spelled?"

"S-a-l-e-m."

"And it's exactly the same packaging?"

"Same colors, same number of letters, same design, everything."

"Then it's obvious. Salem would never sell here. The name is too Jewish."

"Too *Jewish*?"

"Sure. Where do you think the name comes from?"

"I don't know. Winston-Salem, North Carolina, I guess. There's a Salem, Massachusetts, but they don't grow tobacco there."

"But it must come from Jerusalem, originally."

"Jerusalem?" I repeated. "I never thought about it."

"For German ears, it's a Jewish name."

I was dumbstruck.

"They pay a lot of attention to things like that," said Dieter. "I used to do graphics for a big advertising agency in Hamburg. Once they wanted to import an American laundry detergent. They had to call off the whole deal when they learned it was called Puff."

We laughed. *Puff* is German slang for "whorehouse."

"Yeah," I said. "It's hard to know how you'd market it. 'Whorehouse gets your clothes cleaner than any other brand.' "

"Let's go," said Dieter. "We'll find you some Salems." He pronounced it "Sah-lem." It was half past two. "Look," he nodded, "coming in the door. That's Marina. A real Kreuzberg character. She never goes anywhere without her rat, and she always dyes her rat to match her hair." I look closer. Sure enough. The long rat snuggled on her leather-covered shoulder was a brilliant, electric blue.

* * *

*T*he last program on the second television channel is called "Night Thoughts." A balding grandfatherly figure dons a pair of glasses and reads a short homily, or perhaps a poem, from a large open book. My ear was caught, one night, when he said "Now we're going to hear a Russian folktale" before opening the book.

"A rabbi once asked the Prophet Elijah about the differences between heaven and hell," he read aloud. 'Hell,' answered the prophet, 'is a place where everyone has a pot full of the most delicious food in the world. But the spoons there are so long that no one can bring the food to his mouth.' 'And what is heaven?' asked the rabbi. 'Heaven is exactly the same,' said the prophet, 'but there people have hit on the idea of feeding each other.' "

A *Russian* folktale? How many Russian rabbis do you know?

Afterward, as always, there was a moving rendition of the national anthem.

"But that's '*Deutschland über Alles*.' "

"Yeah."

"I thought it was illegal."

"They banned a couple of verses. After the war they wrote new ones."

"But how can you sing the melody without thinking of—"

"You can't."

"I see."

"East Germany has a new national anthem. Eisler wrote the music."

"Didn't anybody want to write a new one here?"

"*Ach was.* Just after the liberation, there were hopes for a change. But the Americans didn't want a new Germany, they needed old Nazis to fight the cold war."

"And now?"

"The national anthem is the national anthem."

"And nobody ever complains?"

"There's a right-wing radio program, once a week, which concludes with the national anthem. Just afterward comes a program by the Greens. They begin with the sound of a flushing toilet. So you hear the national anthem, and then you hear the toilet. Nothing anybody can do about it if it's the trademark of the show."

* * *

The Arsenal Theater shows films which are particularly obscure, providing access to every country and time. In honor of the fiftieth anniversary they featured a program: "International Perspectives on the Nazi Period." I went to see a documentary from a series called *Why We Fight* made by the American War Office in 1942. It was a veritable paean to what it called the free and united Russian people. Smiling peasant women harvested grain, tired scruffy young men defended Leningrad, all under the benevolent eye of their "brave leader, Stalin." American generals described the Russian effort as the war's most crucial. The commentator's voice boomed, the music throbbed with dramatic tones only Hollywood achieves. Printed at the beginning was a warning: "This film has been declared obsolete, but may still be valuable for educational purposes." You bet.

Arthur Miller wrote that modern nihilism was born in the eight or ten years of realignment after Hitler's death. The death camps murdered millions but not the notion of morality itself: that might have survived a view of the chasm in the heart of the civilized world. Not the existence of absolute evil but the slick sudden capacity to come to terms with it—there shuddered faith.

* * *

The bartender had seen me often enough to justify a nod, but he didn't. I drank my wine standing, trying to look at ease. I never visited Dieter before stopping in here for a glass or two first. Should that be a warning?

But part of the pleasure of an affair like this is the border of nervousness which precedes every meeting. I never knew just when I would see him, was never sure how he'd sound when I'd call. Dieter sent me surrealist postcards, full of longing and charm; then I'd hear nothing for days till he called, a little loaded, some early morning. That bred excitement, though, what was the problem?

"It's romance, not passion." The friends' diagnosis annoyed me. I wasn't looking for the love of my life; that was something else I'd left behind. If nothing is real, everything is permitted—and where was that true but Berlin?

"*Zahlen.*" Pay. No please, no thank you. Conforming to the parsimonious language of the kneipe, I counted my change and left. Dieter kissed me at his door.

"Let's go." He brushed a hand through his hair before shepherding me to the street.

"Wasn't that Gunther?"

"Yes."

"I thought you'd thrown him out."

"He started an affair with Anja. Nothing I can do if she lets him sleep in her room. Not that he gives a shit about her. He needs a place to stay. And a bathtub."

"Is Anja in love?"

"Anja is a typical Berliner. Lesbian, keen on very young girls. With a tragic relationship to a father figure." Dieter left me no time to wonder about his breezy dismissal, but murmured something about *Gesamtkunstwerk*. We were on our way to visit Anton. They were planning a show together: Dieter was to paint, Anton would make electronic music.

Skinny, fair Anton made one feel he was permanently looking over his shoulder, even when he sat quite still. His apartment was stacked with abstract canvases in one or two colors, cut in thin asymmetrical shapes. The hashish he offered was stronger than I'd expected; after three or four hits I could hardly speak.

"Have you ever played with a Moog synthesizer?"

We made weird noises for a while before going out to dance next door.

"No-oo Home-land. Who will protect me from Ameri-ca?" Unending drums. After writing that chorus the New Wave group Ideal was banned from Berlin's American-sponsored radio, which didn't prevent the song from being heard all over town, in discos with names like The Big Apple, Las Vegas, California, The Bronx. A couple of drinks and then music, unstopping. I didn't want peace: just pounding, turning, there where thoughts stop. But dancing didn't help, the hashish had rocked my balance. Or was I simply lonely? Dieter's cold quick depictions of the people in his world were dismaying. I searched for a junction through the tempting empty Szene to which he didn't really belong.

"Look," said Dieter, when we'd reached his building, "that apartment belongs to three sadists. The music is turned up loud so you can't hear the screams."

"Three sadists and no masochists?" I made a feeble joke. For who goes to Berlin without reading Isherwood beforehand? Or seeing *Cabaret* at the very least? "Isn't that unfortunate?"

"Three sadists."

"What else do they do?"

"They run the gay disco downstairs."

We climbed the stairs to his apartment. "You know why the landings are so wide? This used to be an officer's house. The law said stairway landings had to be wide enough for two Prussian officers to salute each other in passing. Without touching. Like this." Dieter raised his hand to his forehead, sticking out his chin in a mock salute. Laughing abruptly, he took my hand; we ran the rest of the staircase. For the first time I fell asleep unhappy in his arms.

* * *

*T*he oaks in the Hasenheide Park are high and still, larger than most of the trees left in Berlin. Who wanted to protect them in those winter years when the coal was gone and people dug stumps from the ruined streets to put in their stoves, a little every morning, to keep from freezing to death? Sentimental Communists, thinking of Luxemburg and Liebknecht speaking here to thousands at the revolution that failed? Surely not. Then was it just fortune?

* * *

A small crowd had formed in front of the brass band which was no longer playing.

"It's too militaristic, Charlie, give us something else," said one man.

"It's not militaristic," said the bandleader. "That's good revolutionary marching music. Gets in the blood."

"Marching music. Blood. This is the Eighth of May!"

"Maybe they can't play anything else," shouted a woman.

"Then I want another band."

"*Na*," said a newcomer, demurring. "They're all like that. The good songs." He began to sing:

Una links, zwei, drei
Una links, zwei, drei
Wo dein Platz, Genosse, ist
Reih' dich ein in die Arbeitereinheitsfront
Weil du auch ein Arbeiter bist.

"Exactly," said the bandleader.

"That's different," said the first man.

Problems have surrounded the Eighth of May since the guns ceased firing in 1945. They begin with the name. The Eighth of May delivered the Germans from Nazi tyranny, but to call it the Liberation seems coy. Tyrannized peoples, normally, yearn to shake their own yoke, but few Germans longed for liberation till it was clear they had lost the war. A more forthright designation has frightening undertones: to call it the date of the Occupation is to suggest, with the right, that any form of government would be preferable to those imposed by foreign hands. The Day of the Unconditional Surrender might seem to be neutral, but nobody celebrates losses, so those who choose this term use it to lament the fact that the Eighth of May also signified the division of Germany.

Richard von Weizsäcker may have hoped to end this discussion by becoming the first president of the Federal Republic to refer to the Eighth of May as the Day of Liberation, and to insist that the division of Germany be mourned in context, by acknowledging its roots in the Nazi-caused war. His speech made headlines in 1985, but it didn't end confusion about the proper way to designate or commemorate the date.

Polls show a general preference for silence, but some people organize street fairs celebrating the liberation of Berlin and the hopes of every left-wing group in town. Leaving the bandstand I noted: the Afghans protesting Soviet imperialism looked uneasy, uncertain where they belonged. The man holding the banner reading "Solidarity with the U.S. Peace Movement" was wearing a Communist Party button. The PLO members stood together, shouting in Arabic.

A sign on the streetcorner said WEAPONS FOR NICARAGUA. No. WAFFLES FOR NICARAGUA. In German the difference is only a consonant. "Two marks," said the woman behind the stand, pouring batter onto a griddle. "The proceeds benefit a hospital in Managua." I bought a waffle and continued down the Hardenbergstrasse.

* * *

"I just saw a kneipe on a ship where we can watch the sun go down," said Dieter, entering my door. So I grabbed my jacket and we swept down the curve, stopping to pick handfuls of blossoms spilling out from the trees on the bank. And there was a moment, on the deck of the shabby old houseboat moored to the side of the canal, watching light fade over the lanterns and banners that made up Kreuzberg, the new green that was the color of the leaves hanging over the ship; there was a moment when I drew in my breath. This is what you wanted, always. No matter what happens later or further or somewhere else. Your scruples are misunderstandings.

The innkeeper was fat, and of indeterminable age. With a thick Berlin accent she told us that the bouletten were fresh that day. We ate them together with cheap tangy wine.

"Nice kneipe," said Dieter. "Though they might fix it up a bit. With such a great location ..."

"No," I replied. "It's just right the way it is. If you made it chic and shiny it wouldn't be Kreuzberg."

"Two months in Kreuzberg and you're already its biggest champion? I suppose you're right," he conceded, kissing me across the table.

"Three months. Going on four."

A sign at the entrance advertised dancing, on Fridays, to live accordion music. Two taciturn workers sat downstairs at the bar. We talked of illusion and ambition and Gauguin and Camus and the revolution in Portugal.

"I think you overdo it sometimes with this dark demonic German business," I ventured. The night was so gentle.

"It's true. It's a myth I fall for. Mephistopheles and all."

"All alone? Or do you play it up with me?"

"You're good for me. You've no idea how good." He sighed, ignoring my question. "You challenge my reactions. Make me examine the way I grew up. It isn't always easy." Was Dieter at his most seductive when he talked of the pain of coming of age in this land? Watching stars appear in the sky I could not make more than an abstract sort of distance from this thought. Swans rippled on the water. Turkish music seeped from an empty window. What were regrets to a night like that?

Iron Curtain

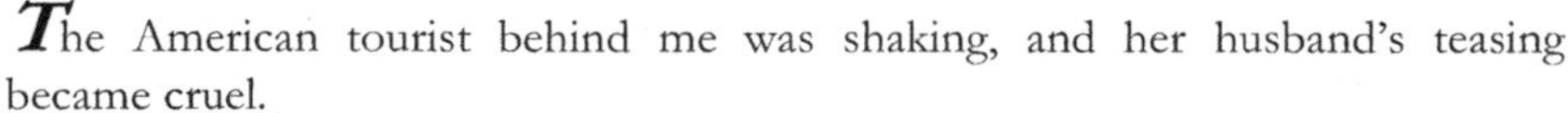

The American tourist behind me was shaking, and her husband's teasing became cruel.

"Who knows, maybe they'll send you to Siberia," he said.

"Shhhh," she whispered, pointing to the camera on the wall.

"Good thing you've got your winter coat."

"They're *watching* us," she whined.

We were standing in line at the East Berlin border. The husband, it turned out, was born in East Berlin. His parents had fled when he was a baby, and now he was going back to his birthplace, that was the point of the trip, for Chrissakes, they had gone to Paris because she wanted to go to Paris and now, by God, they were going to East Berlin.

"I come here often," I told the woman. "Let me tell you exactly what's going to happen. It's nothing at all, when you know. At the end of this line the man looks at your passport. Then you give him five marks and he gives you a tourist visa. Then he rings a buzzer which opens a metal door. On the other side are more guards. Sometimes they ask people to open their bags, but they don't usually search Americans. Then you go to a little booth and exchange twenty-five West German marks for twenty-five East German marks."

"They have different money over there?" asked the man.

"Yes," I replied. "It's a different country."

"And I have to exchange twenty-five marks?"

"You each have to exchange twenty-five marks, and you have to spend them in East Berlin."

"But that's *blackmail*."

"After that," I continued, "you show your passport again, and the guard buzzes you through the big door. Then you're out. Right in the middle of the Friedrichstrasse railway station."

But the woman wasn't listening. "What about the camera?" she whispered.

Overhearing other Americans I normally stayed silent, blushing with anger and shame. The process of crossing the border was usually simpler, and less time-consuming, than the process required of foreigners entering the United States. The very worst thing that could happen to a foreigner at Friedrichstrasse was to be denied entry, and sometimes this happened, on the silliest of pretexts. But anticipating a police state, even worldly travelers shook in their shoes. Perhaps it made the journey more thrilling, for this was, of course, not any old border, but a border between worlds, running straight through a city. It was absurd, but also absurdly easy, to take the subway to behind the Iron Curtain.

There were four lines at the border: one for citizens of East Germany, one for citizens of West Berlin, one for citizens of West Germany, and one for citizens of other countries. Those in the first could only travel if they were over sixty-five or had special permission; those in the second had to apply a week in advance stating particulars and purposes of their visit. For the rest of us it was only a matter of ready cash. When I had it, there were nights when I crossed the border to go to the opera. At Kochstrasse the transit official announced, "Last station in Berlin-West," and the train rolled past an empty station, going to ruin, until it reached the border station at Friedrichstrasse. Then you went up some stairs and down some others until you came to the long hallway with the four lines.

The guards were serious about the passports: they always told me to take off my glasses to compare my face with the passport photo. Still it rarely took long to reach the waiting room of the station, where East Germans stood clustered before the door to the border, waiting to meet relatives who emerged, one by one, carrying flowers and sacks of food.

BERLIN-THE-CAPITAL-OF-THE-GERMAN-DEMOCRATIC-REPUBLIC GREETS ITS GUESTS said the sign on Friedrichstrasse. East Berlin didn't call itself East Berlin, but Berlin-the-Capital-of-the-German-Democratic-Republic. This was rank provocation: under the terms of the treaties Berlin was not to become the capital of anything, but to remain a city under occupation by the four allies. But the 1950 proclamation of the Russian sector as capital of the German Democratic Republic wasn't worth starting a war about. So the sparring remained verbal, the West continuing to call East Berlin what the East just as tenaciously referred to as Berlin-the-Capital-of-the-German-Democratic-Republic. The popular designation for the other side was the same on both sides of the Wall: this was the contraction "Drüben," which means "over there." So the remark "If you don't like it here, then go to Drüben" referred to East Germany if spoken in West Germany and to West Germany if spoken in East Germany. *Alles klar?*

East Berlin had all the bearing of a capital city, for the Russians got the best of the deal when Berlin was divided up. The massive museums and memorials on Unter den Linden formed the center of town, before the war; what became West Berlin was only a collection of suburbs. I was never able to grasp this, however often I studied old memoirs and photographs. The division of the city was final, for those who came after it. People on one side of the Wall meant something different when they said "Berlin" than did people on the other. The half one didn't live in was peripheral at best; in East Berlin, it didn't even appear on the transit maps.

The East had preserved an air of the past: no neon in the air, no store fronts stacked with things. Western visitors found it gloomy, even larger and grayer than West Berlin. How many of the colors in our lives are pieces of advertisements, when it's not the beginning of springtime? At the corner of Unter den Linden and Friedrichstrasse was the Bulgarian Cultural Commission, its show windows displaying peasant dolls and small rugs. Further on were the monuments: a Greek temple, the opera house, the heavy gates of Humboldt University, the dome of the baroque cathedral. Sidewalk cafés set back under trees served sour beer. Streetcars took the place of buses in emptier streets. Behind the National Gallery, another museum in ruins: without the Marshall Plan, rebuilding a city was slow. People dressed in pale fabrics, there was none of the black and red called style on the other side of town. The occasional punks sat with soldiers and professors at long tables in the kneipen. All of them stared when you walked through the door; however plainly you took care to dress they saw at once that you came from the West. Sometimes you'd ask for the menu and the waitress would tell you not to bother, there was only one thing to eat anyway. In other places there was a menu but they were out of everything except something that wasn't listed in the first place. The subway station at Alexanderplatz had paintings where you expected cigarette ads: WE WANT PEACE, MR. REAGAN, said the slogan under the picture of a small girl. Inside the store selling dishware were blown-up photographs, not of sleek customers eating from the dishes with relish, but of smiling workers at the factory which produced them. When you bought an exhibition poster at the Volksbühne Theater it came wrapped in paper printed with quotations of Simone de Beauvoir.

Visitors had to return to the border by midnight. Passports were checked again twice. Sometimes the guard in between asked if you'd spent all your money. If you hadn't, you could leave it in a little savings account at the border, to spend the next time. Or you could keep it in your pocket, they hardly ever looked. Then you were back in the subway. The walls were covered with green-gray tiles reminiscent of a high-school bathroom. Was it voyeurism, wanting to see what life was like where the state owned the means of production?

* * *

"You're Hungarian?" asked the bartender. He had teased me, gently, about my accent. Ordering a beer at the kneipe next door to the Brecht Theater I had failed to roll my *r*'s the way the Germans do.

"No."

"Italian, then."

"Not Italian either."

I let him guess for a while. He ran through a whole list of countries before I told him the right one.

"America?" asked the tall, rather drunken man who'd been watching us. "No. Not really."

"Want to see my passport?"

"American," he repeated, wonderingly. "If you're an American, then I have to buy you a whiskey. Bernhard," he called to the bartender, "one whiskey!"

"We're out of whiskey," said Bernhard.

"*Ach*," he apologized, "you know how it is here. Always out of something. What else do Americans drink?"

"It doesn't matter. We drink all kinds of things."

"But I want to buy you a real American drink."

"A cognac, then. Is there cognac?"

"A cognac, Bernhard."

Bernhard poured me a cognac. "Cheers," said my companion, raising his glass. "And what is your name?"

"Susan," I answered.

"Cheers, Susan. My name, my name is Adolf. Unfortunately, like—you know who. It was really a problem for me as a child."

"Cheers, Adolf."

Like Kant and Hoffmann and Hannah Arendt, Adolf was born in Königsberg, that faraway city which no longer exists, not even in name. Now he worked as an engineer in East Berlin. We talked about history. He bought me another cognac.

"I would like," said Adolf, "I would like to propose a toast for the new year. If I may be philosophical for a moment. I would like to drink to international peace between all the peoples of East and West. Regardless of their politics. This is a wonderful moment. We must take advantage of it and drink to peace in the new year."

"To peace in the new year," I said, draining my glass, trying to understand his emotion. Americans in East Germany were uncommon; one who found her way into a local kneipe and ordered a beer in German, however accented, was a rarity. I felt wonderful, relieved to be in that half of the city where my country didn't supply the occupying army. Here they saved their resentment and scorn for the Russians.

"Another round!" said Adolf, who was beginning to weave slightly.

"You've already had quite a bit," said Bernhard.

I had to spend my East German money before midnight, so I bought a round for the tableful of border guards who sat just behind us, shyly waiting to join in.

"On the house," said Bernhard, presenting me with a foul tasting apricot brandy.

"Thank you," I replied, "but I've got to be going. The border closes at midnight."

"If I were on duty," said one of the border guards, "I would let you through without any problems. What does it matter? Midnight, a quarter past midnight, what does it matter?"

"But you're not on duty," I answered.

"That's true," he said regretfully. "And who knows? Sometime you get someone who's pretty strict.

"So I'd better go," I continued.

"Just one more," said Bernhard, bowing slightly and handing me another apricot brandy.

Back on the other side of the Wall I began to ask around. People in East Berlin seemed warmer than people in West Berlin. Not just friendlier to Americans: that was easy to explain. They seemed nicer to each other. Less formal. Less fearful. Everyone I spoke to confirmed my impression: it was, they said, a well-known fact about East Germany. And most of the people who emigrated from East to West complained, after a time. They could buy what they wanted, they could go where they wanted, and something very crucial was missing. Relationships were colder. More isolated.

Ulla explained it by saying that because East Germany was a totalitarian state, people there had to develop closer interpersonal relations. To protect themselves from the government.

Dieter told me that because East Germany was not a consumer society, people there had been able to develop different values. In which human relationships were not determined by economic competition.

* * *

The Palace of the Republic was the final monument ranged on Unter den Linden, East Berlin's heavy version of the Champs-Elysées. Sprawling white marble, its most attractive feature was a mirrorglass wall which reflected the old cathedral across the street. It was the seat of the East German government, built on the site of the kaiser's palace, part of which was bombed during the war, the rest of which was blown up in a burst of antiimperialist ardor afterward. On the street outside stood a massive equestrian statue of Frederick the Great.

"Berliners," said Dieter, "are full of contradictions. Of course, historically speaking, Frederick was actually very progressive."

Taking my arm, Dieter guided me through the red-carpeted hall, lit by garish chrome. Its marble walls were hung with large paintings, each cut to the same size. Some of them verged on caricature, socialist realism of the worst sort. *The Future* was the tide of a blue and brown canvas upon which a man, a woman and a child pointed toward a city in a valley, gleaming with new technology. Others were more abstract, with bright flesh-colored tones. Teenage couples embraced tentatively on large red sofas. Clumps of old women sat flicking cigarette ashes. In sharp contrast to the vast formality of the row of monuments outside it, the hall was designed to invite casual use by its citizens.

"The beer is undrinkable here," said Dieter, "and we have to use up our East money anyway." So we sat in plush chairs at the bar sipping imported cognac. The East Berliner nursing his beer next to us stared absently toward Alexanderplatz. Cold afternoon sun streamed onto my face.

Away from central Unter den Linden, East Berlin streets were clearly worn. Older buildings were pocketed with bullet holes; the rows of new ones displayed a drabness even more exaggerated than that of the West.

"Do they have to be so ugly?" I asked.

Dieter, usually so mindful of style, answered impatiently. "Nobody was thinking about design after the war. There were millions of people whose homes were bombed out."

I blushed, reminded once again of my good fortune. I kept my mouth shut, my movements awkward, as we reached the huge ugly highrise where Dieter's aunt and uncle lived.

At the doorway everybody apologized for something. Lena was sorry that she had nothing better to offer us: the cake she'd baked two days ago was going stale.

"It's the end of the month," said Hans. "The cupboard is bare."

Dieter tried to explain why he'd come empty-handed. Western media urged visitors to bring food for the starving brothers and sisters in the East. "And then you see the grandmas lugging sacks of potatoes over the border, as if East Germany weren't the potato capital of Central Europe!" Not wanting to look as if he were responding to anticommunist descriptions of East German scarcity, he had broken the first rule of European hospitality and arrived bringing absolutely nothing. Except, of course, a guest.

"Susan comes from America." Dieter introduced me with a clumsy laugh. "She wanted to see how an East German family lives."

Hans looked at me archly. "I'm afraid I can't display my children, they're out this afternoon."

But soft plump Lena led us to the living room and soon we were seated on the sofa, talking with more warmth and wit than I'd encountered in all of West Berlin. They spoke of recent films with the kind of engagement for which the East is famous. The sleepy sophistication so characteristic of West Berlin was absent; in its place was a naive intensity that struck me, oddly enough, as rather American. Everything seemed to matter, and progress held out hope.

Lena served her stale cake with coffee, and asked me where I came from. Though they'd never been to America, they knew more about it than the West Germans I'd met.

"Atlanta?" said Hans. "Wasn't that the home of Martin Luther King?" As I nodded, he continued expectantly. "Maybe you can answer something. We've always been puzzled that the blacks in America have never formed a revolutionary movement. I attribute that to the power of religion; I know the civil rights movement was organized through the churches. But how do you explain the fact that the churches retain their authority?"

The question was a clear one for someone whose life was bound up with the struggles of Central Europe. My glance was drawn less by his very bright eyes than by the long scar crossing his forehead; Hans was, Dieter said, a resistance hero. Yet how could I begin to explain? I could speak of the grinding thrust of the American catechism, ceaselessly imparting its lessons: problems are personal problems, all resolvable by plenty of work and a positive attitude. The ideology of having no ideology keeps American struggles from turning into what Europeans call political ones; but I felt helpless to try to translate. Instead I mumbled something about the power of oratory. Hans waited, disappointed; he had really hoped for an answer.

Lena turned the conversation homeward, asking Dieter for news of his family. She was shocked to hear that his brother had been jailed for stealing a motorcycle.

"Wait a minute," I said. "Don't they put people in jail for stealing here?"

"Of course not," she answered. Stealing was treated as a psychiatric problem, like alcoholism. In a state where private property was kept to a minimum, someone who stole was viewed, quite simply, to be not in his right mind.

In the years when the division of Germany seemed final, careful conventions came to govern family visits. Everybody seemed to walk on eggshells. Sophisticated West Germans tried not to treat the Easterners as poor relations, civilized East Germans fought the view of westerners as rapacious or condescending boors. The clichés were hard to parry. Try as they might to talk of the ordinary, conversations turned into cultural comparisons. Forty years had altered the fabric of the everyday. Not until the border opened would they see how deep the alterations lay. The two Germanys could be viewed as a gigantic laboratory: nowhere else on earth was there such a chance to study the changes which opposing political systems have wrought on one people's lives. For the families affected, those changes were too loaded with decades of resentment and guilt to be anything but an object of the politest kind of chitchat. To risk more would be to risk plunging into the cold war, whose stereotypes flickered above and behind the exchange of information; the cold war, not just any old family conflict.

We were interrupted by the entrance of Hans and Lena's pale daughter, fourteen and very shy. She'd returned from an unsuccessful attempt to get tickets for a discotheque.

"There are so few here that they're booked in advance," Dieter said to me softly.

"Next time," her mother comforted.

"Susan comes from a Jewish family," said Dieter, apropos of absolutely nothing. I looked from him, to Hans, to Lena, to my knees.

"Ah," said Hans quickly, "and are you religious, or is it just your family background?"

"That's the thing about being Jewish," I answered. "You can't always separate it. I'm not Orthodox. I wasn't raised in a very religious family."

Hans stood to open a door to the next room, revealing a wall of books and a grand piano. He picked out a large volume and brought it back to the sofa.

"Maybe you know this painter. He was Jewish too. From Russia."

I paged through the colored plates. "Not bad," I said, "but he stole a lot from Chagall."

"Not stole," said Hans, "learned."

I passed the book to Dieter. What had he wanted from his announcement? In an instant I had been made colorful, a little risqué. Hospitable from the start, our hosts had become a shade warmer, a shade more interested. If a shade more strained.

"A sip of cognac?" asked Lena. Dieter looked at the darkening sky.

"But we can't let you go empty-handed," said Hans, returning to his library. "Let me see what I've got which might interest you." He gave me a volume of Confucius and a very hearty handshake. "Next time let us know when you're coming, and I'll invite a few philosophers. If I can't find any Kantians, would you settle for a Hegelian?"

"Sure."

On the street there were just enough lights to find our way to the subway. Over a factory was a large red banner: THE WORKERS OF THE BERLIN BREWERY COMMIT THEMSELVES TO ACHIEVING HIGHER QUALITY IN THE KARL-MARX-YEAR. Nineteen eighty-three was celebrated in East Germany as the hundredth anniversary of Marx's death. The fiftieth anniversary of the Nazi takeover, which made so many waves in West Berlin, passed with a brief ceremony. This was part of East Germany's claim that it had settled accounts with the Nazi period years before, in the act of its very founding.

"I like your aunt and uncle," I said to Dieter.

"I know what you mean." We strolled in silence past the brewery. After a moment he said, "It's hard for me to visit them. I hardly ever do." Seeing Hans and Lena reminded Dieter of all he had missed as a child. His home was crisscrossed by obstruction, bounded by petty rules: there was no room for the easy friendliness Hans and Lena took for granted. Nothing given, nothing taken. His parents could only meet the end of their war with dull defeated stoicism; and this clung heavily to the simplest of gestures. Had fortune granted him his mother's brother for a father, Dieter's inner life would have been a completely different one. In the shrug of the shoulders which stilled his rueful wishes, I saw an echo of the torpid self-control he'd been taught as a child.

"How is it that they keep in contact?" I asked him. "When one was a Nazi and the other in the resistance?"

They didn't see each other often, and they avoided political discussions when they did. Of course there were families which the war tore apart: ex-Nazis who denied the nephew who'd sold the Fatherland, ex-socialists who forbade their wives to see the brother who'd joined the SS. But the Second World War was not a civil one, and the feeling that only the dead are wholly innocent creates a kind of blunted tolerance for betrayal, on all sides.

The subway, when we reached it, was nearly empty, its walls hung with bright posters warning against nuclear arms. The lines at the border were short. In a few minutes we were on the other side.

"Finally back in the free West," said Dieter. "Now I can breathe again." His sarcasm was weary and distracted.

* * *

Torn between wistfulness and uncertainty, Dieter's stance toward the East was unusual. Among West Berliners good words for East Germany were rare. Not everybody's East German uncle was a resistance hero: most East Germans muddled through the war no differently than their West German relations. Still, the violence of West German feeling about East Germany, even on the left, was surprising.

Werner stung me with contempt one summer evening when I was waxing rapturous about Berlin.

"This is the most self-obsessed city in the world," he muttered.

"Because its possibilities are unlimited," I answered. "Just the fact that you can take the subway to the East and—"

"East *Berlin*?" he snorted. "East Berlin is dead. There's nothing going on there at all."

Even if that was true, I argued, there was something fantastic about the fact of it. You could go to hear *The Threepenny Opera* with Mackie Messer saying, "Compare the crime of robbing a bank with the crime of owning a bank." Then you walked out of the Berliner Ensemble and there, around the corner from where the play was written fifty years ago, were portraits of Marx in the store windows. It was a completely different set of possibilities.

"You like seeing pictures of Marx in store windows?" Werner laughed incredulously.

"Look, it's hilarious. Last week I saw a picture of Marx in the window of a fur store. Draped in red. But—"

"East Germany has betrayed every important idea Marx ever had. And all the hopes that were placed in it after the war. Now it's simply a repressive petit-bourgeois state which pays lip service to socialism and only really cares about keeping up with Western consumerism, which it will never be able to do. It would be tragic if it weren't so ridiculous."

Didn't it matter, I asked him, that East German policy toward the Nazis was far more decisive than that of the Federal Republic? Everybody knew that the latter had reintegrated old Nazis into every level of government in order to fight the cold war. But at bottom, Werner insisted, the East Germans were no better. The censorship in East Germany was dismally reminiscent of fascist times.

"Heiner Müller stays in East Germany despite it, because audiences care about what's said more than they do in the West."

"Heiner Müller is their literary superstar. He has the best of both worlds. Talk to some of the writers who don't get published."

There were, I argued, many ways to censor things. There are countries where ideas seem important enough to censor directly, and countries where they are simply washed away, broken up in a flood of shiny distraction. The second method is far more successful, producing citizens who believe they have freedom of thought, and simply stop thinking. Eastern Europeans, by contrast, are skeptical and savvy, skilled at sorting out possible truth from a range of misinformation.

Werner looked thoughtful. "I was at a conference last year where a Harvard professor said there was more freedom of thought in Eastern Europe than he'd ever experienced at Harvard. Something about the range of opinions, the lack of pressure to specialize."

"So..."

"So if the best you can say about East Germany is that it's no worse than the USA, then you'd better talk to someone with a better opinion of the USA."

Werner's bitterness was not unlike that of many American leftists in the late thirties, whose violent anti-Soviet feeling reflected all the pain of a lover's betrayal. That a country founded on socialist principles should resort to repression and violence felt just about as tolerable as a knife in the back. The history of Germany gave that knife an extra twist. After the war, many looked to East Germany as the answer which would spring from fascism's ashes: its founding and flourishing could show that there was hope for a better society—on German soil. East German failures came to seem, in this light, a betrayal of the past as well as the future, undermining every morsel of confidence anew.

When East Germany began to crumble, revelations of corruption seemed to confirm Werner's anger. Yet like most of the left, he viewed the prospect of reunification with disgust. "This had nothing to do with Berliner contradictions. The flag-waving crowds, the swarming realtors, were no alternative; many hoped that a revolution within the GDR could provide a third way. If its failures were evident, its virtues were less so.

* * *

*J*obs, education, health care and day care. Nobody homeless or hungry or ragged. No violent crime. No mind-eating drugs. Theater, music and art for millions of citizens who took them very seriously. Not to mention my favorite fact about the GDR: any mother of children under the age of sixteen received a day off from work, every week, if she wanted to pursue continuing education.

So what are you saying? Was the Wall just for show?

For more than three decades hundreds of East Berliners went to work in West Berlin every morning, and returned on the S-Bahn at night. They were privileged exceptions, with access to the West, but for many years most East Germans chose to stay in the East. Their decision rested on a mixture of conviction, inertia and hope for a change. Those who wanted to leave faced two alternatives. Getting out legally was uncertain. Many lost jobs and friends after filing for an exit visa that could take many years, if it came at all. Getting out illegally was risky. At some borders the guards didn't fire. At others they did.

The electric company sent Ulli to connect my new radiator. Without impatience or condescension, he carefully explained how it worked. After he'd finished, he stood in the doorway, not making up his mind to go.

"You're not German, are you?" he finally asked me.

"No. I'm from the U.S."

"I wouldn't have guessed. Not from the accent."

"But you're a Berliner. I can hear it in your accent."

"Yes," he said, "from East Berlin." Later, perhaps, I might have guessed. The rough easy Berliner dialect, like many old things, was better preserved in the East than in the West. At the time I stood there shyly, wondering how to look. Ulli proposed that we meet in the kneipe when he finished work.

Ulli spoke with the gruff sort of gentleness, bordering on naivete, which was peculiar to East Germans—both those who had left and those who stayed. Over a beer he told me his story. He was twenty-seven and faced with endless frustration. From a bureaucracy repeating slogans which seemed hollow. From a society whose point had been lost: there were no struggles, no hidden enemies, just an absence of sparkle around the eyes. From a stream of unattainable possibilities broadcast daily by the West. So he'd hidden himself in the back of a truck bound for Bavaria. The driver had helped him, and he had been lucky, crossing the border without incident. In Munich he claimed the West German passport automatically given to East German refugees and took the train back over the border to West Berlin.

"I couldn't live anywhere else. I was born here."

"Here?"

"Here. It is the same city. Sometimes."

It would be years before he would be allowed to return to East Berlin to visit. So he arranged every year to meet his family for a vacation in Prague, the only place everybody could reach without visa problems. Many East Germans did this; it became a routine.

"But you're not sorry you came to the West?"

Ulli paused. He rolled a cigarette, weighing his words. "There's a lot I don't like about it."

"Like...?"

"People are cooler here. They're not responsible for each other. Nobody feels that he's part of a society." That explained, Ulli thought, the brash defiant hopelessness peculiar to young West Berliners. "Over there we have protest, rebellion, but 'No Future'? Never." In the empty space of the kneipe his wistfulness expanded. "And people own too much here, more than they need. I can't stand the fascination with buying things."

"It's worse in the U.S.," I told him.

"Really?"

"There's much more to buy, and the advertising is much more sophisticated. Coming to West Berlin was a relief for me. Though I didn't know how much I wasn't missing before."

The thought made him laugh. "West Berlin is bad enough for me.

"So are you sorry you came here?" I pressed him.

"West Berlin is funnier. There are problems in the West, different problems in the East. Life here is funnier."

Ulli had worked for the electric company in East Berlin, so it was easy to get a job here doing the same thing. He liked the work, and it paid well, more than he could spend. Later, maybe, he'd go to the university. But first he wanted to see the world; the chance to travel was, after all, one of the reasons he'd come to the West.

I asked him where he wanted to go.

"To Israel, first. I want to know what the people there really think about the invasion of Lebanon. Just forty years after the Holocaust they've become the oppressors. I don't trust the reports in the media, East or West. So I'll go there myself this summer."

I wondered why I never had conversations like this with electricians back home. Or anybody else, for that matter. This is how the world might be. You might just decide that the most important thing in your life this year was to find out the truth about something. Not to write it up or talk it out or use it for anything at all. But how had I forgotten this, and for so long?

The night was late when we parted. I crossed the canal to my building, unlit and imposing. On the occupied house by the bridge the handmade neon blinked NO DEMOLITION.

* * *

Before the subway doors close automatically, a Berlin transit official waiting in a glass-enclosed chamber looks to see that the passengers are safe inside. Then he speaks into a microphone: "Stand—back!" Anybody left on the platform has to wait for the next train. At the Kochstrasse station the announcer added: "Last station in Berlin-West." In the East there was no microphone, and the official waved a little flag.

Between the subway tracks and the room at the border in the Friedrichstrasse were four shops selling duty-free liquor and cigarettes, perfume and Levi's jeans. They belonged to East Berlin, which had a natural interest in acquiring Western currency. Since the shops were placed before the border, you didn't even need to cross: you had only to take the subway to the Friedrichstrasse, buy Marlboros and Rémy Martin at nearly half the usual price, and catch the next train to wherever you were going in West Berlin. West Berlin had a natural interest in preventing this; I heard there were plainclothes detectives back at Hallesches Tor to keep you from doing just that. I never saw one, but the thought served to keep my biweekly shopping excursions more dramatic than, say, trekking out to the suburbs to buy discount clothes at Loehmann's.

* * *

Traveling back and forth across the border taught me never to take a perspective for granted. Words had different referents, meanings turned into their opposites. Just one example: My American friend Leslie and I went to see a play called *Eisler* *and the House UnAmerican Activities Committee* at the Berliner Ensemble one evening. In the kneipe afterward two East Berliners overheard us speaking English. Curious, they introduced themselves, asking what we'd thought of the play. They had found it quite provocative. It seemed a good sign for the future that such radical plays were being produced.

"Radical?" I asked.

"Eisler is always presented as a hundred percent communist from head to toe. What he said to the HUAC was more equivocal than we'd been taught to expect."

"That's funny." I told them. "For me it was radical too. Because I'd never even heard of Hanns Eisler before I came to Berlin. His music isn't played too often, since he was expelled from the States. And nobody talks much about HUAC either, these days."

Georg, the older of the two men, smiled. He was a professor of English at the Humboldt University, happy at the chance to converse with native speakers. "That's the advantage of living in Berlin," he answered. "If you want to, you can be better informed than anywhere else in the world. The truth is always somewhere in between."

I nodded agreement. Years of Ivy League study had proved less enlightening than the daily opportunity West Berlin offered me to question every assumption by comparing Eastern and Western descriptions of the world. But what of *their* chances? We questioned uncertainly. Neither Georg nor his friend Erich had ever been to West Berlin. Permission to cross the border required fame, or connections, or a job with the railroad. People who had none of these got their knowledge of West Berlin from radio and television. Several times a day the West German networks broadcast the day's program listings very slowly, for East German viewers who had no access to Western newspapers listing the schedule. George explained this with a smile of withered anger. Neither Leslie nor I knew how to reply. It was hard to avoid feeling that we were unbearably privileged tourists.

"The Western press completely exaggerates the problem," said Erich. "Of course I'd like to go to West Berlin. I'd like to go to Rome. But it's not essential to my *life*. Other things are more important. Like knowing that everybody can get an education and a job and a place to live. Like knowing that I live in a society whose basic principles I can support."

Georg demurred; he was dubious about the state's belief in any principles. A few weeks before, the wife of the television star who hosted East Germany's leading weekly anticapitalist news commentary had been caught shoplifting in West Berlin's biggest department store.

"But that's just the point!" said Erich. "We've strayed from the principles we were founded on. If we'd stop trying to imitate Western consumerism and develop our own identity, those things wouldn't happen."

Erich believed his state to be open to criticism and evolution; most importantly, perhaps, he believed it to be *his* state. Georg found Erich's idealism to be faintly ridiculous, and Erich shone with a vulnerable hopefulness which made him seem younger than his thirty years. He worked at the opera, he told us, as assistant to the assistant director.

"We wanted to go to the opera tonight," I said, "but it's always sold out when they do *Figaro*."

Figaro, said Erich, was his favorite opera too. Tickets were no problem; he'd be glad to get us seats for the next performance.

"How do you like West Berlin?" asked Georg.

"Not much," said Leslie. "The people drive me nuts. Nihilistic at best. No Future."

"What's that?"

"No Future," she repeated. "From a song by the Sex Pistols. It's the slogan of the hour."

Georg asked her to write the words on a scrap of paper. "Hey, look!" he called to two men at the next table. "This is what they're saying in West Berlin."

"That's news?" I asked. "But it's written all over the place."

"That's not the kind of thing they show on television," said Georg.

"Do they mean it?" asked Erich.

"Hard to know what they mean," said Leslie. "They're so damned cold."

"It isn't like this," I told them, "where people just talk to strangers in the kneipe. In West Berlin they sit there and stare."

"They don't *talk*?" Erich was incredulous.

"They don't talk."

"But I'd tell them a thing or two, if I went to West Berlin. Or maybe I'd just walk into the kneipe and laugh."

"Here's to that," said Leslie, raising her glass. "*L'chaim.*" Had she been entirely sober, she wouldn't have said it. Leslie is an artist who designs costumes and stage sets, but all she drew were cattle cars, her first months in Berlin.

"*L'chaim*," said Erich softly.

"Am I hearing things?" asked Leslie. "Did you just say '*L'chaim*'?"

"My mother was Jewish."

Astonishment kept us silent for a moment.

"How did she survive?" I had to ask.

"My father wasn't Jewish. That kept her safe for a while. Then she went into hiding. Her family was taken to Maidanek."

Later I would learn there are many of them. Many? Don't ask for numbers. Who keeps those kinds of statistics in this land? All I know is that I kept meeting them, in the East and the West, children of German Jews, assimilated enough to be cut off from Jewish tradition, not assimilated enough to be protected from the Third Reich. They'd survived by forging papers, by the uncertain protection of a non-Jewish spouse, by emigrating to someplace safe, by enduring a concentration camp. The details were always vague; at first I thought I wasn't hearing well enough. But soon it was clear that these people knew no more than they told me, for the one thing they shared with the offspring of their parents' oppressors was a childhood that had been filled with almost unbearable silence.

At a quarter to twelve it was too late to begin to learn any of this; Erich walked us to the border and arranged to meet three weeks later, when *Figaro* would be presented again. Leslie embraced him as we parted.

* * *

There were people in Berlin, East and West, who could be brought to laughter with the sentence "Let's go straight ahead." Late at night, to be sure, and only in certain moods. You'd be driving through the city and you'd take a wrong turn to wind up not at any old dead end but at the Wall, looming cold, a little forlorn, and somebody would say, "Come on, let's go straight ahead." Nowhere else in the world could this constitute a standing joke.

* * *

It was heavy-handed humor, like the attempt to live normally, as if one were timeless, stateless, simply one among many. On the day appointed, Erich met me at the Friedrichstrasse station and showed me the ruins in the quiet streets behind Unter den Linden on the way to the opera.

There he turned me over to an usher who led me to what was more or less the best seat in the house. The curving boxes and elegant balustrades, so different from the severe functionalism of the opera house in West Berlin, were none the less delightful for seeming out of place there. The Rumanian diplomat next to me turned his program, full of notes about the history of the production, over and over in his hands. Listening to "Voi che sapete" I closed my eyes.

After the performance the usher appeared again, taking me under the huge stage, where a back door opened to a wide café. I smiled politely at the eighteenth-century footman who greeted me warmly; only when he laughed did I realize, embarrassed, that it was Erich, who worked as an extra in the second act. Around us members of the orchestra, dressed in tails, swept by ladies-in-waiting wearing blue satin swirls; I thought I recognized Susannah. Erich led me to a half-empty table. Had the seat he'd arranged for me been alright?

"Couldn't have been better. It was a wonderful performance, much better than the *Figaro* in West Berlin." I expected he'd like to hear this and in fact, it was easily true.

Erich smiled, pleased, but thinking of something else. He drew a photograph with crumpled edges from his pocket. It showed his mother, who had died the year before. Her small soft mouth betrayed nothing.

"Tell me," I asked, "you said your mother was Jewish. According to Jewish law that means you're Jewish too. Why don't you say so?"

That seemed to Erich too much to say, an attempt to create clarity where there was none. His parents left their children free to choose whichever religion they wanted, or none at all. His sisters hadn't been interested in the subject, but when he got older he had joined the Jewish Community. This was an act of keeping faith with something, but it was hard to say what. He went to High Holiday services and occasional talks at the Community Center. The Jewish Community in East Berlin was very small, with a few hundred members, most of them elderly and conservative. There were many more Jews who lived there, but they had nothing to do with the Community.

"Because they're afraid of anti-Semitism?" I asked.

"Oh no," said Erich. "Most of them are Communists. For them Judaism is just a religion, and they don't believe in God."

Andreas and Peter joined us at the table, reminding us that we were somewhere beneath the stage of the Deutsche Staatsoper. They too had been part of the production, and wanted to hear a westerner's view. Andreas argued that the other East Berlin opera's *Figaro* was better than this one, less traditional.

Peter apologized: Susannah seemed to be getting a cold. Suddenly hungry, I ordered a sausage. The first bite was sickening and I sat trying to crumble pieces of meat into the tiny napkin while the others weren't looking. Erich's white footman's wig slipped gently over one ear, his makeup began to streak under the bright light. We all spoke gingerly, looking for balance, somewhere between Mozart and the vast East and West.

Just before midnight they brought me to the border; a triumphant May evening, perfect night for a walk. Through the columns of the Brandenburger Tor I could see the Tiergarten, where I'd breakfasted with Dieter that morning. By daylight the city seemed manageable, its absurdities nearly forgotten. Not every Berliner stays up all night.

"How do you get home from here?" Erich was solicitous. "By subway?"

"Yes, I don't live far, you know, it's just"—I pointed—"over there." Drüben.

We all laughed that shrug-of-the-shoulders Berliner laugh. None of my companions had ever seen the other side of their city.

* * *

Westerners often complained of being used by East German friends; they came to feel their visits were welcomed for the little Western luxuries they were asked to bring. My experience was nearly the opposite: I rarely left an East Berlin home without a present from my host. Yet visits became rarer, and formal; something about it was hard to keep up. The thirty marks one had to pay to spend the day in East Berlin played a role in limiting travel, but it wasn't the crucial one. The fact was that the two cities were separate, and if life in each was uniquely conditioned by the other, it wasn't in a manner which really gave you access to either. Even for the young and privileged, the strain of traveling between two worlds became hard to bear. I lost contact with Erich when he changed apartments; after two years of sailing regularly across the border, the Wall become something to show to visiting uncles.

Settling down meant taking the division for granted. Though it was open to most of them, not many more West Berliners visited the East regularly than East Berliners visited the West. In the everyday world of most West Berliners, other continents seemed closer than all the resources of East Berlin. I'd been thrilled by the daily chance to compare Eastern and Western media, but after a while I rarely took in East German radio or television. And this was not because I found them wanting but because I had to narrow my world: Berlin presents too much possibility, sometimes. I spent years coming no closer to East Berlin than the duty-free cigarette stand in the subway station.

Until Mitch Cohen lent me a memoir he wanted to translate, the story of a Berlin Jewish doctor's daughter who'd become a Communist, emigrated to France, was arrested for resistance work and sent to Auschwitz, from whence she escaped. Stirred by the hopefulness which suffused the book, I asked Mitch to take me along to meet her.

The border was crammed full of young tourists with backpacks. Hearing us speak English, the guard took us for two of them. But in the thirteen years since Mitch left Sacramento for Berlin, he'd aroused the attention of the East

German authorities; perhaps for a book he edited in which East German writers published without permission, perhaps for having too many friends who gave up and came West. Computers work wonders: there was a minute, a phone call, the sound of one and not two visas being stamped, and the guard's brusque manner became a self-righteous chill. "Herr Cohen, your entry into the German Democratic Republic is undesirable." I was quite suddenly alone on the other side of the world.

Not unshaken. I sat down on a park bench, staring at the green paper bag in my hand. Mitch and I had debated, an hour earlier, about what to bring. Not fruit, said Mitch, people are always rubbing East Germans' noses into the fruit you can get in the West. Don't be silly, I'd said, people visit with fruit in the West sometimes too. If they don't bring wine or flowers. Alright, said Mitch, but not bananas. Why not bananas? I asked. Bananas are the cheapest kind of exotic fruit you can rub somebody's nose into. We had settled on peaches. Peaches are different, said Mitch.

It was later than expected; there was nothing to do but to take the peaches to the address on the scrap of paper Mitch had given me at our hasty parting.

"Frau Segal," I said nervously to the short buxom woman who opened the door, "you don't know me, you must be surprised, I'm a friend of Mitch Cohen's and he didn't get over the border—"

"He didn't? But I called the State Department! Come in, come in. What a shame about Mitch. Would you like a drink?"

When I was settled on the sofa with a vermouth, Lilli Segal asked me quick questions about my nationality, profession, family. She and her husband were professors of physiochemistry currently investigating AIDS. Moving constantly, with plump grace, she showed me her research files: on AIDS, the reactions to her memoirs, a new book she was writing about crimes committed in the name of medicine.

"Starts with the Nazis, but it takes off from there. Did you know that whole tribes of Indians were sterilized in the U.S. and Canada in the sixties?" As she was searching for the reports, the doorbell rang. She paused to admit Marthe, a round-faced younger colleague.

"I know you hate white flowers, Lilli, but I thought these might—"

"Yes, those are quite colorful," said Lilli Segal, producing a vase. "They'll do very nicely." Through the eyes of the West, where fresh cuts of dead blooms are trucked in daily from Holland, her flowers looked sadly bedraggled. I remembered the kilo of peaches in my hand.

"Lovely," said Lilli. "We still have quite a problem getting fruit here." She scanned the article Marthe had brought. "I can't work with people who refuse to do research on animals," she snorted.

"*Na*," said Marthe. "We now have a very good course on the ethics of animal research—"

"I'm all for ethics," said Lilli, "but I'm allergic to people who talk about cruelty to animals. When I think of how the SS treated their dogs and how they treated us ... I knew a doctor who wanted to do his Ph.D. on tuberculosis, so he infected twelve boys with tuberculosis, and twelve guinea pigs. For every boy there was a guinea pig. As the Russians were nearing Auschwitz, the guards hung the boys. Alright," she concluded, "I'd better see to the lunch. Think you'd be happy with a fish soup to start?"

"We'll be happy with anything you cook," said Marthe, "unless you were thinking of frying locusts."

"No point in throwing pearls before swine," said Lilli.

Chatting with Marthe, I looked around the sunny room. The longest wall was covered with books in five languages. A glass cabinet held seashells and trinkets of a long research stay in Cuba. On the wall beside the window, overlooking endless rows of pink and gray high-rises, hung the skeleton of a small prehistoric bird.

"May I smoke here?" I asked Marthe.

"Oh sure," she said. "There's the ashtray. Lilli and Jascha smoke too, when they have time."

At the table I remembered that Lilli's memoirs boasted of her cooking: the fish soup she'd whipped up as we were talking was very good. I raised my spoon for a second mouthful and held in my breath. While cooking, Lilli had removed her jacket. Now I could see her arm, bare and flabby, an old woman's arm. The number wasn't rigid, machinelike, but slapped on sideways like a careless gash. I was no longer hungry. But look away, I cursed myself, or look at her face, look at the soup plate, look at Marthe. What in all the world could be more boorish? — To arrive uninvited, be welcomed unknown, and spend the meal staring at your hostess's Auschwitz tattoo? —My eyes wandered unwillingly, again and again; the sick feeling in my stomach collided with the smells of sweet steaming food.

"You wanted to know about vergangenheitsverarbeitung?" asked Lilli. She told me things I'd heard before. East German authorities were vigilant toward any sign of resurgent fascism: an anti-Semitic remark could cost someone his job. There were, nevertheless, ugly cases; she had recently helped a Gypsy family whose son had been taken from them through the mindless discrimination of a Leipzig teacher. Racism had not been demolished, but it was fought resolutely when it appeared.

Marthe demurred, uncertainly. Expressions of racism were officially forbidden, but she feared them nevertheless. She had taught her children not to reveal their Jewish ancestry after they reported a classmate's anti-Semitic remark—

Lilli exploded. "That's where you're a bloody idiot!" she shouted. "If you don't fight, you're lost!" The neighbors, she told us, called a recent house meeting to discuss what to do about the swastikas some kids had drawn on cars in the neighborhood. Lilli had shocked them by announcing that any kids *she* caught drawing swastikas could be picked up in the hospital. If they wanted, they could have her arrested afterward. There was, she insisted, only one way to deal with—

"Lilli," pleaded Marthe, "When the children themselves are affected, what are they supposed to do!"

"Learn to defend themselves, and the Jews in the Soviet Union would be better off if they did so too!" She regaled us with tales of her own confrontations. There was the time, for example, she defied Soviet officials who threatened her with internment. "I had to laugh: they think they can scare *me* with the basement of the Soviet consulate?"

"You're a special case," said Marthe. "You have dual citizenship. Most people couldn't fight back in those days, under Stalinism."

"And there wouldn't have been any Stalinism if the Russians weren't used to letting people walk all over them! Really," Lilli chuckled, "those Russians. One has to learn to say no."

Marthe struggled silently; Lilli was clearly her mentor, and she had too much affectionate awe for the older woman to voice a reproach. Still I wondered: were Lilli's privileges the result of her refusal to waver, as she clearly believed? Or could she allow herself the luxury of chutzpah because her privileges were unassailable: who would dare deny her right to travel, no matter what she said? Circumspect Marthe was not among the privileged East Germans: she had never traveled in the West, and only rarely to other Eastern countries. Our generation has no Old Guard; being a hero, and proving your mettle, must find other forms. — Yet Lilli's courage was undeniable. She had been younger than Marthe, younger than me, when she scorned the offer to survive Auschwitz by accepting privileged work in the camp's hierarchy. Could the whole world be gained if we all just stood fast?

While I was musing, Lilli had cleared the soup plates and brought a platter of shish kebab. We talked of glasnost and Gorbachev and why East Germany seemed slow to change. Lilli said the younger generation had been bought off with consumer goods. "If you own your own home at the age of thirty, of course you have an interest in the system remaining as it is. Then they keep out Mitch Cohen for writing a poem or something, and it looks like a police state. Idiots." She passed homemade cake and coffee. "And now," said Lilli, "we might take a walk. You've been to East Berlin before, but perhaps there is something I can show you?"

I nodded unhappily toward the ticking clock on the wall. "My husband is away, and I have to pick up my son from kindergarten."

"Too bad," said Lilli, "but I know how it is. I raised two kids without grandmothers myself. I'll walk you to the border, then. Wait a minute. Did you see any books you'd like to have?"

She led me back to her living room and swept through the library, putting books in my hands. "Now here's something that might interest you, but what is the one I was thinking of? Marthe, help me, you know the one I mean. It's called *Next Year in Jerusalem*, but who is the author? You don't know either? I can't believe it, I always had a perfect memory. I must be getting old."

Lilli Segal was seventy-eight. On the way to the border she walked as quickly as I do, but for the pauses she made to continue one or another of the conversations we'd begun upstairs. My thanks were hurried. It was an unlucky day at the border. The pretty blond guard was in no mood to wave me through, though I stretched out my U.S. passport hopefully; there were six books under my arm. Had I bought them in the GDR? They were gifts? From whom? One of the books was Lilli's own memoir, and I showed it to the guard.

"I've heard of her," said the woman. "A GDR author."

"A professor at the university," I offered innocently, convinced that all Germans were more impressed by that title than any other. An old comrade, I thought acridly, but said nothing more.

So you were visiting her? continued the guard. And she gave you her book, and the rest are from her own library? I must look at the dates—there's a law against removing old books from the GDR but these look—that's alright, they're all recent enough. And how do you know this woman? How old is she? And what do you do in West Berlin? Now if you will please open your bag and put everything on the counter....

Keys, coins, papers, pictures, tissues, pens, tobacco. I smiled chastely and mastered my gnashing teeth. Wouldn't you know it: the one time I had to hurry, they gave me the kind of examination that appears in the tabloids. With relief I watched her finger my notebook, undecided, and return it to the counter unread.

"You may pack your things," said the border guard, "and wait here while I take your passport and papers to the next room."

I was desperate, and pleaded simply, one woman to another. "Will it take very long? You see, I have a little son, he's not even three years old and I'm already late to pick him up—"

"It won't be long," she said kindly, and, in fact, it wasn't. Five minutes and four doors later I was back in the West. Outside, the Wall looked more ridiculous than ever; just at that spot it was no taller than me.

But it was the West which seemed lifeless after a day with Lilli Segal. For days afterward I wavered between increasing dejection and hope.

Free University

When I met her she was sixty years old and very beautiful. Margherita von Brentano came from a noble family, long entwined in the history of German culture and power. She was well-known in Berlin for her outspoken and critical support of left-wing causes. During philosophy lectures she paced the floor, chain-smoking, waving her hands for emphasis.

A few weeks after I'd shyly introduced myself to her, someone tapped my arm after a lecture. "Brentano thought I should get to know you," he said. I was more confused than flattered as we went out for coffee. What could Brentano possibly know about me? All I'd done in her presence was to blush and stammer. "Listen," said James, "if you made it through the Nazi period, you had to be a *Menschenkenner*. Your life depended on making snap judgments about people."

Several months later Brentano read the first part of my dissertation and tried to quell my growing disgust with philosophy. Of course it could be remote, empty, and pointless. Sharing my misgivings, she urged me to stay nonetheless. "If people like you give it up, there will be no one but pedants left in the field." She asked me to be her assistant for the Kant course she was giving the following term. Insisting it would help my self-confidence as well as my German, she left me no choice but to agree.

* * *

German universities strike American observers as vast and impersonal institutions. American universities seem like high schools to Germans. German students come and go to lectures that interest them. There are no course exams or final papers; their academic success is determined by two batteries of tests whose subject and timing they can roughly control. With no tuition fees to worry about students are free to spend whole semesters pursuing a subject which suddenly becomes important. They do so alone, as they do everything else during their studies; the personal engagement which we call teaching is not expected from even the most popular professors.

Built just after the construction of the Wall ended Western access to the old Humboldt University, the Free University, West Berlin's largest, resembles a temporary airport. Its center is a low gray building the size of two football fields, whose dismal corridors stretch on to identical classrooms. Even people not usually inclined to agoraphobia can panic if lost in it. In the middle is a coat checkroom, a soda fountain and a bank of Xerox machines. Search the streets surrounding the university and you'll find two mediocre bookstores and one of the dumpiest kneipen in town to serve a "campus" of fifty thousand students.

Nothing in Dahlem invites them to stay; they disperse after classes into the city sprawl.

This is more than a failure of planning. Even for students, most intellectual life takes place outside the university. Here tradition plays a role: with some notable exceptions, creative thought in Germany was seldom undertaken by professors. Moses Mendelssohn couldn't even get elected to the Royal Academy, and it would be more than a century after the death of the "German Socrates" before Hermann Cohen received a chair at the Marburg University. Besides Jews, German academics were hostile to anyone left of center; universities are state institutions, and professors are civil servants. After the war there were sporadic attempts at reparation. The University of Frankfurt, for example, offered chairs to Adorno and Horkheimer, who were both Marxist and Jewish. Yet the latter's lukewarm response to the sixties protests their work had inspired just confirmed suspicion that the power bestowed by a university inevitably corrupts.

Power? For Americans the academic is most often a figure of fun; it is hard to imagine that "professor" might have an imposing, let alone a threatening ring. In Germany the little prefix "Dr." can get you right to the boss, past a suspicious secretary who refused to connect you without it. Germans who receive Ph.D.'s go to city hall to have the weighty designation officially entered in their passports as a change of name. The sense of authority which the words "Professor" and even "Doctor" convey is ambivalent. For the man in the crowd it has much to do with being a solid citizen: in the service of the state academics earn very generous salaries. Thus many major thinkers, and their less talented admirers, continue to eschew both solidity and salary to search for something outside academic halls.

* * *

Though full of ambivalence, I soon felt grateful that Brentano had persuaded me to teach for her. Having to stand before a class and convey the excitement lying buried in those old books forced me to remember why I'd spent half my life studying philosophy. For the first time in months I could hear questions about my work without recoiling. Loving wisdom may take many forms; but mightn't doing philosophy, in the right sort of way, be one of them?

The students who met with me once a week to talk about Kant were more independent than American students, and oblivious of authority. I found something to like in each of them—the moderate punk with the strand of green hair in her eyes, the acne-faced woman with tentative questions, the arrogant, handsome young man who'd just returned from working in West Africa.

* * *

Hans-Jürgen made himself noticeable the day I started teaching. He seemed younger than the other students, but he probably wasn't. His blond hair looked dyed, and he dressed expensively. His remarks were quick, sometimes bright, and fully unconnected. He interrupted the other students; I frequently had to intervene. By the second meeting they rolled their eyes in an amused but unmistakable gesture whenever he began to speak, which was often. Hans-Jürgen was, in short, what we call a problem student back home.

The hour had been spent discussing the political consequences of Kant's conception of reason; I'd compared Kant and Marx, railed against Hegel. So it was only natural that the talk should turn to questions of political engagement when several of us went afterward to drink coffee at the university cafeteria.

"But what's the point these days? We have no control over the decisions they make in Bonn. Look at the missiles. Even the politicians don't have much of a say about that; it's all been decided in Washington." Rainer's bright blue eyes were pleading nonetheless.

"That's just the sort of resignation that can doom the peace movement from the beginning," said Karin, pretty and determined. "Look how many prominent people have promised to blockade the missile sites. And it isn't even summer yet."

"The peace movement cares about the missiles but they don't care about me!" That was Hans-Jürgen. Karin and Rainer exchanged glances. "Besides, I find politics boring. I'd rather go to Dschungel. The people there are better-looking."

"I like to go to Dschungel too, sometimes," I told him. "That needn't exclude being politically active."

"The peace movement is full of granola eaters. People who worry about the environment. I'd rather stay in my room for a week than go to a meeting with *them*." The other students turned away, weary of Hans-Jürgen's chatter. I wondered wistfully about obligations; I'd much rather talk to them.

"Heil Hitler!" said Hans-Jürgen suddenly, raising his hand in the Nazi salute.

"I don't find that amusing, Hans-Jürgen. Not in the least. There are things one can't play around with."

"I find it very amusing. My father was an SS officer. Once I took out his uniform and wore it to high school. You should have seen how all the petit-bourgeois teachers reacted!"

"How did they react?" There was no point in giving this boy a lecture; what on earth would I tell him? All I could do was ask questions. For his sake? For mine.

"They called a big conference about me. The principal made a speech about democracy. One teacher—some old 'sixty-eight leftover—wanted to throw me out of the school. But then where would they put me? My mother had to come."

"And what did she think about it?"

"My mother never thinks about anything."

Mercifully, we were interrupted before I had to think of something else to say. Walking alone to the subway I was shaking: what was I, in the end, what the fuck was I doing in this country? Had my faith in the Enlightenment no limits?

Was it a philosophical temptation which kept me here? The temptation to understanding, to show the sense behind the shock of words? This kid was the product of particular conditions (oh reason, reason) and, as he stood, the living incarnation of nihilism. — So you wanted to see whether philosophy has something to say about real nihilism, the hard stuff?

* * *

The story wouldn't go away. I hadn't realized before what teaching the little group had meant to me. Meeting once a week to pour out my theoretical soul before them had helped dissolve the last of my unspoken fears about living in this land. There was no Nazi lurking behind every sweet blond smile. The new generation was new. They moved me, amused me, annoyed me and interested me in the same ways that students anywhere else would do. I'd taken them to heart.

I was not about to let this be ruined by one boy who was, without a doubt, severely disturbed. Still...

"A student in my class said 'Heil Hitler' to me today," I told Dieter eating pizza at a sidewalk table on the Goltzstrasse. "I was kind of shaken up by it."

"He said 'Heil Hitler'? What did you do?"

"Not much. Listened to him, mostly. He's clearly got problems. He was trying to shock me."

"You should have thrown him out of class."

"It was after class. We were sitting at the cafeteria drinking coffee. That would have been the wrong response anyway. He needs to be in therapy. That was obvious the first time I saw him."

"Why are you being so cool about it? You should have yelled at him. Told him that you're Jewish. Shown him that there are people who are emotionally affected by that kind of shit."

"But that's just what he wanted. He said the most provocative thing he could think of in order to get a rise out of me. And whether or not I'm Jewish is beside the point. The thing is wrong, period, no matter whom he says it to."

"You don't understand," said Dieter. "One has to react more strongly. That kind of thing can get out of hand."

The next day I told James the story. Politically conscious and historically knowledgeable, an American who'd lived ten years in Berlin, he was surely a person who'd have a balanced perspec—

"Bring charges."

"What?"

"Bring charges against him. You'll have to go to court."

"Take him to court for saying 'Heil Hitler'?"

"It's illegal. I once brought charges against an old Nazi and won. I was sitting in the Café Kranzler, and the man at the next table said that Hitler should have gassed all the Jews. I took him to court. I said that my grandmother was Jewish, and it was a personal injury." James's Scotch-Irish eyes lit up when he smiled.

"But *James*. This isn't an old Nazi. This is an eighteen-year-old kid. Nineteen at the most. He's severely disturbed. Almost borderline psychotic—I don't know, I'm not a shrink."

"You can say that all the Nazis were crazy if you like."

"But he isn't a Nazi at all. He's simply using Nazi symbols to get attention, because it's the easiest way to frighten people here. Like the kids who draw swastikas because they're illegal—it has nothing to do with political conviction."

"Are you sure of that? Do you know how many neo-Nazis there are here? Do you realize how powerful their ideology still is?"

"Maybe not. But I've taught philosophy before. I trust my intuitions about students."

"Ever read Jean Améry?"

"No."

"Jewish writer. Concentration-camp survivor. He killed himself a couple of years ago. Améry wrote that the past will only be overcome when the Germans begin to identify with the victim rather than the perpetrator. It's an important statement. We were brought up to think that no decent human being could do anything *but* identify with the victim. That's not true here." James twisted the pack of matches in his hand. "You'll see when you've lived here awhile. I don't even bother with them anymore. All of my friends here are Arabs."

Was everybody's reaction so at odds with my own? I began to ask around. Some were against bringing charges; a legalistic mentality was of a piece with Nazi bureaucracy. Others were against shouting matches; emotional aggression was of a piece with Storm Trooper methods. All were in agreement that I was mistaken in treating the incident as a matter of one boy's personal problem.

"But I understand this kid. I know why he said what he said. I *want* to understand him—"

"Understanding for fascists," said Werner, "is the last thing we need any more of in this country."

Finally and thoroughly uncertain, I called Brentano. She had taught at the university for twenty-five years, her political credentials were impeccable and it was, after all, her course. We arranged to meet on Thursday. But on Thursday I was in bed with a fever. I canceled the appointment and the class as well, shelving the question for another week.

* * *

I entered the classroom with a handful of notes about Kant's theory of natural science. Before I could begin to discuss them, Rainer said: "Hey, tell us the story about the 'Heil Hitler.' Who said it? What happened?"

"What?" I was stunned. The students were perfectly still. For the first time, Hans-Jürgen was absent.

"Brentano said somebody had given you the Nazi salute in class. We didn't know anything about it."

I cursed my indiscretion. A garbled version of the incident must have reached Brentano before I could speak with her. At the beginning of the last lecture, students told me, she had furiously challenged whoever dared to make anti-Semitic remarks in my seminar to say "Heil Hitler" to *her*. No one stepped forward.

"But who was it, Susan? When did it happen?"

"I can't tell you. I'm sorry."

"I'll bet I know who," said Karin, looking at me through narrowed eyes.

An hour later I stood at Brentano's door. "Come in," she said, gripping my hand warmly, "I want to talk with you. Who was the student who said 'Heil Hitler'?"

"I don't know if you've noticed him," I answered. "His name is Hans-Jürgen. He's young—"

"Hans-Jürgen." She put her head in her hands. "Hans-Jürgen."

"Then you know him?"

"I told him to go to a psychiatrist the first time I saw him. He spent an hour in my office talking about his family. If it had been anyone else ... But he was sitting right in front of me when I spoke to the class last week! He looked around the room and didn't say a word."

"Not surprising."

"If it had been anyone else, I would have thrown him out of the class and considered taking legal action. But Hans-Jürgen.... Tell him to come and talk to me."

"If I see him again. He wasn't in class today."

"I'll write him a note if he doesn't come next week. I must have his address somewhere." She rummaged through a stack of papers on her otherwise empty desk, then quickly opened two or three drawers. "I'm sure I have it somewhere."

* * *

He never showed up in the class again, but it wasn't the last I saw of Hans-Jürgen. Sitting in the Café Einstein a month later, I felt a hand on my shoulder.

"*Susan!* I saw you from the bar and I just *had* to come over and say hello. You must have thought I'd been unfaithful to you, didn't you? But I'd never be that! I simply haven't had a minute to spare for philosophy these past weeks. I've met a director who's launching me into a film career. We flew to London last Saturday. I'm making *piles* of money. I'll come and see you soon, though. Will you be teaching next term too? And now I've just *got* to run." He was out the door before I could say a word.

"Who was that?" asked James. "Hitler Youth?"

"Yeah." James can be so dry that it hurts, sometimes, and my smile was uneasy. I couldn't get past the feeling that I'd done this boy wrong, though I couldn't say for the life of me what doing him right would have looked like.

"You didn't tell me he was gay," said James.

"I wasn't sure before," I answered.

* * *

You have to look hard in Berlin to find pure theoretical discourse. Michael Theunissen said his grammatical musings in philosophical anthropology were motivated by the need to determine whether philosophy after Auschwitz is possible. Lecturing on Nietzsche, Jacob Taubes held hundreds spellbound by asking whether Goebbels had been right to find confirmation for diabolical anti-Semitism in passages of *The Gay Science.* Years before Victor Farias's revelations Brentano devoted weeks of her seminar to the question of Heidegger's Nazism.

"Sometimes," she confided, "it's a relief to teach Aristotle's *Metaphysics.*"

But it isn't merely a matter of certain texts; the very disciplines themselves are open to question. Rather: the very idea of preserving and bequeathing a past is met with skepticism. Its treasures have been, at the least, devalued. Those monuments of humanism which did not positively lend themselves to abuse by the Nazis did not, in the end, do anything to stop them.

Contemporary elitism and a vestige of belief in the power of education would have us believe that Nazism arose from a vast and benighted German proletariat. In fact, the educated upper classes produced the highest percentage of Nazi party members. Opportunism and cowardice played a role in many decisions to join the movement: professors had a great deal to lose by opposing the state. But fear of forfeiting all the cozy privileges which attach to German academic life was hardly the only motivation for supporting fascism. Heidegger was merely the most famous of the many who happily heralded the beginning of a new era in the German universities. Contemporary accounts describe the radiant faces of humanities professors brought to life through sudden conversions to Nazism. Photographs show students throwing banned books onto bonfires with joyful resolution. Was it precisely a weariness with thinking which led so many academics to yearn for solution and faith?

Few of their successors would give a single explanation for the triumph of fascism at the universities. The simple fact of it is an inheritance condemning them to eternal vigilance against anything which hints of repetition. This fed the frightened reactions to one boy's scream, this made the politicization of discourse a moral imperative. The refusal to retreat to purely academic matters, the call to remembrance of that which others try to forget: mostly, it was moving. Still there were days when I couldn't shake the feeling that the Nazis were summoned to give intensity to hours which would otherwise pass in oblivion. Flagging conversation could so easily be breached with a little shiver of aestheticized horror. Academics were no guiltier of this than the countless intellectuals who've made their home outside the university, but they were no freer of it either.

* * *

The seminar was a minor institution, attended by artists and actors and assorted literati as well as the legions of ageing graduate students who transcribed every word. The walls of the professor's study were lined with expensive complete editions of nearly everything; his lectures leapt gently from Giotto to Marx to modern psychoanalytic theory. I went, one evening, as to a monument. The subject under discussion was a new film which used montage: photos of a female prisoner arriving at the Auschwitz ramp; footage of contemporary policemen explaining intelligence techniques; shots of an underwater machine making endless waves; detailed Allied aerial photos of concentration camps. The film's main theme, said its director, was the fact that the Allies neglected to bomb the gas chambers or the railways which led to them, while making air raids on factories a few miles away.

The circular singsong of the professor's voice suited the film's movement perfectly. "Preservation and destruction, destruction and preservation, whereby one naturally can't preserve what's been destroyed, still the whole is a perpetually returning simultaneity. Your film," said the professor to his eager former student, "is a metaphor of protest against this coupling. The observation of Auschwitz was impossible because it would have impaired the frictionless ebb of this essence. Destruction and preservation, preservation and destruction..."

Rapt silence filled the room. Pretty women dressed in red miniskirts, hair slicked back to show the skulls behind their attentive faces. More than anything else, the professor wanted to please; he beamed with delight when quiet murmurs confirmed his cleverness. In vain I sought the charisma which had captured so many Berliners I knew. Perhaps the secret lay in his eerily lilting voice.

"Horror is the terror which communicates itself," he intoned. "Your problem is the problem of all artists: how do we find an appropriate picture of the horrendous?"

The director nodded. He had been careful, he said, not to produce a film like that kitschy *Holocaust* with its trashy trivialization of world history.

A test case for two cultures. *Holocaust* displayed all the weaknesses of Hollywood: personal anecdote took the place of real understanding of politics or history. German intellectuals viewed it as another example of American ignorance. Yet the series had achieved something which years of more informed vergangenheitsverarbeitung had not. Broadcast in 1978 on West German television, it unleashed a storm of emotional discussion among the populace at large. Amid all the scholars' scorn, Gunther Anders praised the film precisely because it reduced the abstract fate of 6 million to the story of a particular family, enabling millions of postwar Germans to shed tears, for the first time, for the people next door. Where does theory become betrayal? Maybe tearjerkers are needed in a land where rage is so easy, mourning so hard.

The seminar brooded with uneasy silence. One student stammered tentative discomfort; he'd clearly been taught that grief was passé. Still, he was trying. "Perhaps I'm too sentimental, or maybe I still believe in mourning, but somehow I feel a personal foundation to be missing in the film we saw today."

"The professor, however, pronounced his verdict quickly. Films like *Holocaust* were "mass events for Kleenex, the tears roll down the Kudamm." Again he crooned, "Horror is the terror which communicates itself."

Three tape recorders switched off as the seminar concluded. On the way to the subway a student caught my look of dismay. "Sometimes it's more exciting," he said consolingly. "Were you there the time he talked about Godard?"

Ruins

At eleven o'clock on a Sunday morning I waited with a hundred others for the opening of the exhibit "Kreuzberg 1933: A Neighborhood Remembers." Its purpose, said the catalogue, was not to point fingers at the guilty, but to answer one question: "Would we have been capable of resistance?"

The first speaker at the opening was a well-fed historian and Social Democratic Party (SPD) official. His speech concerned the present. Good old-fashioned antifascism is no longer enough, he said, for the threats to democracy have grown subtle: surveillance by anonymous bureaucracies, consumer culture and a media which obscures the actual social relations. "We have not worked through our past, but merely repressed it," he concluded. "Because working through the past requires active confrontation with our fathers."

The audience applauded warmly, but his speech was nothing new. Willi Boos, the second speaker, was transfixing. "I am not a historian," said the little old man whose life was spent in the factories of Berlin. "I can only tell you a little about my life back then." His story mirrored thousands of others. As a boy, he joined the workers' sports club. "Of course we were left-wing. We were workers." Initially a Social Democrat, his father grew disillusioned when the SPD came to power and sent police to shoot demonstrating workers. He joined the Communist Party. Boos recalled Rosa Luxemburg speaking in the Hasenheide, hundreds of thousands behind her. "*Berlin bleibt rot*" said the papers. Berlin stays red. How could this enormous movement fail to stop the Nazis? He tried to explain. Hunger, misery, lethargy, terror. The left was divided. Nobody thought life could get any worse. The Nazis took power and ruled with fear: every day it was harder to know who could be trusted. Boos's voice, already shaking, broke down as he told of the colleague whom the Gestapo caught committing sabotage at the munitions factory where he worked during the war. "You have all seen pictures of the Nazis' victims, but I cannot describe how he looked when they'd finished with him." With great dignity he wiped away tears and continued, seeking neither to exaggerate nor to excuse his own behavior during the Third Reich. Like many others, he engaged in small acts of resistance: forging documents, encouraging delays at the factory. Like many others, he could have done more.

Slowly, the audience rose. They were young and old and they wanted to talk; small groups formed inside the exhibit hall. The elderly seemed anxious to tell their stories, but the burden of openness which the little man had catalyzed was quickly exhausted.

People scattered neatly to look at things in glass cases. Photographs and documents describing the Nazi acquisition of the Kreuzberg hospital: the firing of Jewish doctors, the closing of the marriage-counseling and birth-control clinic.

A section called "Nazi Kitsch" displaying swastika-covered eggcups and matchboxes. Advertisements for the latest hairstyles: because they are esteemed by all other women, Germans have a duty to keep their hair fashionable. Pictures of a department store with a sign reading JEWISH BUSINESS: ANYONE WHO BUYS HERE WILL BE PHOTOGRAPHED. Snapshots of SA troops beating up people trying to enter a theater showing *All Quiet on the Western Front.* The city responded by banning the film as a threat to public safety. Concert programs of the Worker's Music Association featuring a "Socialist Cantata for Choir, Soloists and Orchestra." Brochures of the Social Democrats, urging voters not to allow "that Austrian foreigner Hitler" to determine Germany's fate. The last legal posters of the Communist Party: WHO VOTES FOR HITLER VOTES FOR WAR.

Kreuzberg in the early thirties.

In the park outside the exhibit hall Turkish teenagers sat on a bench playing unfamiliar stringed instruments. Half-dressed residents of the occupied house on the corner leaned yawning from the windows. A young family was barbecuing a picnic in a trash barrel. I walked to the Wall and leaned against it, smoking. The graffiti reading TURKS GET OUT had been freshly painted over; now the thick orange letters read NAZIS DIE.

* * *

Once I returned to the exhibit to see what had become of the large white panels which were placed around the room. On each was printed a question; space and Magic Markers were provided for viewers' responses. One month later most of the panels were as empty as they had been on the morning the exhibit opened.

What did you know about the resistance? What did you think of it?

Nothing

I'm sorry, nothing

Was it possible to live unpolitically?

Yes

Yes

Yes

Yes

Did you (or your parents) clean out the bookshelves in accordance with the Book Ban?

Of course not

My father put the banned books behind the bookcase

My parents were poor sows, we couldn't afford to buy books

My grandfather was arrested for hiding banned books

Would you act differently today than you did then?

Yes

Yes

We were forced to act as we did!

Never in my life—I'd rather die

I'd rather do it again than die, but it was unfair

Only one panel had been covered with responses.

Is "Jews get out" the same as "Turks get out"?

Both slogans conceal the social contradictions between capitalism and the workers

Turks and Jews are human beings too

Here I can only say: Turks get out

The Turks should only expect this if they don't conform to German ways. Who wants a Turkish man making advances to her?

Long live Adolf Hitler!

"Turks get out" is worse because we've been through this once before. People should have learned something.

Neither the one nor the other has gone up in smoke.

* * *

You might call it another Berliner contradiction. Small talk can seem relentlessly intellectual, but words like "Enlightenment" or "reason" are suspect. Dieter's friend Jürgen looked wary when I used them; he'd only meant to ask politely about my work. It was Sabine, the poet, who bluntly objected: Enlightenment thinking led to fascism.

"Nazi mass murder could never have been carried out without technology," added Dieter.

I tried hard to argue that the kind of reasoning which produces technology was only one aspect of reason; there were other, more essential conceptions of reason.

"I meant something else," said Sabine. "It's instrumental thinking which allowed them to forget they were dealing with human beings. Full of hate and love and sorrow."

"The Nazis were masters at manipulating mass emotion too," I replied.

"It's true," said Dieter. "There was a lot of mysticism in Nazi propaganda." He had a way, in discussion, of hedging his bets.

"But you can't react by going back to Kant," insisted Sabine. "*Eichmann* appealed to Kant at his trial."

"The devil can quote scripture too. The judges at the trial protested at that one. Kant doesn't say you have to obey *every* law. He says you have to obey the law which human reason gives to itself. And that has to do with treating people as ends, not means."

"Isn't there a deeper sense in which Sabine's right?" asked Jürgen. "Eichmann wasn't emotional. He didn't hate Jews personally. He carried out plans coldly and rationally. That's how the Nazis operated."

"Listen. I know that the notion of reason has been coupled with domination and order. In this country especially. All I want to argue is that there's another way to look at it."

"Could be," said Sabine. "I think other things are more important. Reason is male-oriented anyway. It's the basis of the whole patriarchal society."

"A Green Light for Reason," said Jürgen. "That's the new slogan of the Berliner Transit Authority. They want us to ride the subway more often."

"The dialectics of Enlightenment," said Dieter. "Do they read Adorno in America?"

* * *

Wanting a bicycle I put in an order with Gunther, who was trafficking in what he insisted were not stolen goods. He now lived on a literal junk heap.

"The finest address in Berlin!" As he swept his hand across the horizon I had to agree. The bombed-out lot was private property, belonging to someone he knew. It was heaped high with every imaginable kind of object: rocking horses, old books, welding tools, basketballs, costume jewelry, empty picture frames. Located on the Potsdamerplatz, once the center of Berlin, the Wall was just behind it. Every Saturday Gunther peddled the things he collected in the course of the week at the Flea Market across the street. "I retire to my chambers when it rains," he told me, pointing to a portable shack he'd constructed from tin sheeting and old canvas. "Only the bathroom is missing. But what could be better than pissing in the open air?"

The dump contained an order invisible to strangers; Gunther found a bottle of schnapps and a volume of Goethe in an instant, offering me some of each under the warm blue sky. He read very well. Affable and gracious when sober, he regaled me with stories of his past, most of which were probably true. The childhood in the Harz in a family of nine. Fleeing west at the end of the war in the face of the Russians. Leaving his apprenticeship in the coal mines to go to sea. Becoming an actor by chance in Vienna. Losing a million marks through an obscure form of fraud. Wrecking his next career as a photographer by drinking so much that he never made a deadline.

"Now let me show you the bicycle. This one I saved for you. The trademark alone is worth two hundred marks. Exceedingly rare. For anyone else I would have sold it separately." Gunther pointed to an artful, antique-looking shield on the fender. The dark green frame shows signs of rust.

"But I don't care about the trademark, Gunther. I care about whether it rides."

"Of course it rides! Try it yourself," he motioned. "We'll just polish it up a bit." From a tool chest I hadn't noticed before, he produced oil and rags.

"You paid Gunther two hundred marks for *that*?" said Dieter, looking disdainfully at the bicycle the next day. "The old swindler."

Dieter may have been right, but I didn't care. The bicycle worked well enough and besides, the first thing that Gunther did with the money was to invite me to a lavish lunch. I followed him to the supermarket; he rode a bicycle made for a dwarf or a circus, which looked as if it would topple over any second under his bulk. We squandered a hundred marks and came back wobbling with sacks of steaks and potatoes which Gunther cooked on the wood stove. Cooking utensils were missing, lost somewhere in the junk heap; he cut the meat with a large rusting ax.

"You been seeing much of Dieter these days?" Gunther asked.

"Umm-hmm." I was guarded.

Gunther, said he, just wanted to warn me. "The man lies like a master. And he's tightfisted as hell. Underneath all that revolutionary avant-garde chit-chat he's just a petit-bourgeois kid from Stuttgart."

"I'd like to stay out of your fight."

"What fight? The man thinks I'm going to kiss his ass because I need a bathtub. He can take his bathtub—"

"How did you meet Dieter?" I wanted to change the subject.

"Let's see, it was 'seventy-four, no, 'seventy-five, at an S.E.W. May Day party. He was drunk, and I, well, I never turn down a drop or two." Thus reminded, Gunther passed me the bottle of brandy.

"Are you a Communist, then?"

"Me a Communist? Of course not. But the First of May has to be celebrated."

"Not in America it doesn't."

"The First of May isn't a holiday in America?"

"No."

"But it's International Workers' Day. It's a holiday everywhere else."

I shrugged my shoulders.

"Hear that, you hirelings of state capitalism?" Gunther shouted suddenly, swinging the ax in the air. "But don't think for a minute that you're any better!" I looked mystified in the direction he was waving. "The border guards." he pointed. In the little white tower just on the other side of the Wall were two sentries posted before machine guns. "I try to give them a little something every day," said Gunther. "It's a terribly dull job. Escapes are attempted so rarely these days."

* * *

***"N**o young German could develop a normal relationship to you," said Dieter, staring at his feet.

"Develop?" I asked, summoning, for the occasion, all the bold optimism I ever possessed.

"Perhaps it can be developed," he conceded, "but it will never be there from the start."

I'd been the one who had wanted to talk. Three months it had been, very nearly, three months of late nights and slow mornings, looks across champagne glasses, hands held in the park. Beethoven and lovemaking under his paintings. But there were the lies, for example, pointless lies which I'd learned that he'd told. No that wasn't the point. Was it his way of tottering between public and private, the wrinkle of heart under gleaming skin? My uneasiness hovered unsteadily, it had no anchor. With every passing week I became increasingly vulnerable, and increasingly mistrustful. I couldn't say why.

When I finished speaking there was nothing to be heard but the drip of leaves and the motorcycles on the distant Kudamm. The *Biergarten* was deserted, it had started to rain. We sat sheltered in a wooden pavilion. Dieter stood up as though to leave, but returned a few minutes later with two glasses of beer.

"How shall I explain it?" he began. "Knowing you confronts me with myself. It brings up rage, it brings up sorrow. I can't really deal openly with you without dealing openly with my parents. And that I don't know how to do."

"What do you mean?"

"Look. Every time I see you I think of Dachau."

His eyes were without expression, withdrawn to a distant pain. The place was very still. I doubted my right to speak. Could I tell him, for example, that he had to forgive his parents for being Nazis? In whose name?

I took a deep breath. Did I say too much? We have to *talk* about anti-Semitism, acknowledge its depths. Demystify the Holocaust, not to shrink in horror from this particular history, these very words "German" and "Jew." Of course you're full of clichés which are lying in wait while you're looking at me. But racism is universal too. There are parallels. (Parallels.)

From politics I moved to psychology, groping for old intuitions like a cripple who'd lost his crutch. I could see him recoiling: he lived fraught with fear of a darkness within. You can't go on this way, I told him. If you look exactly at your own worst fears of what you might be capable of doing, you'll find it is less than you thought.

"I'm a German," he replied, "and when Germans flip out..."

He couldn't finish the sentence. I was close to tears. Had he meant to scare me? And what's an intention when collective guilt is peering in the window, the blond beast knocking at the door?

"Don't mythologize," I answered. "We've got to *think*."

"It's cold," said Dieter. It was true. We were both shivering in the wet night without flame. He reached as though to take my arm but drew back. Perhaps he was only stretching.

"If you could give me hope..." He met my eyes and waited.

Dawn was breaking over wet leaves by the time we reached the Nollendorfplatz. It seemed we'd been silent for hours.

* * *

*T*hree black soldiers drinking beer on the subway, Otis Redding on a ghetto blaster, loud. Two teenage girls giggling, intrigued and shy. A couple of other young Germans showing pleasure with quiet smiles. The rest of the passengers' faces ranging between irritation and fury: Berlin subways are normally hushed. I snapped my fingers to the music and spoke loud American English, oblivious to conflicts about identity. For a moment it felt like home.

"Where ya goin' tonight?" asked one of the soldiers.

"Kreuzberg," I said.

"I like Kreuzberg," he said, "but there are too many Turks there."

"But..." I was too astonished, for a second, to continue. "The Germans say that about the Turks the way some white Americans talk about blacks."

"I know," he answered. "I can't help it. Maybe it would be different if I spoke their language."

"Our protectoral powers" was official Berlinese for the military presence, but common people used the term with contempt. Was it an occupation? The Allied law allowing for Berliners stopped without passports to be shot on sight was still on the books, but nobody thought of enforcing it. There were occasional attacks on U.S. military installations, but normal resentment of the army was muted. Still, the soldiers told me they felt it all the time. "I'm here to protect the Germans," said one. "I'd lay down my life for them if I was told to. Think they care? All you hear is 'Ami go home.'" Said another: "A German fellow asked me the other day whether I'd kill him if I was told to. Sure, I said. I follow orders. I don't make the politics. I'm here to do my job."

At the Wittenbergplatz we parted with a smile and a wave.

Standing on the platform, waiting for the train. Two hundred years after young Moses Mendelssohn, hunchbacked and poor, begged for entry at Hallesches Tor, there's a Jew left in Berlin talking about reason?

* * *

Friday dawned and demanded; at the market people shivered, cursing the unseasonable rain. Only the vegetable brothers took their time; wind and damp impressed them as little as the mood of a surly customer. In the line before me stood an Indian couple with a small child; the woman, wrapped in a thin sari, held an eggplant in her hand.

"Do they eat eggplants in India?" asked the little brother. The woman looked blank; after a time her husband replied.

"Yes," he said. "Often."

"More than other things?" continued the vegetable man. Did the silence reflect their poor German, or was the question unanswerable? He tried again: "More than zucchini?"

The Indians were silent. "The green things," said the brother, pointing; he was busy weighing tomatoes. There was no response. He wrapped the tomatoes in paper, put them aside, and picked up a zucchini. "This—zucchini," he said slowly. "Do they eat them in India too?"

"Ah yes," replied the Indian. "We eat them too."

The vegetable man packed up the eggplants. "Are you going to stay in Germany for a while, or are you just visiting?"

A little pause. "We stay here," said the husband.

"But then you'll learn a little German?" The sentence was hearty, falling somewhere between a question and a demand. The vegetable man gave a handful of loose grapes to the Indian child who took them, unsmiling, in his small fist.

"And where are you from again?" asked the vegetable man, turning to me. "Italy, was it?"

"USA."

"Ah yes. Long way away. I bet your parents aren't too happy that you're here." He glanced at his brother, arranging apples with a frown.

"Not particularly." If you only knew.

"Hard decisions."

"Yes."

"So what'll it be today?"

"A pound of pears."

"Try some grapes. Sweeter than candy. And the raw material won't give you a hangover, like the finished product."

"OK, I'll take a pound of grapes too."

Along the wet canal bank the merchants shouted: "Come, ladies, my eggs are the biggest!" "Two heads of lettuce for a mark, come get 'em!" "My bread is frr-esh! For your table!" One ageing vendor simply cried, "Hey, people! I need money!" On his table lay long thin strands of pink gladioli, a few carnations. He smiled hopefully. I wonder what his chances were. A few feet away stood two large flower stalls, bursting in abundance and color.

* * *

At the Flea Market that weekend, I told Leslie of Dieter. Our last conversation had shaken me hard. I was moved by a torment I'd never imagined, the uneasy sorrow wracking sons of the land. (Sins of the fathers. Sins of the fathers.) I could cry for his pain. And yet, and yet. All the responses felt wrong.

For Leslie my conflict merited no sympathy: "Why do you want to have close relationships with these people anyway?" Her husband Bob had been more sardonic: if I was tired of Dieter, he could introduce me to an actor who also looked just like an SS officer. Feeling condemned to alienation from the last of the groups I might possibly belong to, that tiny set of American Jews living in West Berlin, I lapsed into silence and gloom.

We turned to examine the stand selling piles of hundred-thousand-mark bills, relics of Weimar.

"But this is too good to be true! Imagine finding you on my doorstep!" It was Gunther, with a large jug of wine and a colorless young man in tow. "Come along, girls. We're on our way to pay a visit. Have you ever seen the Afghan Embassy?"

"I've seen the Spanish Embassy. The Italian one."

"Then you don't know what you're missing. Bernhard" — he pointed to the young man — "will drive us there."

In Berlin's first days as the capital of Germany, magnificent embassies were built in the Tiergarten. After the war ambassadors took up residence in Bonn. What to do with the vast splendid buildings which remained in Berlin? Nobody expected them to be needed in the future, but they couldn't be demolished, for an embassy is foreign territory, property of its respective government. Nor did the respective governments care to pay the expenses of keeping up a second embassy in a city which was no longer the capital of anything. So the embassies became a stop on the underground junket, weirdly lyric, locked and moldering. Another testimony to our not-quite status. (Not-quite capital. Not-quite ruin.) No salvageable past, no foreseeable future. Walking round the battered buildings was soon a lovers' cliché, for Berlin cast the spell of the moment. You might see them, between kisses, telling tales of the quarter: wasn't it ironic that only the Italian, Japanese and Spanish embassies survived Allied bombing quite whole?

I wondered what the Afghans had done with such a large embassy. Bombs and neglect had left the immense neoclassical building largely in ruins; three pigs, a donkey and a number of ducklings were nosing through the weeds outside. We were there to visit a painter who Gunther said had occupied several rooms of the embassy. "The reception hall makes a wonderful atelier."

"Are the animals his?"

"His girlfriend takes care of them."

"Have they lived here for long?"

"A year or two. The Afghans have other worries."

Gunther's knocking failed to produce a response. He walked to the back of the building and began to yell.

"Uli, you swine! I haven't come to borrow money, I've come to pay it back."

"Maybe he really isn't home," said Bernhard.

"Rot."

It was impossible to break into the building; all the ground-floor windows had been boarded up. Leslie and Bernhard began a halfhearted game of Ping-Pong on the table set up on what used to be a lawn. Gunther gave up on Uli and turned his attention to the jug of wine. It was nearly twilight before we piled into Bernhardt's Volkswagen to head home.

"It's a shame," said Gunther, "that you missed the inside."

* * *

We met in the Tiergarten, sparkling green after an early storm. Dieter had been to the KadeWe, and proudly spread plastic containers full of seafood salad and pâté on the thick damp grass. It was a farewell splurge. He was leaving the next morning to spend six weeks bicycling through Portugal. I pulled a bottle of champagne from my bag.

Punk couples, old couples, all holding hands on the clear summer's day. Dieter took off his clothes and stretched out in the grass. I followed him shyly: the Tiergarten is set in the center of the city, Berlin's Central Park. He laughed at my awkwardness: "The only people who pay any attention to nudity here belong to the U.S. Army." I followed his glance. Hovering over the meadow just above the tree line was a helicopter circling the rows of naked sunbathers. "Or do you suppose they're looking for Russians?"

We paused, locked fingers. Dieter turned onto his stomach.

"Can you cream me in?"

"What?"

"Cream me in." He looked at my blank face with impatience. "With the *sun*tan lotion." I blushed, opened the tube and began to rub his brown back. After nearly a year, linguistic battles no longer dominated my days. Still there were moments when language failed utterly in the face of the most ordinary demands.

"You're very pale," said Dieter, surveying me critically. "Let me do your back." He kissed my shoulder lightly. I relaxed again under his hands.

Drinking champagne, we chatted about the summer. I had no real plans. A woman I knew had invited me to her parents' house in the Luneberger Heide; perhaps I'd take her up on it.

"Luneberger Heide." He sighed. "I can't wait to get to Portugal. Away from all these deep, dark Germans." Dieter laughed at himself heavily, but it was unmistakably laughter.

Hours passed where nothing troubled the peace but a wayward Frisbee, retrieved by a diffident nude man.

"C'mon," said Dieter, "I want to look at Brandenburger Tor."

We packed the remains of our lunch onto the bicycles and rode the short distance to the gate, symbolic center of imperial Berlin. Now it belonged to the East Germans who had, however, thoughtfully arranged things so that Westerners could see the old monument quite clearly. Behind the wire stood a Soviet tank on a pedestal and a plaque, in German and Russian, commemorating the Liberation.

"There," said Dieter, pointing to the street. "You can still see the tire marks."

Black streaks of skidded rubber looked burned into the pavement. "What happened?" I asked.

"Somebody killed himself yesterday by driving his car into the Wall. It was in all the papers."

"Oh."

"Eighty miles an hour, right next to the Brandenburger Tor."

"I guess that's the way to do it, if you're going to do it in Berlin."

"They've strengthened security today. It's bad press for the East when West Berliners start using the Wall to commit suicide."

The day was ending. We bicycled along the Wall, not stopping till the end of Kreuzberg. The evening was so quiet we could hear the televisions in the houses on the other side. Under the weeping willows Dieter began to sing "Avanti Popolo."

"Teach me the words," I said.

His voice was deep and potent; I wouldn't hear it for a while.

* * *

Celle is the sort of German village which appears on travel posters. Its half-timbered houses were built in the Middle Ages, but they've been so carefully restored that the town looks like a Hollywood set. Four miles away, at the edge of a bleak pine forest, stood the plain modern house where we sat drinking beer. Ulla was gentle and attentive; nobody knew quite what to say. The five of us were united temporarily by acquaintance with Ulla and desire to leave Berlin. Richard thumbed through a book of color plates of ancient vases. I looked over his shoulder. I had brought things to read, but couldn't bring myself to unpack them.

In putting my bag in her father's study, Ulla meant to be especially nice: everyone else at the house party had to share a room. But next to the bed was a Nazi monograph with pictures of all the boys in uniforms and swastikas, along with pictures of them, old and well-to-do and unhappy, at a reunion forty years later. The book was right out there, next to photographs of Greek statues and expensive editions of Plato, for the old man was a philologist, and all he had left after his worldview was shattered in 1945 was the good old German nostalgia for ancient Greece.

Ulla had told me this quite casually while driving back from the train station at Hannover. She'd never spoken about her parents before. I hadn't thought it out in advance, just made some wrong assumptions. Ulla was on good terms with her parents, good enough to invite a party of people to their house while they took their annual vacation. Mustn't their pasts be acceptable?

Apparently not. I was a weekend guest at the home of a Nazi a couple of miles from Bergen-Belsen. It was too much. They may have to forgive their parents, but I didn't; I couldn't. Now the Nazis were gone, soaking up the Grecian sun, and Ulla's politics hadn't changed. She worked for the women's committee of the Green Party, went to demonstrations against missiles and racism. Still I felt, unfairly, deceived: I wouldn't have come if I'd known.

"You've never seen this part of Germany?"

"No. I've traveled a bit in the south."

Ulla wanted to show me the landscapes of her childhood. We packed a picnic and I followed politely through acres of plain pines to the muddy shore of a small artificial lake. Nothing adorned the place, no broad bank, no sweeping sky, no graceful tree, no gentle hill. My companions talked about nature and tried to look casual as they took off their clothes to swim.

I sat on the strand, feeling torn. After months of meeting people whose family relations seethed with blunted rage, Ulla's easy toleration of her parents' failings was almost refreshing. I had heard her speak warmly of her brothers, her niece: something in their lives was powerfully intact. Yet the price was immense. She accepted a father who didn't even have the decency to keep his Nazi memorabilia under wraps.

It is impossible to know how many families tend such skeletons. Evidence was destroyed in conviction or fear. Since the weekend at Ulla's I have visited other households whose heads had been Nazis. There nothing more offensive than a portrait of Goethe graces the walls. Faces stay dull, unrevealing. Perhaps what's in the actual closet doesn't matter.

Back on the terrace we slapped mosquitoes and ate spaghetti. A neighbor's dog whimpered across the road. Ulla returned from the cellar with a second bottle of wine.

"Oh, sorry," she said, after tasting. "I'll get another bottle. I meant to get something dryer. It's so dark down there I could hardly see."

"Wait a minute," said Richard. "This is an extraordinary wine."

"I don't like sweet wine," said Ulla.

"Let me see the bottle," said Richard. It was a 1939 Sauterne.

"Oh," said Ulla. Her smile was a little embarrassed. "My father was in France during the war."

"Mine too," said Wolfgang. Half-glances, half-smiles. Breaches and bonds which I'd never share.

"And he's kept a case of this down there all that time?" asked Richard.

"I guess so," replied Ulla uncertainly. "Maybe he was saving it for a special occasion. I didn't mean to open it. My parents just told me I was welcome to make use of the wine cellar."

"You can't put it back now," said Wolfgang, laughing. "Cheers. Maybe we should see what else he's got saved."

Did I join them? Of course I did. As Wolfgang pointed out, the bottle was already open, and who would have been helped by my making a scene? The Frenchman who'd been plundered forty years before? (All armies plunder.) The young Germans sitting in that desultory night? I filled my glass again. It was the very best Sauterne I ever tasted.

Before breakfast the next morning I asked Ulla to take me to the train station.

"You haven't even had a chance to rest," she said, "and you're already going back to Berlin?"

"Sometimes it's like that," I answered.

* * *

Fleeing Germany for Italy is a very German thing to do. I didn't care. There was a seat on a flight to Rome and I took it, spending two dutiful days on the Campo dei Fiori before taking a bus south to the Amalfi Coast. And there I sat in what is surely one of the loveliest places in the world, wondering why it failed to move me. Rocky cliffs hung with grape arbors and pink-white houses sweep down full of drama. The sea below merges with horizon to give a view of blended nothingness: call it infinity. I stopped in cafés and tried to stare intensely. The days were too hazy. Or maybe there wasn't enough bougainvillea on the mountainside.

Mornings tossing in the Mediterranean waves I let go of all the tumult I had come to sort out: Germans and Jews, Americans and Europeans receded temporarily under those crazy cliffs. Afternoons I read *The Ambassadors.* The novel was even more appropriate than I'd remembered, but gave no answers. For all his brilliance, James could no more *state* the problem than I could. Is that what they mean by a question of style?

By twilight the promenade was full of people, familiar bright loud. At the café on the water swarms of pretty, exuberant children lay, unaware, their hands on mine in passing. An old man, his handsome face lined, shouted genially to his cronies with a baby in his arms. Behind him the sound of church bells, buses honking and braking round precarious curves. Boccaccio gardens, sky turning bold. Moons on the water. The night could take me with her.

* * *

For all its being famous Capri is still the most beautiful island I know. All the balances are right: between wild and tended, dry green and warm golden, bright and hidden, mountain and sea. There are corners, smelling of wet moss and hot marble, where you might be the last person on earth. The colors are perfect; swimming off the island feels like tumbling in light. Evenings I sat on the terrace, drinking cold wine like clear water, trying to learn to do nothing.

Antonio spent three years at Oxford before coming home to run the little pensione where I found a room. He was delightfully chauvinistic: "Why should I go anywhere else? Capri has everything. If I want to be alone, I can be alone here. If I want to be with people, they come from all over the world. The landscape is beautiful, and it's not superficial beauty, like your American landscapes. Capri has history. Every stone on this island means something."

What is the history of Capri? Emperors traded other islands for it, men of fame or wealth from many countries retired here to write and reflect. There are plaques on the houses they lived in. The most famous historical site on the island, however, is the Villa Jovis, once the palace of the Emperor Tiberius. The ruins aren't bad, and the setting is spectacular: the long walk to the top of Capri takes you to the end of the world, preciously lonely, commanding sky and sea and the whole of this perfect island rolling down from your feet. And what do you know about the Villa Jovis? It's in all the guidebooks, put more or less politely: Tiberius used to bugger his slave boys here, and throw them off the cliff when he was done. (Which cliff? That one?) What role does this thought play when you're sitting alone here, taking in the view? Does it bestow mystery? Tradition? Depth?

Theodor Adorno, stuck in Santa Monican exile, wrote that California is Italy without soul.

* * *

Ute invited me for coffee a few days after I returned to Berlin. She speaks good Italian, knows all the places I'd seen.

"I'd move to Rome in a minute if I could," she told me. "I love everything about it. The Italians are wonderful."

"I liked it there too," I said.

"They're funny about the Germans, though."

"How's that?"

"Their picture of Germany is a little one-sided. They go on and on about Goethe and Schubert. I have to remind them that's not all there is to Germany. Unfortunately."

When they talked to me about Germany, they asked how I stand it, living in a country full of old Nazis, barbarians and boors. Who knows what they say about Americans? They don't say it to me.

Unlike other folks, Germans hold flattering remarks to be base and craven; German honesty obliges them to say only unpleasant things to peoples' faces. That's what Heinrich Heine wrote from Paris in 1854.

And Americans say there is no such thing as national character.

* * *

"I was so afraid you wouldn't be here." Dieter shoved a tentative arm under my shoulder. A sunbeam played in the lone window.

"You're the one who was in Portugal."

"That's different. It was just a vacation. I was afraid you might give up and go back to America."

"No," I answered. "There's too much I want to do here. Too much I need to learn."

"I had the feeling you were homesick."

"I am homesick. Often." But no place felt like home. Some had reproached me for settling in what they saw as enemy territory, and I was anything but at ease in it. But the flaccid comfort of the American intelligentsia was no imaginable alternative. After being surrounded by people whose souls shook for contemplating tradition, how could I return to a life in which culture was simple: it meant opera, cathedrals, and gourmet cuisine? After hearing Berliners in any kneipe worry about the possibility of art after Auschwitz, how could I listen to anguished debate about the possibility of philosophy after Wittgenstein?

"I guess you can't." Dieter stood up to turn over the record. Quiet reggae. On the way back to bed he looked carefully into the long wardrobe mirror. Free, we are free, across the canal the church bells chimed.

"You know, honey..."

I turned. Were we as close as all that?

"While I was away, I was thinking. We have to go further. You must help me."

"Help you?" I asked.

"By telling me more about...Jews, for one thing. By confronting this German-Jewish history. I mean..." he paused. "The feelings between us...have something to do with all that."

I looked up sharply, spilling coffee on the rumpled blanket. How much could we admit? Dieter's pull was the pull of his land; he might have been its emblem. And what was he seeking in me?

"To talk more directly," I answered slowly. "I don't know."

"Don't know what?"

It was so quiet in the building. Even the pigeons had left the courtyard.

"If one could say the word 'Jew' here without thinking 'Holocaust'—that would mean something. I don't know if one can."

"But Americans are optimists," answered Dieter. "Don't you think we can try?"

Angelita; or, International Solidarity

Angelita and Wolf met in Moscow. The cleverest, the toughest of ten children, she'd made her way from her father's farm in the Dominican mountains to the university in Santo Domingo. There she became a Communist and was chosen to spend a year at the International Party School, last relic of the Comintern. Wolf had traveled the shorter distance from Berlin, where he worked for the railway. After their year in the Soviet Union they married. Their son Raoul was born in Berlin.

The two of them were the driving force behind an organization called Central America Solidarity. I was sick of observing my country through others' eyes, while patiently insisting that there is another America, heart and soul opposed to official policies. Eldridge Cleaver might be selling trousers nowadays, but I grew up with his words in my ears: "If you're not part of the solution, you're part of the problem."

Central America Solidarity, a coalition embracing several shades of political opinion, was the most energetic of the local organizations I had visited. It was also international: half of its forty-odd members were Latino, among the rest were numbered a Filipino, a Yugoslavian and a Kurd. In addition to calling demonstrations at appropriate moments, the group was devoted to three projects. One was the maintenance of a guerrilla radio station in El Salvador, another, the construction of a health center in rural Nicaragua. The third was the support of the University of El Salvador.

"With your experience," said Angelita, "I think you should join the university group."

"Oh" — I faltered, very disappointed — "I've spent so much time in universities, I'd sort of like to get away from them. I was hoping to do something more practical."

"But thinking is practical," she answered surprised, opening her eyes a little wider. Sharing her easy conviction, government troops had attacked the University of El Salvador in 1980, killing thousands of unarmed students and faculty. Most of the buildings were destroyed, what remained was occupied by the army. Yet the university continued to function, holding semilegal classes in basements and garages. Those present were risking their lives.

Daydreaming Enlightenment, so hard to conceive. I had spent years trying to demonstrate the connection between theory and practice; was it only philosophers who needed to be shown? "But what," I asked, "can we do to help them?"

"They're counting on international pressure to reopen the university. There are already campaigns in Italy and Spain. For five marks you can become an honorary member of the University of El Salvador." She showed me a stack of mud-colored certificates the size of diplomas. There was a space in the middle for the new member's name; at the bottom stood the words "With Culture to Freedom." "When the university is liberated, they're going to build a monument showing the names of all the people who helped them. "Meanwhile," said Angelita, "I hope to raise enough money to build them a library."

"Can't you keep this fucking place a little cleaner?" The door opened suddenly, Wolf entered the room.

"Raoul spilled the cocoa on his way to bed." Angelita's voice flattened, searching for calm. "And the bell rang before I could find the mop and now we're—"

"Ah," said Wolf, noticing me.

"—talking about the university group," she finished with the slightest air of triumph.

Wolf shook my hand, smiling behind his ragged beard. His small eyes maintained a promise of innocence.

Angelita turned back to me. "You could really be useful," she continued. "I mean," she paused, "you're a philosopher. That's an important profession." Enjoying her shrewdness, I suppressed a smile. "Besides, it's the project I'm working on. I'd really like to have you with us."

Not unwillingly, I gave in; this was a woman I wanted to know.

"Shall we drink to it?" asked Wolf. "I've got Russian vodka. The very best." Three little glasses came down from the shelves. Behind them stood the complete works of Marx and Engels. On the right were framed photographs of a large family smiling under Caribbean trees.

* * *

She was short, and always in a hurry, but it never made me nervous, for her haste contained a kind of calm at the center. Our conversations were broken by the beat of the everyday: Raoul's need for a sandwich, a stop at the laundry, the perpetually ringing telephone. Angelita left an impression of never quite being able to concentrate. Then she would quite suddenly utter a fairly stunning bit of insight. Her observations were always personal. Pressed about political theory she defended a vague sort of democratic socialism, boasting that the Dominican Communist Party was the world's most independent. "We were the only ones to criticize the invasion of Czechoslovakia, and the Soviet Union respected us for it too!" As we got closer she confessed she would never have joined the German party, then caught herself with a groan. It hurt to betray her comrades by criticizing them to an outsider; it hurt more to belie her own internationalist principles, which refused to allow for national failings on so grand a scale.

It seemed we were always in motion. "Do you want to meet Alicia? She is"—Angelita sighed—"a prostitute. No political consciousness. She's a wonderful seamstress. I've been trying to convince her to make a business of it. But she has two kids at home in Santo Domingo, it isn't easy." Taking my arm, Angelita steered to the side of the subway station, just avoiding three stout matrons determined not to stray an inch from their course. "I never remember: if they're on the left, you're supposed to keep right, or what? Alright," she shrugged, "it's quarter to three. Would you mind if we stopped at Karstadt's? They're supposed to be having a sale."

Behind the department-store escalator two tables were piled high with children's clothes. We joined the women who stood before them, gravely looking for the proper size. "I'll never forget how my mother divided an egg once. After the invasion it was all we had left. She gave me one half; my little sister got the other. So I understand Alicia, you know? But it isn't an answer. She drinks now."

"What about these, Angelita?" I held up a pair of jeans.

"He'd never wear them. Four-year-olds get very picky. I've found something." She took two pairs of pants to the counter and asked the cashier for the price.

"What?" barked the woman, irritated and blank. Angelita's German was indeed rather bad. Still, her question had been perfectly intelligible, even if the endings were wrong.

Unflustered, she set her mouth only slightly. "I said, how much are these pants, please?"

"There's a sign on the table," said the cashier. "If you people know how to read."

"Bastards," I said. "C'mon. There's a cashier on the other side of the store."

"Do you think they'll be any different?" Angelita smiled. "Let's go. I've got to take the leaflets to the office, and I promised to visit Alicia before I pick up Raoul."

* * *

Though its daily paper could be found at most newsstands, the Communist Party played less of a role in the affairs of the Federal Republic than in those of any other continental European country. Other Eurocommunists had the luxury of abstraction, but Germans had an instance of real existing socialism right on their hands. Perceived as agents of East Germany, its members were prohibited from holding public office, which includes teaching positions of any kind. Sometimes they joined other leftist groups in coalitions where they weren't particularly welcome; otherwise they maintained their own feckless rites. The entertainment at their annual party was a sort of Las Vegas manqué: acrobats in sequined suits balanced trays of champagne glasses from their mouths, squeaking swing bands played to middle-aged working couples dancing cheek-to-cheek. In the beer garden on the terrace there were hearty handshakes; everyone addressed each other as "Comrade" and nobody knew all the words to the "Internationale." It seemed anything but threatening.

The Charlottenburg party office was housed in a new building with red window frames. Over the Xerox machine hung a portrait of Lenin, hands in his pockets, walking by the Neva. Wolf was pacing in the corridor when we arrived.

"You're almost twenty minutes late!" he shouted. "Think I have nothing better to do than wait for you?"

"We were meeting at the university. It ran late," said Angelita.

"Everything runs late when you're around. Latino time. No wonder," he sneered, "no wonder your comrades never get it together politically, down there."

She shouted something in Spanish. I intervened. "Angelita is late because she does so many things. I don't know how she manages at all."

"I do a lot too. That's not the point. It's a matter of temperament. Speaking of getting things done," he returned to her, "I don't suppose you'll get around to cleaning the office today?"

"I have to pick up Raoul from kindergarten."

"But you expect people to work in a shit hole like this. Very commendable, exploiting your own party. They pay good wages. You think you'd get twelve marks an hour washing floors for anyone else?"

"*Olla, gringa.*" It was, thankfully, Mario.

"*Gringa*?" I grinned. "The comrade from San Salvador to you."

"At the meeting," explained Angelita to their puzzled faces, "Susan made a speech on behalf of the University of El Salvador. The moderator looked at his program and her dark hair and introduced her as the comrade from San Salvador."

"Congratulations," said Mario.

"We collected four hundred marks," reported Angelita. "She was only fazed for a minute."

"Where are the leaflets?" The story had deflated his ire, but Wolf was still fidgeting.

"In my bag," said Angelita. "No, not that one, those are Raoul's new pants." She scribbled a note, arranged a meeting and parted from her husband with a nod.

"There are Turkish bouletten on the corner," she told me when we'd reached the street. "Do you want one? They put rice in them. I haven't eaten all day."

"Angelita," I said, "can't you get a better job?"

"That's what Brigitte says too. She thinks it's disgraceful that a graduate of the Party School in Moscow should work as a cleaning woman. But what can I do? My German is bad. Wolf paid for a language course which I never finished, years ago. Eight hundred marks, so now he's mad. I couldn't sit down and learn all those cases." The Turkish youth serving sandwiches through the window smiled broadly when he saw her. "Want a bite?" Angelita offered me her boulette. "The best job I had here was with the Red Cross. It only lasted a couple of months, though. The supervisor of the refugee homes didn't like us inspecting conditions." She waved to the Turk, turning to go. "Cleaning's not so bad, it's just boring. But they're pretty relaxed about the hours I work."

* * *

Brigitte was twenty-seven and very thin. Writing a dissertation on the PLO made her the most educated member of Central America Solidarity, and she never succeeded in suppressing her pleasure about it. At big meetings she took notes, especially when Wolf was speaking. Marlene was a feminist lawyer whose house was full of plants and whose husband always smiled. We all met regularly to prepare forthcoming events. At Angelita's house there was invariably something to eat.

"I had to cook anyway," she would shrug.

"You buy avocados?" asked Brigitte one evening, surveying the table with an upturned brow.

"Oh." Angelita smiled, a little embarrassed. "That argument. Maria's strict too. But we eat avocados every day at home, and—"

"I don't buy fruit from South Africa, and I don't buy fruit from Israel," said Marlene. "I think one ought to be consistent."

My stomach tightened. I asked cautiously, "You think one should boycott avocados because they come from Israel?"

"Of course," said Brigitte.

"Do you boycott U.S. products?"

"Maybe one should," said Marlene.

"But it would be very impracticable," concluded Brigitte. "Besides," she said, "it's a different case. The State of Israel is founded on Zionism, and Zionism is the ideology of racism and oppression."

"There's a socialist Zionism too. The original goal of Zionism wasn't to oppress anybody but to create a state where the Jews could live as a people like any other."

"But the Jews aren't a people at all!" cried Brigitte impatiently.

"Brigitte," I said, "I am Jewish. And I will tell you that the Jews are a people."

"You see?" she said brightly. "I would never have known that you were—of Jewish extraction. And it doesn't matter to me at all. For me, you're just an American."

"But it matters to me!"

"But you're not religious?"

"No. A little. Not really."

"Then your family background is irrelevant. Judaism is a religion. Only Nazis and Zionists think it has to do with nationality."

"Listen to me!" I was losing patience, and composure. "You're talking about a question that's been debated for hundreds of years. It's *complicated.* The Jews aren't a people the way other peoples are. We can't be. We have a different history. Still there's something I have in common with every Jew, no matter where he comes from, that I don't have with any random American."

"I don't," said Marlene, "understand what you mean."

"I do," said Angelita, who had been silent, watching very carefully.

"Angelita," said Brigitte, "you don't know anything about this subject. You can't possibly understand what she means."

"Yes she can," I said.

"All right," said Brigitte, suppressing a sigh. "Explain it to us."

"She means she feels isolated," said Angelita.

"But she wouldn't feel less isolated if there were a few more Jews around!" cried Brigitte in exasperation and scorn.

"The hell I wouldn't."

"There are no typical Jewish qualities," began Brigitte, more patiently. "All the studies agree. Even the allegedly typical Jewish appearance—dark hair, crooked nose—is simply a feature of one particular group, the Eastern European

Jews. The rest is just Nazi propaganda. Do you know," she said instructively, "there are even blond Jews!"

"Most of my cousins, for example."

"Then you see," said Brigitte, "the idea that there is some kind of characteristic Jewish identity is nothing but a racist myth."

"What I see," I said slowly, "is that we are already exterminated. As a people. The few of us who are left over can stick around. If we're real quiet about it."

* * *

"I only wear makeup when I'm furious," said Angelita, looking at the mirror with satisfaction.

The reception for the rector of the University of El Salvador had been a qualified success. Touring Europe to raise support for his beleaguered university, he had been well-received in England and Holland. After failing to prod the Berlin universities into offering official support, Angelita had to wangle a room for the press conference from a vocational school.

"They're afraid of offending the occupying powers. But I'm ashamed," she said, "that we couldn't do better. Do you realize what a risk he's taking?"

The rector was a stocky, modest man with a small moustache. His predecessor had been murdered, and this tour was a gamble. It might bring enough international publicity to deter the military from further violence. It might produce the opposite effect.

Perhaps it was on his mind as he answered reporters' questions under dull fluorescent lighting, evoking another world. On the floor of a rented basement in San Salvador, quiet students pored over shared textbooks with an ear to the door. After classes they continued to staff the countryside literacy programs which the university initiated.

"And terrorism?" asked a journalist. The army's pretext for storming the university was a photograph of a papier-mâché rifle in a student theater production.

"In a country like El Salvador," said the rector, "education itself is subversive." Angelita translated with shining eyes.

Mario and I had prepared kettles of stew to serve after the conference at two long tables hastily shoved together in the bare white room. There was plenty of wine and plenty of toasting.

"Here's till we meet again in a liberated El Salvador!" called Brigitte, moderated that evening by unaffected ardor.

Dinner eaten, we pushed back the tables. Angelita and Wolf stood glowing, reconciled for a moment in each others' arms. A scratchy tape recorder played Dominican and Salvadoran music. We danced, gay and turning, long into the night. A deep sense of joy overtook me: my life was unutterably *contingent*, and this was a truth I'd been lucky to learn. But it was no night for reflection; I let myself be taken, easy and grateful, into pairs of strange arms.

"Excuse, please." It was the rector. "May I dance?"

"But of course."

"You I want to especially thank." His English was stiff and slightly nasal.

"To thank me? Whatever for?"

"Excuse me. It is to me very moving when a North American wants to help with our struggle. That way we do not feel so lonely."

"It's you I have to thank." Somewhere, I recalled, there were academics who say they wonder about the existence of the external world. But how could I begin to explain?

"You should come to San Salvador for a visit," he urged. "It would make us very happy." Maria, at his side, agreed.

Raoul fell asleep in a corner; those of us remaining were rather drunk. In Spanish, then in German, we sang the "Internationale." The rector had a tear in his eye.

* * *

"Susan," asked Angelita the next morning, "with you and love—it's not so easy, is it?"

"What do you mean?"

"I mean..." she was suddenly shy. "Well—you don't just go to bed with anyone, so lightly?"

"No," I answered, "I don't, really."

"I've been watching. I thought you might—it's funny. I'd always heard that American women go to bed without thinking about it. Like changing shoes."

"Really?"

"When I first went to Moscow, I was very nervous. I didn't want people to think I came from a backward country. So I went to bed with Wolf the second time we met. Afterward I felt so bad that I wanted to hide my head in a hole in the ground. "*Tja*," she said, smiling again, "he told me later that he hadn't expected it. But I just didn't know."

* * *

At the bottom echoed longing. Once there'd been a man who wrote poetry. He was killed in a murky accident, but things between them had gone wrong before that. Angelita was vague about the details though she told me hundreds of stories about her relatives back home. Her stance wasn't stoic, but she handled her own misfortunes the way she handled the dishes that had to be washed, dried and put away till morning.

The discordance was under the surface. West Berlin in the eighties fairly burbled with support. The fashion for Latin America extended beyond predictable murmurs of support for any cause directed against U.S. policy. Five or six stores in the center of town alone survive by selling knickknacks from Central and South America, and there are just as many kneipen featuring salsa and empañadas. The Berliner clientele stands swaying, wistfully applauding Latino "warmth" and "spontaneity" in something of the spirit with which Nietzsche wrote of Heine's "lightness."

I was late to the first of the Spanish lessons Angelita offered to the members of Central America Solidarity, and excused myself with a joke: "I figured this was the right spirit for beginning." "That doesn't make sense," said Brigitte. "If you come late, you'll have less time to learn." Angelita laughed all past explaining.

Friendship with her was a pull to the side. Arriving in Berlin I'd fought the equivocal lure of an *Ausländer* camp. Bitching about the Germans was the workaday pastime of thousands who lived there, voluntarily or not; it seemed specious, racist and boring to boot. Through Angelita it came to seem inevitable. Not because she did it; the few occasions she complained were suffused with wry compassion. Years later I learned that the Mexican owner of the shop selling Mexican trinkets on the Kudamm was forbidden by her German husband and his German partner to have a voice in running the store. Here I saw nothing so lucid, or rotten, just daily condescension and distrust.

They meant well, they tried hard. (Meant too well? Tried too hard?) They simply failed to see when this light-brown woman who spoke lousy German and worked as a maid was head and shoulders above them: not just in humanity but in discernment. So gradually and despite all intentions, the decisions in the group devoted to the welfare of Central America were made by its German members.

It would be another year before Angelita gave in to despair, bought two plane tickets, and took Raoul to Santo Domingo.

Hot Fall

The words "Hot Fall" embodied a threat: the peace movement swore that the missiles wouldn't be stationed with ease. No one knew whether the violence implicit in the expression would materialize, but there was nowhere to go without thinking of war.

In September a group called Doctors Against Nuclear War set up a table in front of the Kaiser Wilhelm Memorial Church. Every day on the Kudamm, they passed out leaflets with the heading: THE LIVING WILL ENVY THE DEAD. At the university ninety professors called for an illegal strike; some pressed for joint action with union leaders. Banners hung from the windows of many apartment buildings. Some of the slogans were funny: NO NEW ATOMIC WEAPONS UNTIL THE OLD ONES ARE ALL USED UP! There were others, grimmer than the leering skull which adorned them: DO YOU WANT TOTAL WAR? The question came from Goebbels; nobody in Berlin could read it without thinking of old newsreels showing thousands of civilians, right arms raised to the podium, shouting in answer, "Yes!" So many of the banners (old sheets, torn curtains) fluttering on the streets that fall read simply NO!

"It's the largest popular movement in this country since the Nazis," said Brentano ruefully.

"Do you think it will succeed?"

"There's a chance. I don't know."

The Parliament would meet in November to decide whether to accept the gift of 202 Pershing missiles from its principal ally. ("Occupier," came the mutter, smoldering anger growing louder, those days. My eyes to the ground.) The peace movement wanted to preempt them with a referendum: "Atomic weapon-free zones" were created throughout the country. It was hard to know what to say when the Philosophy Department voted to declare itself weapon-free; nor had anyone thought of proposing to station the missiles in Kreuzberg. Still I bought a yellow sticker that said KREUZBERG IS AN ATOMIC WEAPON-FREE ZONE to put on my door.

There were, of course, other voices. "I think the anti-Americanism today is just shameful," said the dentist. "I want you to know that not every German citizen feels that way. Some of us appreciate the protection your country provides us." She thought she was doing me a favor; I tried to disappoint her cautiously. (It's hard to argue vigorously with your dentist.)

"But I support the peace movement myself. I don't think the missiles will protect anything. On the contrary."

"Oh, but..." She laid her drill on the table. "You are still very young. Let me tell you a story. I was just a child when the Russians came. My mother was hiding in the cellar; it was my grandmother who opened the door. 'If you come one step further, I'm going to telephone Stalin.' Ah, she was clever, my grandmother. 'See?!' she shouted. 'You—here? I telephone Stalin.' Now that soldier didn't understand a word of German, but you can bet he was out of the house in a minute when he heard that. Telephone—Stalin. Which just goes to show," she concluded, picking up the drill, "that you can only deal with the Russians by using force. That's all they understand."

It was the Russians, and nobody else, who reopened the theater, in June '45, when most of Berlin still lay buried in rubble. And what was performed, those first months of occupation? ("Liberation." "Occupation.") *Nathan the Wise*, Lessing's plea for enlightenment and tolerance, starring his best friend Moses, alias Nathan, everybody's favorite Jew. That, too, was the Russians' idea: searching for roots left in German culture on which one might hope to rebuild a civilization. (Auschwitz they had liberated in February.)

"You're forgetting the rapes."

"I'm not forgetting them."

"The Russians raped thousands of women, those first weeks in Berlin. The men were all gone."

"Twenty million dead."

"What?"

"Twenty million dead Russians. Shot starved burned hung beaten gassed. It's just a fact. There wasn't a family in the Soviet Union who hadn't lost someone to the Germans."

"My mother didn't kill any Russians."

* * *

*T*he clock showed a mere 7 A.M. Barely awake and wondering I picked up the ringing telephone. The caller didn't identify himself; his voice sounded distant on the crackling wire. "Erich will meet you at the border at Friedrichstrasse on September sixteenth, four P.M." It was an anonymous message from East Berlin. Sleepy cold-war spy stories played in my ears until I counted the days and realized it was quite simple. Erich had no telephone, and must have received my letter inviting myself to High Holiday services. I had wanted to celebrate with someone, and he was the only Jew I knew in this city. (This city.)

But if Erev Yom Kippur was in ten days then today was Rosh Hashanah, and suddenly I wanted to go to services, even foreign, and alone. There was a synagogue across the canal. For the first time in my life I knew the dates of even the minor Jewish holidays; they were marked by the presence of a police van guarding the gate. On Friday nights the lamps were lit. I hadn't seen other signs of life there.

No longer able to sleep I washed, dressed and called the central office of the Jewish Community.

"Fraenkelufer?" Synagogues have no names here, they are called by the streets where they stand. "You don't need a ticket if you want to go to the Fraenkelufer. Shabbos, they're happy to get a *minyan*."

Are they looking out for neo-Nazis? Perhaps the PLO? Synagogue security is tight in Berlin: a withdrawn young man with an Israeli accent searched my bag at the door. Afterward he was not unfriendly. "L'shana tova," he said, pointing to a staircase. "L'shana tova," I replied, going up to the balcony reserved for women.

Slowly, the synagogue began to fill up. With relief I watched small children enter, adults with faces which might belong in American cities. Nobody was in a hurry: latecomers interrupted praying men with a handshake, children ran down the aisles, only slightly subdued.

"L'shana tova," said an elderly woman. "That is my seat."

I rose, embarrassed.

"But you may sit in the seat next to mine for a while. Frau Friedmann always comes very late." The entire first row of the balcony, where I had placed myself to lean down to see the service, was in fact empty. Fumbling a little, I switched seats.

My new neighbor took out a prayer book and placed it on the ledge before her. "This is your first time at the Fraenkelufer, no? Most of the young people go to the liberals in the Pestalozzistrasse. The cantor is famous. So he was in the movies. *Nu*? With that organ, they might as well be in a church."

"This is a lovely synagogue," I ventured in reply.

"This is nothing. In the old days this was one wing of the synagogue. They used it as a little chapel. Seating was different too." I followed her finger, tracing air. "The main synagogue was burnt. More they didn't leave."

Below us the cantor stopped singing. An older man stepped to the altar, and spoke all of the words I had most feared to hear.

"The Holocaust, like the destruction of the Temple, was God's punishment for our failure to keep the Law," he began. My neighbor was silent, examining her fingers; the other faces were too far to see. "We must never forget, we survivors—and each one of you knows how narrowly you survived—that almost everyone abandoned the Jews. Even those people who resisted the Nazis. The exceptions—there were some exceptions. They came from the little people. The ones who had nothing. The others? They left us to rot. Which is why," he concluded, "to criticize Israel is to cut your own flesh. Whatever they do, we must stand behind them. We have no one else to count on."

Had I the right to judge? My survival was never in question. (Three generations on American soil, from Odessa they came, my forefathers, and Galicia.) No the question is wrong, the issues are separate: it's thinking that's needed, and none too soon. But it was thought that failed me, sad blankness took its place; I listened dumb, to the chanting below.

* * *

Dieter never wore a watch. Every few minutes he leaned his head out the gallery door to look at the church-tower clock. The opening had been set for seven o'clock. It was his first one-man show.

"Look," I said, "let's open a bottle now. It'll do you good."

Dieter shifted a stack of catalogues, forming an asymmetrical pile on the table by the door.

I tried again. "Nobody comes anywhere on time in this city. It would be too authoritarian." Dieter gave a little snort of ersatz laughter.

By eight o'clock I was busy, opening bottles, answering questions. They had turned out in numbers, it would be a success.

"But the Salome trend is declining..."

"Three weeks in Corfu, it was much too brief..."

"You haven't seen *Class Enemies*?"

"Anton is working at the Schaubühne...."

"How do you suppose he came up with that title?"

Dieter stood in the center, glass in hand. The tension in his face had turned to excitement. Edging my way through the crowd I could see his relief.

"My girlfriend, Susan," he introduced me to Tina, and said in my ear, "I've got to talk to the man by the window. That's the reporter from *Zitty*."

Stunning Tina cocked her blond head to the side. One shoulder was bare, the other covered in red.

"You're an old friend of Dieter's?" I tried.

"I knew him in Stuttgart," she replied.

"And how do you like the paintings?"

"Better than the stuff he used to do. He's gotten away from Beuys's influence."

"I really like them," I said.

Tina glanced around the room, twisting a jagged earring. "You're not German, are you?" she asked.

I shook my head.

"Where do you come from?"

"I'm American."

Tina stared. "Amis," she said.

I stiffened and said there were all kinds. And as for the politics—

"I don't care about the politics. It's the people that get me. They're so superficial."

"Ever read Nietzsche?"

"Nietzsche?"

"*The Gay Science*. He said the Greeks were superficial—out of profundity."

"Oh," said Tina.

"Noncommittal," said Dieter. I felt his hand on the small of my back.

"What?"

"The *Zitty* reporter. They never say for certain. But I think he'll review the exhibit."

"Great."

"Your glass is empty," he said with a smile. "It's time to celebrate!"

By the rivers of Babylon
Where we sat down
And there we wept
When we remembered—

"Nothing like Bob Marley," said Dieter. "Jürgen brought some music. Come. Weren't you in Jamaica once?"

Days and nights. The gallery was emptying, leaving spots of lipstick on clean cheeks. The press and possible buyers had come and gone. Dieter was humming, elated and generous. Only friends still remained.

"Good opening," said Jürgen, "but what are you going to do with the rest of the champagne?"

"Start in on it. Oh," said Dieter, turning to me, "I nearly forgot. This is for you."

In a used-book store he'd found a memoir, written in the last century. The author's name was Blumenthal. "What he writes here about Berliner Jews looks pretty interesting."

Gratefully uneasy, I looked at the chapter he showed me. Dieter was trying hard. To speak more directly, of Germans and Jews: he'd said that he wanted to learn.

My eyes traced words on a page, but tension kept me from understanding them. Dieter's older colleague Thomas peered over my shoulder. "Yes, that was the sad part," he said, shaking his head. "They really viewed themselves as Berliners. Hard to imagine now, but—"

"You were saying you just attended that synagogue in Kreuzberg, Susan?" Dieter broke in with a hasty cough. He was warning Thomas, protecting me. Intervening to be sure that no word went wrong. Making everything clear from the start.

"Oh," said Thomas, "so you're..." he paused, staring.

"Jewish," I said.

"Really. Well." He searched his pockets for matches. "You know, I've never really been sure. Is it—are they a religious group or something like a nation?"

"Depends on who you talk to. Both, I think."

"So you, uh, you follow the religion?"

"Not very strictly. I go to synagogue for the holidays. Last week was the Jewish New Year."

"Ah, they, I mean you have a different calendar?"

"Starts in the fall. Like the academic calendar."

"Really. Interesting. And, ah, I suppose you support the State of Israel?"

Our voices were level, quite easy, really. Breathing was even and pulses were slow. His glance revealed no shame or tension, mine betrayed no fear. It bore every formal resemblance to an ordinary conversation. That's what Dieter had wanted.

* * *

Erich was waiting on the other side of the border, looking relieved that I'd gotten his message. "We have to take the S-Bahn to the synagogue. There's not a lot of time."

The silence was a reprieve after the flaunty teeming streets of the West. Our conversation felt clumsy. East-West friendships moved fast, if at all, for all the commonplaces which let you slide into familiarity were absent. (Chance meetings. Telephones, often. The question: your place or mine?) But something else was in the air that day too.

Plain and out of the way, the small synagogue was the only one left standing in East Berlin. "Is there a balcony?" I asked. "We're not that *frumm*," he said, "or that full. Everybody sits downstairs." I followed him into the main room where he pulled a yarmulke from his jacket pocket. "But not in the same row!" he said quickly. "The women sit on that side."

Divided by an aisle, then, I spent much of the service glancing at Erich, who knew even less about praying than I did. The congregation was old, the service was short: no rabbi, no speeches, no display.

"We could go back to my house, if you want, until you have to get to the border. I mean, it's Yom Kippur. We can't really go to a kneipe."

Erich lived in one room with a coal oven and a kitchen. There are thousands like it in the working-class corners of West Berlin. Its colors were runny, mustard and brown. Next to the window was a large bookcase packed with neatly ordered volumes.

I had brought him another. Its author, Edgar Hilsenrath, was a German Jew who survived a Nazi ghetto in Rumania, and his book *Night* was the most powerful I'd ever read on the subject. Erich had never heard of it. He thanked me for the gift.

"I've never been so shaken up by a book. Ever. It's about something worse than a concentration camp. In Rumania. They deported thousands of people to a couple of ghettos. They sealed them off, so that hardly any food got in. They rounded up and shot everybody who didn't have a place to sleep at night. And then they kept pouring more people in. So the Nazis were superfluous; they let the Jews do to each other what the SS did elsewhere. Well, almost."

He looked at me. "My grandmother was at Maidanek. That's what she said: the worst thing was not what the guards did. It was what people were forced to do to each other."

For days I had wanted to ask a question, since the moment when the inconceivable image bored into my head to stay, I suppose, till the day I die. It was too fragile and terrible to trust with just anyone.

"They interviewed Auschwitz survivors on the TV last week. Did you..."

He nodded very gently. "With the chain..." Enough. Enough to know that he was left with that image as I was. Enough to know that he too spent nights thinking: It could have been me, could I have done *that*, would I have survived? It didn't matter that we couldn't say more, unable to repeat the story of the woman forced to drag her friend through miserable death. Silent understanding: is that what I missed in this land?

We shared it for minutes. Then Erich rose and took a book from his shelf. "I want to give you something too." Called *Jakob the Liar*, the novel about the Warsaw Ghetto was written in East Berlin. Erich inscribed the flyleaf before putting it in my hands.

"How do you live here, Erich? You were born in Berlin, but—"

"Listen," he said. "This isn't West Germany. The Nazis hated Communists as much as they hated Jews. So the antifascism here is genuine. It's not something they trot out on special occasions to put the Allies at ease."

"But—"

"No but. Are you asking if I feel at home here? It's my country. I try to defend it. I support the principles it's built upon."

"But—"

"How could I possibly feel at home?"

* * *

*T*he kneipe in the Oranienburgerstrasse was smokier than most. The mirror behind the bar reflected bottles, blunted anger. The tables in the back were painted a lewd green. They were taken by real punks, and people who find them authentic. "Berliner contradictions," I muttered with a weary smile. It was after midnight, and Dieter was waiting.

"Central America keeping you busy?"

"I don't really understand your contempt."

It wasn't contempt, he answered precisely. He just knew the Berlin political scene too well to take it seriously. Of course, I was new here, and they must be delighted to have a token Ami to show.

"I don't mind that."

"If you don't mind being used ..."

But I didn't feel used; I had too much in mind. Living abroad had made me aware of my country's power; I felt responsible for abuses. And that wasn't all.

"So what else is driving you?"

"Thinking about German history."

He shrugged his shoulders. "Do what you like. I'm just surprised that you want to spend your time collecting a couple of marks for Nicaragua."

"El Salvador, actually. It isn't much, but it means a lot to them. It's painful to see how much it means to them. Besides," I said, "it's hard to make comparisons. But I once heard a Berliner talking about the German resistance. He was asked if it had been worth risking one's life for a little petty sabotage. It hadn't stopped the Nazis; only the Red Army did that."

"And he said?"

"The resistance in this country accomplished one thing: that postwar Germans needn't feel *boundlessly* ashamed."

"But the talk about resistance is always exaggerated. A couple of college students guillotined for printing up leaflets in Munich. Here and there somebody hiding a Jew. There wasn't very much."

"I know that too." It was hard to talk there; the blue-haired waitress stepped on our feet, and the music was noisy. "But you sound so defeatist today."

"Defeatist?" Dieter reached for my hand. "I'm just sick of everything about this country. Sick of everything about this continent." He sat up straighter. "What would you say if I asked you to come with me to an island?"

"Which island?"

"Any island. In the South Pacific, preferably. I've got money saved. It would last us a year, at least."

"Are you kidding?"

"No."

Someone had called me the week before, asking for advice about fellowships to study abroad. I began explaining options, the advantages of going here or there. He interrupted quickly: I had misunderstood him. He was just looking for the quickest way to get to New Zealand. Away from the bombs.

"I know how he feels," said Dieter. "This is the prewar age." He waited for an answer. "What do you think?"

"I don't know, Dieter. Berlin is enough island for me at the moment." I looked at him closely but couldn't find disappointment. Then again it was hard to tell what Dieter meant, sometimes.

Something about the posture was familiar, or was it the haircut? The young man at the bar was wearing a jacket emblazoned with a large U.S. flag, which in Berlin that fall was almost as provocative as wearing, let's say, an SS uniform.

"Your face is absolutely white," said Dieter. "What's wrong?"

"I just recognized someone. The student from last spring."

"Who?"

"The student who said 'Heil Hitler.'"

"Oh."

"I have to say something to him."

"Umm-hmm."

Hard to say why I was trembling, ever so slightly, as I made my way to the bar. Facing the mirror, Hans-Jürgen could see me approaching. He turned quickly and clapped a hand on my shoulder.

"Hey, you thought I meant it personally, that business with the silly 'Heil Hitler.' But I don't have anything against Jews—"

"I didn't take it personally, that wasn't the—"

"My aunt is half-Jewish, in fact."

The light was lurid, and I felt rotten. There were so many things to do at once: To apologize for the way the incident had been handled. To explain that I'd never viewed it as a personal matter. To try to make out that it was, nevertheless, nothing to laugh about. Hans-Jürgen offered me a cigarette; he didn't want to listen.

"Where'd you get the jacket?"

"Oh, that?" he answered. "I had it specially made. Pretty sharp, eh? Everybody's just *appalled* when they see it. They start yelling about the Pershings. Me, I'm easy. Let the missiles come. What do you think?"

What I think, Hans-Jürgen, is that you are a mess, in a thoroughly unpolitical way. But it's not much consolation, being vindicated. What I feel is helpless, down to my shoes I feel it, and I cannot remain.

* * *

"W*ould you rather have a little less, or a little more?"

I had asked for a pound of bananas, the pointer on the scale showed a pound and a half. The vegetable man offered to break up the bunch.

"That's alright," I told him. "Make it a little more."

"What else?"

"I'll take some tomatoes."

"Tomatoes are expensive, twelve marks a kilo. It's the only kind I buy these days. The ones from the Canaries rot in twenty-four hours."

There were perfectly good tomatoes for half the price at the next stand, but I never contradicted him. "So when will you get tomatoes I can afford?"

"Hard to say. There's a harvest coming in Morocco sometime."

"Then give me some parsley. No, not that much—"

"Oh, stop yammering," he replied, putting the parsley into my bag with a wink. "Stick it in water, it'll keep for a week."

"How much are the cucumbers?"

"Two twenty-five for the big ones. These here are one seventy-five."

"I'll take a little one."

"Are you crazy?" He held the cucumbers side by side. "The little ones, in truth, looked rather shriveled. "Who would take one of these, when—"

"Alright, alright, you've convinced me." I counted out coins; no one was waiting behind me. "The market's almost empty. Is there a holiday soon?"

"Holiday," he snorted. "There are so many unemployed people, they all need vacations."

"Wouldn't mind leaving town myself."

"You will," he answered. "I see that already. You'll go home, and what's more, you won't come back. You're one of the ones who won't come back. Some day, just like that, you'll be gone."

"I don't know."

"But I do," said the vegetable brother. He picked up the sign stuck between tomatoes and wiped out the words KILO 12 MARKS. With a stubby piece of chalk he wrote 100 GRAMS 1.20. "Sometimes you have to work with tricks," he confided. "Folks are *so* feeble-minded—" He stopped in mid-sentence, eyes caught and choked. His glance was held by a youngish man whom I recognized as a steady customer. Quick as a shot, the vegetable brother let his expression run: from a look that acknowledged he'd been caught to a look which assured the young man that he was excepted from this general law of human nature. The vegetable brother was almost as canny with silence as he was with words.

* * *

"I wanted to get back last night," said Dieter, "but the train was delayed. Somebody threw himself in front of it."

"Killed?"

"I suppose. Train was stopped for three hours, so I missed the connection to Berlin and had to spend the night in Hannover. That's a horror-city. So bourgeois, it's hard to believe. Eight hours in Hannover," he shuddered. "Wouldn't want to get stuck there again."

"Dieter," I asked him, "how was it in Stuttgart?"

He shrugged his shoulders. "What you'd expect, I guess. The old man was lucky. Didn't have time to feel a thing. It'll be hard for my mother. She's practically deaf, though she doesn't like to admit it. She was very dependent on him for getting around. I thought a lot, while I was there, about the importance of our sense of hearing. Vision is primary for me. But still..." There were lines at the corners of his eyes.

Not too many: too much has died in this land.

I reached for his hand, helplessly. "And you?"

"I haven't had anything to do with my father for twenty years." Dieter paused, smoothing his hair with his hand. "And he'd been dead since the war ended, inside."

"Yes, but—"

"Heart attack's an easy way to go. Come on," he said, "we'll miss the concert if we sit around here."

The black and white poster promised APOCALYPTIC EROS. Inside the roomy kneipe, a fussy gay man and a very pretty woman were reading bad poetry, in three languages, to the accompaniment of an occasional saxophone. Dieter drummed on the tabletop with long fingers.

"Holzberg was supposed to come," he said, looking toward the door. "Don't know what happened. This isn't much to come out for. We could have heard Nina Hagen at the Metropol."

I shivered. He was talking about his father. More exactly, he was not talking about his father. I knew that pushing him would elicit a few scraps of dogma: family relationships belong to petitbourgeois assumptions which have no place in the modern world—unless, *per impossible*, you just happen to be blessed with the right kind of family. Pushing him a little harder would lead to tears. But for whom? Could I believe his tears for others when he hadn't shed a one for his own father? And I knew he couldn't cry for his father's death because his father couldn't cry for the deaths of millions. His father had caused the deaths of millions. No that was absurd. Perhaps he hadn't caused a single one. He spent the war in Norway, where the Occupation was kind; that's what he'd told Dieter. That's what Dieter told me. Oh wretched silence. You never could be too sure about those things.

Booing and hissing may greet premieres at the opera; even well-bred Berlin audiences are not deferential. That night no holds were barred. "Enough of this trash!" yelled a thin-haired man. The pretty woman on stage paused, then began to read something in French. "I don't understand a word!" shouted a second. I tried to catch the woman's eye in sympathy but gave up after a while; smoke hung in the room, and she seemed only slightly unnerved. The saxophonist looked undecided.

"You're in Kreuzberg now," called a woman from the corner. "Here we have other problems."

* * *

GENOCIDE WILL BE DECREED TODAY

*T*he homemade banners were no longer confined to the occupied houses. There were more of them every week, in quiet houses on quiet streets. One day in November radios and televisions blared from windows all over town. It was a rather defeated form of protest. Polls differed somewhat, but they all agreed that if a public referendum were held, at least 76 percent of the German population would reject the stationing of the missiles. So there was no referendum; the question would be decided by Parliament, after the debate being broadcast that day. Nobody had any doubts about the outcome.

The demonstration on the Kudamm was small and merry; it was bitterly cold. A young man carried a sign reading BETTER TO FREEZE TODAY THAN BE INCINERATED TOMORROW. People holding torches encircled an accordion player singing "*Und weil der Mensch ein Mensch ist.*" On the sidewalk farther down, a girl was playing a tuba. From the crackling loudspeaker of a crawling truck one could make out the voices in the parliamentary debate. The demonstration was meant to be spontaneous; no one was certain of the route. Handing out leaflets for Central American Solidarity, I placed myself behind the Social Democratic Karl Liebknecht Youth Club because these teenagers were clearly doing the best job of shouting.

Auf die Strasse sprechen die Massen:
Kohl und Genscher, ihr seid entlassen!

Their faces were so fresh and exuberant, one could almost believe them.

"I don't need one!" The old man on the sidewalk rejected my leaflet with a cry of pain. "I don't need to read anything! I'm a Jew!"

I smiled at him, confused. "But so am I," I said.

"That you don't need to tell me. I see that already. And that's why I will have nothing to do with you."

The man was nearly shouting; I wondered if I'd heard him wrong. A small crowd of women formed a circle around us.

"What's going on?" demanded one. "Don't give her a hard time!"

"Is he saying something against Jews?"

The old man brushed them aside, taking my arm. "I want to show you something."

"Wait a minute—"

"You're going to see," he insisted, and lead me to the front of the demonstration, where he pointed a finger at a young woman wearing a sandwich board. On it was a painted skull.

"Those are the people who murdered my whole family!" he cried. "Can you imagine what I feel when I see that? And you, a Jewish girl, together with these—"

Slowly, dizzily, I began to understand. The skull was an SS symbol. It took a moment before I found my breath.

"You're mistaken," I began. "That's just what they're not. Did you hear the loudspeaker, just a minute ago, warning people to remember Nürnberg?"

"What's to remember? You hadn't even come into the world. But your father, surely, or your relatives—" He turned, abruptly, to leave me on the sidewalk, where the women who had wanted to defend me approached.

"What did he want from you?"

"Are you alright?"

"What was he saying?"

"He was"—I stopped and wondered, not knowing what I was meant to explain—"confused," I answered, overwhelmingly weary.

The loudspeaker sputtered. In faraway Bonn they were voting; the missiles would be stationed. The sign on the back of the truck read HIROSHIMA-VIETNAM-GRENADA. Next to it a poster purporting to be the advertisement of an American travel agency: "VISIT EUROPE WHILE IT'S STILL THERE!"

* * *

"You forgot it was *Thanksgiving*?"

My mother's voice was warm and faint on the telephone. In the background I could hear my brothers making gravy, laughing loudly, breaking glass.

"They don't have Thanksgiving here, Mama. And I've been pretty busy."

"Tell me what you've been doing."

"Writing some. And there's a lot going on politically."

"We heard about the demonstrations against the Euromissiles. There were protests here too. Did you see *The Day After*? It's a movie about nuclear war."

"I read about it."

"Go see it, if you get a chance. It was on television here. Of course, it was awful being interrupted every ten minutes by commercials, but..." she sighed, "That's the way the world is."

"But that's not the way the *world* is! They don't have television commercials here. Not even in *West* Germany."

"They don't? Well, I can't say. Do you want to speak with your brothers?"

I did, of course, feeling lost and remote, far more than an ocean away.

* * *

There were no men in the train compartment. Sitting next to the window was a Turkish teenager whose long black hair was held tightly in place with a plastic clip. Across from her were two plump and elderly West Germans wearing ugly hats. Opposite me, next to the door, was a quiet old woman whose shoes (or was it the cut of her suit?) revealed she was East German, traveling to visit a child who lived in the West. We were heading toward Köln.

"Ugh," said the plumpest of the West Germans. "I'll be glad to get over the border. It gives me the shivers, just riding through."

"I know just what you mean," said her companion. "The way they look at your passport..."

"It's not so bad nowadays," said the East German.

"You can't tell me anything," said the first woman hastily. "We worked in a Russian camp after the war. What we suffered, let me tell you..."

"I'll never go there again," added the second. "I've seen enough of Drüben."

"Lots of fields in this region," said the East German, very pointedly. The compartment fell silent.

Outside the window, on a very gloomy day, men and women were pitching squash into an open truck. Are there harvest songs, like those in New England, about all being safely gathered in? Nothing evokes safety, here: staring through the unwashed glass I wondered how often that patch of ground had changed hands.

The Turkish girl unpacked a platter full of carefully wrapped pastries. Before taking one she offered the platter to each of us.

"Oh! Well, I don't mind if I do!" said the first West German. "Eh—did you make them yourself?"

"No," said the girl. "My aunt made them last night." She spoke perfect German, was anxious to please.

We chewed quietly.

"Were you, eh, were you born in Turkey?" asked the second West German.

"In Düsseldorf," said the girl. "My parents came from Ankara."

"*Ach* so," said the first West German. She looked at her companion. That night they would tell their husbands that they traveled from Berlin with a Turkish girl who was quite in order, really.

"And do you, eh ..." The second West German searched for something to say. "Do you cook Turkish at home, or German?"

"Both," answered the girl with an eager smile. "It all depends."

The stink of the train toilet was comforting, like anything familiar. I paced the corridor, smoking. Dieter was in Köln, trying to sell paintings. He'd be waiting on the platform, I could count on his face.

* * *

If you look to the left there are grave shadowed mountains, a long sweep of bay. If you look to the right there are cream-colored towers, and plastic signs in orange and brown: OBERBAYERN IMBISS, TOP BRITISH DISCO. Keeping your head turned left requires some practice, depending on the sun and the time of day. On the ever-sunny terrace by the harbor I stared at the coastline, wondering if ordering white wine instead of coffee would increase my depression or dull it.

El Arenal de Majorca.

"It's a package deal," said Dieter. "Off-season, and absurdly cheap. The hotel will be full of German tourists, but the interior is unspoiled. We can rent a car and drive into the mountains. What do you say?"

I had said yes.

Two weeks of plunging over coastal roads, seeking hidden coves between cliffs, watching the horizon, praising the light. Nights we sat in one or another of the desolate bars in the squalid tourist haven. On New Year's Eve we escaped to Palma, the capital city, where we found a crowd of people on a chilly plaza. A band played "Viva España" and we danced too, with the desperation peculiar to the holiday. The Majorcans sang, drank, and ignored us.

Our conversation staggered.

For all the misgivings I'd had before, seeing him there was a blow. Dieter was stiff and flustered, graceless and raw. Off German soil, he was helpless. Talking to shopkeepers? Slow torture. I saw his wish to be different from all the other tourists who were wrecking the coastline. I felt his hatred of all things broad, rich and Aryan. I watched the frustration before his own paralysis turn sullen, finally, distrustful and proud. All that passed through his eyes in the time it ought to take to say "*Una cerveza, por favor.*" But he ordered in German, very quickly resigned.

The waiters did not smile, and they did not frown.

"You should really see Portugal," said Dieter, fingering his wine glass in an empty bar. "I, myself, am much more drawn to the Portugese. The Spanish are so macho."

"How do you mean?" I asked, no longer very credulous.

"Think of the bullfights!" he answered. "But that's merely an expression. You can see it in their faces, if you know how to look. Or the way that they move."

The water by the harbor was cloudy, the afternoon sun faint. Dieter returned to the hotel to read *Saint Genet.* I was glad of the chance to sit alone, unequivocally wretched.

Staring at the harbor empty-eyed I recounted what I didn't like of Dieter Brock. He had a remarkable way of being didactic without being particularly informative, holding forth in a manner both dogmatic and abstract. He was arrogant, and flat. His remarks about friends were singularly cold and anecdotal: never once had I heard him betray a note of compassion. His reactions had become predictable. Should I try, however gently, to discuss my apprehension, he'd apologize profusely for all of his behavior. A moment later his face assumed a cast of unsinkable depression. After a time he'd talk vaguely of his past, demanding and refusing comfort.

I touched only skin.

One night in a moment of dread which rang genuine he'd confessed that he feared there might be nothing else. Dieter was made out of moments: one spasm of ache and outrage for his country's devastation; one eye scanning a room for a glimpse of Brian Eno through an avant-garde crowd. — Holding a hundred parts together with circumspect theater: positively Faustian I had found it, not so long before.

"*Uno otro vino blanco, Señora*?"

Nothing had prepared me; still I should have seen it coming, should have listened to the undertones. My questions had been worthless: I'd forgotten all I'd ever learned of reading between lines. I had heard the "Dachau" and not the "baby." I had taken everything for what it seemed. He might have been playing, he might have been desperate; with me he was fleeing, and it had to misfire. I was as moved by his trial as disgusted by his failure. I was anything else but in love.

Perhaps he'd been right, that night in the garden: it wouldn't be different with anyone else. Whenever they see me, there's blood in the air. Perhaps he'd forgotten. I never would know.

It was clear on the island. All this would soon become a scrap of stories to tell. But to whom? I wondered, and ached. I was already marked. Was there a corner of New York, perhaps, where someone understood what I'd come to understand here? I dismissed the longing like a foolish child: it was time to learn to live alone.

Dieter wasn't reckless; his passion and frenzy were checked for display. He saw the wind was changing and he drew in his sails. No point in affecting affect when the object would be gone. Our last days on Majorca were distant and demure. There was no scene to be made, no boat left to rock. We returned to Berlin with unspoken relief.

Ten days later I met the man I knew I would marry.

Garlic

*M*y first visit to Burger King was an act of despair. I had been two months in Berlin and thought I wasn't going to make it. There were so many reasons. On top of everything I'd just fought with Thomas and Ingrid, who showed no signs of going to Indonesia. Burger King. You spend half your life, these days, telling people that there's more to America than *Dallas* and Coca-Cola and missiles, that's just the stuff we make for export, and then you sit down in a foreign city and eat a *Whopper mit Käse*? I thought it was giving up, that afternoon. I fought the fantasy of slitting my wrists all over the most awful of Thomas's intricately morbid paintings by telling myself that it would be cowardly to commit suicide before determining whether or not I could learn to speak German. Then I walked out of Burger King and went to see *Faust.* The movie, the famous one, with Gustav Gründgens.

Things change. Eating at Burger King never lost significance, but later it was moods of defiance which took me there. It happens to be true that, gastronomically considered, a *Whopper mit Käse* was better than the rest of the fast food the city had to offer, but I knew that saying this was an act of provocation, producing suspicion in the faces of the best of my friends. Berliners eat *currywurst*, a thick hot dog cut up in pieces, with spicy ketchup piled on top to give it a flavor. There are also bouletten, hamburgers, really, but you eat them cold, dabbed in mustard, with a little piece of bread on the side. *Currywurst* and bouletten are traditional specialties. Now there's also the *Döner Kebab*, a hot sandwich in Turkish bread with six or seven pieces of tough beef the cook cuts from a spit in the window, shredded lettuce and onions on top, if you're lucky, a slice of tomato. In left-wing circles it's politically incorrect to say you find *Döner Kebabs* too greasy; there's even a rock song which begins with the words "Kebab dreams in the city of the Wall" and ends "Deutschland, Deutschland, it's all over / We are the Turks of tomorrow." As one of the Turks of yesterday, I could say what I liked. Burger King is better.

Impatient? A hamburger is a hamburger, grilled or fried, with mustard or ketchup or both, if you like, rare or medium rare or well done. If Berliner cuisine is really so bad that a *Whopper mit Käse* is better than the local substitute, then go to the Burger King.

How much meaning is too much meaning?

Let me tell you some stories about garlic.

* * *

***"M**y parents never allowed us to eat garlic," said Dieter over dinner one night.

"Why not?" I asked, not particularly curious.

"Garlic is Jew food."

"Jew food?" It took a minute before I was able to try to joke about it. "I wish it were. Jewish cooking is too bland, usually." Laugh, kid. So that's what explained the emphasis in his voice as he repeated "I really like garlic" while cooking the broccoli. I once met a man who told me his parents, old Nazis, wouldn't buy oranges from Israel. But no garlic, not a bit of it, all those years after the war?

* * *

> I asked my father if all Jews were rich. My father told me that there were also lots of poor Jews, especially in Eastern Europe.
> "And in Germany?" I asked.
> "Here too," said my father, "but not so many as in the East."
> "Our teacher told us recently," I said, "that all Jews eat garlic."
> "We don't eat garlic," said my father.
> "Why?" I asked.
> "Because it gives me heartburn," said my father.
> "And the other Jews?" I asked.
> "In the East," said my father, "they eat a lot of garlic. But the goyim there, they eat it too."
> "What are goyim?" I asked.
> "Those are the non-Jews," said my father.
> This talk between me and my father took place in the presence of our servant Grete, who happened to be in the living room. Grete said, "My old boyfriend the streetcar conductor, he was in Italy once. And they eat garlic there too."
> "That's true," said my father. "The Italians eat a lot of garlic."
> "Even more than the Jews in the East?"
> "I believe even more," said my father.
>
> —Edgar Hilsenrath, *Bronskys Geständnis*

Hilsenrath was nine when the Nazis forbade children like him to continue going to public school.

Was the idea that all Jews eat garlic as much a part of Nazi propaganda as the idea that all Jews are rich? What makes up an ideology?

* * *

***S**hela learned the hard way when her obstetrician, suspecting premature labor, sent her to lie in a hospital room with five other women in similar circumstances. On her husband's first visit he brought a bowl of white bean salad, a change from the hospital food. With him were friends, loud and expansive. Their talk filled the room with slow strange accents and buoyed her for an hour. When they departed she was all the more alone in the normal aimless quiet of the crowded room.

"That's some bean salad," said the sullen young Berliner in the next bed.

"Would you like some?" offered Shela. "There's plenty left."

"The very nerve!"

Unwary Shela replaced the aluminum foil and put the bowl in the corridor refrigerator. Not ten minutes later a nurse hurried to the room.

"Is this *your* salad?"

Shela nodded.

"You *are* planning to finish it soon?"

"I just had some, but..."

The other women on the ward exchanged glances. It wasn't quite a gloat, just a confirmation of providence.

"You *will* finish it soon, that's right?" The nurse coerced a nod from Shela as she patted down a bed.

When shifts changed, the night nurse entered the room.

"May I ask which of you ladies put a bowl of..."

Invisible fingers focused on Shela.

"It's bean salad," she murmured. "My husband brought it."

"Your *husband* brought it?"

"She said she married a German," came the fluster by the window.

"And how long—"

"I'll finish it soon," sighed Shela, beginning to understand.

"Because it's asking an awful lot to expect a room full of pregnant women to have to smell..."

"Garlic," went the whisper clear through the room, filled with the pleasure of seeing justice done.

Not an hour went by before a third nurse approached her. There was no longer a need to question: the entire hospital seemed aware of the culprit's identity.

"There's a ... smell in the refrigerator," the nurse announced. "I was wondering if I could—"

"Throw it out," said Shela. "Throw it out and leave me alone." She turned her face to the pillow, but the tears wouldn't come.

* * *

Angelita and I were shopping for the benefit. It's a form of political life so common in Berlin that we had to reschedule our benefit twice so as not to conflict with other groups. A large hall is rented, a foreign band is engaged, the organizing group sells food, drink and books about the cause of the evening, there are short speeches during the breaks between the music, and you have a few thousand marks for the Kurdish nationalists or the Turkish dissidents or the Chilean refugees. Our food had to be Central American, so Angelita was in charge. I was there to help carry the onions and beans and beef and eggplants she piled into the cart. And forty heads of garlic. We were cooking for four hundred people.

"I don't know what the Germans have against garlic," said Angelita. "We eat it all the time in the Caribbean. Here they call foreigners garlic-eaters. As if that were a reason to hate them."

"I know," I said, "and it started with the Jews."

"Really?" said Angelita.

"I didn't know it either till I came to Berlin. But the Germans call Jews garlic-eaters too."

Angelita, Marlene and I spent the next day cooking. I hadn't seen Marlene since the day she'd said she wouldn't eat the avocado from Israel. Chopping vegetables, we tried to sound relaxed.

"Here, taste this," said Angelita, reaching a ladle into the enormous pot on the stove. "Do you think it needs more garlic?"

"There are people," said Marlene, "who don't like garlic. But I think differently. I really like garlic."

"So do I," said Angelita.

"So do I," I said.

"Then chop up some more garlic," said Angelita, handing us each another piece. "But very fine. It has to be chopped very fine."

"I know how to chop garlic," I replied. "Told you yesterday." We laughed together as two women in a foreign country can do.

Marlene and I were chopping garlic, enough for four hundred people, enough so they can really taste it, when Karl entered the room. The first time Karl spoke to me alone, he asked if I came from a Jewish family. Yes, I'd said, happily surprised, nobody here ever recognizes it. My mother was Jewish, he'd told me. Told me the minute he got a chance, but Karl was a Communist, a printer turned party functionary, and when I brought up the subject sometime later, he said it meant nothing to him.

When Germans enter a room they shake hands with everyone in it. Marlene stopped chopping, and Karl shook her hand. Then he took my hand, and instead of shaking it, or kissing it, he put it to his nose.

"Mmmmmmm," murmured Karl, inhaling lustfully, gracefully, and walking out without a word.

Ten minutes later Marlene and I were still chopping garlic. "Ooooooh," she burbled, wiping away a stray piece. "My fingers are so *sticky*."

* * *

*I*t isn't memory, and it can't be blood. Still, nothing comes from nothing. A little research reveals that garlic was well known as an aphrodisiac in the ancient world. It was one of the fruits for which the children of Israel, fed up with manna and missing the fleshpots of Egypt, cried out in the wilderness. Among thirty-four entries which the Talmud devotes to the subject there is this one: "Our Rabbis taught: five things were said of garlic: It satiates, it keeps the body warm, it brightens up the face, it increases semen, and it kills parasites in the bowels. Some say that it fosters love and removes jealousy."

Along with the public reading of Torah and baking bread for the poor, eating garlic on Fridays was one of ten regulations instituted by the prophet Ezra. This was no mere culinary suggestion. Promoting love and arousing desire, garlic was to aid the Sabbath lovemaking pious Jews hold to be a *mitzvah.* Accordingly, the Aryans were not the first tribe to eschew the eating of garlic. This honor belongs to the Samaritans, a rigorous sect from Babylonia, who held the tradition of encouraging lovemaking on the Sabbath to be in violation of the Torah's prohibition on lighting fires. Hence Mishnah refers to them, rather quizzically, as the non-garlic-eaters.

* * *

One evening I was invited to dinner by William, an American in Berlin for a year. The only decoration in his kitchen was a small framed drawing of a head of garlic.

"Yours?" I asked.

"Everything belongs to the woman whose apartment this is."

"You know about the Germans and garlic?"

"I heard something—"

"So the apartment belongs to a German woman? Mid-thirties? Progressively minded? Subscribes to the *Taz*? Vacations in Turkey? Record collection strong on Biermann and—"

"I've never met her. I'm just subletting."

"But she's German?"

"Yes."

* * *

The best of intentions expose the most seams. The introduction to a thin volume entitled *Cooking with Garlic* begins this way:

> The glorious victory of garlic in our everyday cuisine can no longer be hindered. Anyone who has enjoyed southern food in a relaxed holiday atmosphere has encountered the taste. And why shouldn't we conjure up a holiday mood with a little kitchen fragrance to spice up our workdays? To be sure: there is, alas, no proven remedy against the smell. For not only your breath betrays to your neighbors what you have eaten; garlic oil is secreted through the pores of the skin. Many things have been recommended to combat it: chewing parsley, juniper berries, coriander seeds, cloves, and coffee beans. Only experimentation will determine what really helps you.
>
> I received the most refreshing solution in an interview with a top manager, a real garlic fan. "When I have eaten garlic, I confess to it, and ask my partner to endure it with composure, or to remain six feet away from me. This takes the wind out of their sails and creates a relaxed atmosphere at the same time. It's that easy!"

* * *

And yet perhaps it's called for, this painful forced show. In 1989 there began a rash of neo-Nazi computer games among West German schoolchildren. Among them was an "Anti-Turk Test" with questions like the following:

Why can't Turks speak German?

(A) Because they have rotten teeth.
(B) Because they eat garlic.
(C) Because they have no tongues.
(D) Because only Germans can speak German.

When the correct answer is chosen, the words "Bravo, Nazi!" appear on the screen. For the wrong answer, the computer prints, "Off to Auschwitz!"

* * *

This time, Sarah and Jesse had decided not to reveal it. With mixed feelings, naturally, but the last day-care worker had said, "If I'd known you were Jewish, I wouldn't have taken your son." It was a matter of protecting him, and besides, they were leaving the country soon. Afternoons they sat with the other parents on the playground, smiling uneasily, hoping to fit in.

"Your child is the only dark-haired one in our day-care center!" said Inge brightly. "Such cute curls too." Sarah stroked her son's head and swallowed hard.

"Have they ever asked why he's circumcised?" asked Jesse one night.

"I know," Sarah answered. "It really stands out when the kids are naked. No. They haven't."

"Afraid to ask."

"I don't think it occurs to them."

"The children ate an awful lot of garlic yesterday, didn't they?" asked Petra, looking hard at Sarah. At the cooperative day-care center, parents took turns cooking lunch.

"I put some garlic in the lentils," said Sarah, straining to keep her voice level. "We use a lot of garlic at home. I never really notice how much."

"We are very antigarlic," said Petra. "I notice it right away."

"Really?" Angelika was an easygoing schoolteacher with political convictions. "We use a lot of garlic ourselves."

"But I don't notice it with you at all. With them"—Petra pointed to Sarah with a little smile—"I smell the garlic."

Sarah returned the smile, and shivered.

* * *

"You're collecting garlic stories? But there are thousands," said Margret. She was brought up in London but returned, years ago, to her parents' home town. "Let me tell you about my boss at the press agency. Once when he was slightly loaded, he told me that Germany had lost the war because International Jewry found out what they were doing to the Jews. 'After that,' he said, 'We had no chance. How could one expect us to stand up to International Jewry?' He didn't mean to be offensive; I was supposed to take it as a compliment."

"And the garlic?"

"I was coming to that. I had lunch with a colleague at a pizzeria on the corner. When we came back the boss was standing in the doorway. Ten feet away. He yelled at Gabi. 'Garlic!' he cried. 'In my office I expect some consideration for the people who have to work with you all day. In Margret's case it's excusable. I remember, before the war, the Jews ate a lot of garlic. But from a German employee I expect a sense of responsibility!'"

"How long did you work there?"

"A couple of years. If I were going to quit over a thing like that, I might as well pack it up here."

"I suppose."

"In Silesia in the thirties there was a mixed Polish-German population. Those who were in favor of German annexation stopped eating garlic. From one day to the next. *Heim ins Reich*. It was a movement."

* * *

There were no better Germans than the German Jews: no more passionate performers of Beethoven, no more ardent readers of Goethe, no more patriotic soldiers in the First World War. In hindsight this might seem merely craven, and pathetic; but the stalwart Jewish hunger for classical German culture magnifies the tragedy of the Nazis' success. That it was hunger is undeniable. No other two peoples were so bound at the soul, wrote the philosopher Hermann Cohen in 1915. My last story, however, took place in 1987.

The rabbi had nominated Michael for the post of cultural director of the Jewish Community; he was very unsure if he wanted the job.

"You know what the Community is like. Stock conservative. Who's interested in culture? They'll want me to spend my time organizing Women's International Zionist Organization tea parties."

"If they're interested in hiring you it means they want to change."

"To what?"

"To the way it used to be in Berlin. Think of Einstein playing the violin at the Jewish Community Center!"

"And how," asked Michael, "am I supposed to produce that?"

"We'll bring him back," I said recklessly. "Bring back Einstein."

Ambivalent or not, Michael had already passed the first stages of review. At home in the Berlin cultural world and the Jewish tradition, it would be hard to imagine a better candidate for the job. All that remained was the interview with Heinz Galinski, the man who has, since shortly after his release from Auschwitz, been the director of the Jewish Community of Berlin.

Michael paced the waiting room in his one good suit. A door was opened; the secretary told him to enter.

"*Pfui*!" said Galinski, standing up behind his desk. "It smells of garlic here." He walked to the window and opened it wide, heedless of the March chill. "Has someone been eating garlic?" He looked hard at the newcomer.

Michael had been prepared for nearly anything else. He answered slowly. "My wife made fish soup last night. It could be that she put some garlic in it."

"So you eat a lot of garlic?"

"Well, yes."

"You'll have to change that, if you intend to represent the Jewish Community of Berlin."

The rabbi sat mutely in the corner, observing his protégé.

"You Jewish?" asked Galinski.

"Yes."

"You married?"

"Yes."

"Your wife Jewish?"

"Yes. And our son Benjamin is Jewish too."

Galinski didn't smile. "Just how," he asked, "did you imagine this job?"

Michael fingered the notes, made the night before, in his jacket pocket. "There's a lot one could do to, uh, enliven Jewish culture in Berlin. I know a group who'd like to create a Jewish theater—"

"Theater!" interrupted Galinski. "He wants theater! Who does he think is going to pay for it?"

Michael tried again. "The Community provides a lot of social services for the Russian immigrants," he began. In 1987, half the official members of Berlin's Jewish Community had been born in the Soviet Union. "But I think one could do more to utilize the cultural resources of the Russian members—"

"The Russians!" Galinski exploded. "Once more the Russians! When am I going to hear something else?"

The job was given to a certain Uwe Hammerschmidt. He has a neatly trimmed blond beard and is said to be thinking of converting to Judaism.

* * *

I called Alexandra the next day. "Michael is an idiot," she told me. "You can't go to an interview smelling of garlic. For a job doing anything besides loading trucks, that is."

"But he'd eaten the garlic the night before! And had a bath and a shave in the morning!"

"Doesn't matter. It won't do."

"Alex," I said, "the Germans are meshugge about garlic. I've never seen anything like this anywhere else."

Alexandra's outburst was unprecedented. "I don't know what you're talking about! Did I ever tell you about the time I was in New York to organize that exhibition? One museum refused to lend us a painting they'd already promised in writing, and it was just because I showed up in tennis shoes and my colleague had eaten garlic the night before."

"Alex, I don't—"

"It was an Edward Hopper painting. We really needed it. I should have worn an expensive silk blouse with little pearls, that's what they all wear there—"

"It's true, there are certain dress codes—"

"Although the Americans look terrible, I've never seen such a bunch of schlumps in my—"

"But they don't make an issue about garlic—"

"Oh yes they do, not in your academic circles but elsewhere, American society makes me sick!"

"Alex, I don't like it all that much either, I live here, you know—"

"So stop complaining about the Germans! My mother would have made a wonderful SS guard if she hadn't been Jewish! Three times a day she sends my father to the gas. What do you want me to tell you about garlic?"

* * *

Stories have ways of getting around. Six months later Galinski saw Michael coming out of the library of the Jewish Community Center.

"You there!"

Michael stopped, unsure just what Galinski recognized or remembered.

"Do you have anything to do with the ... garlic stories?"

"Garlic stories?" said Michael. "Not my line. My wife collects garlic stories. She's writing a book."

"You aren't the source of the garlic stories?"

"I believe, Herr Galinski, that you must be the source of the garlic stories."

"When I find out who has been telling garlic stories about me, he will be expelled from the Jewish Community."

Sesenheimerstrasse

Midafternoons I could hear the Bulgarians practicing. They lived downstairs. She played piano at a dance academy; he played clarinet with a police band. I greeted them informally, without knowing their names. I didn't catch them the first few times we met, after a while it was too late to ask. I greeted their daughter all the more eagerly when we passed on the stairs. "*Hallo*, Marie-Therese." "Say *hallo*, Marie-Therese," prompted her mother but Marie-Therese would stare, exquisite brown eyes holding an edge of blankness, verging on anger at their center, and clutch her mother's hand.

My window, looking out to the hinterhof, was the one in the apartment from which you could best see the tree. It bore flowers in the springtime, and chestnuts in the fall; most of the year it offered a sea of bare branches or dull green. These were usually sheathed in rain. The first year was deceptive. All those days lying naked in the Tiergarten, lots of sun and the air was good. I hadn't known that Berlin weather was mostly variations in gray. Or hadn't I cared, when I lived for the night?

* * *

The room looked different the first time I saw it. Faded curtains, the color of old olives, hid the chestnut tree and the slanting roofs across the courtyard. Next to the window were taped blownup photocopies of portraits of Baudelaire and Poe, fraying at the bottom. Claudio's best painting, *Three Bums*, lay framed but unhung in a comer; there was a mattress on the floor. Every other available surface was covered with books, piled high as they would go without toppling: Joseph Roth, Petrarch, Cervantes, Dostoevsky, Walter Benjamin, Gershom Scholem, many I'd never heard of at all. It was January 1984 when I met Michael. After Benjamin was born, we made it his room for a time; it was the quietest in the house, and I used to show him the tree, early mornings, when he was tiny. "Look at the buds," I told him. "It's springtime." He turned his head to the sound of the wind. Once he could walk he began to gravitate toward the middle room, which had been mine. I wanted a desk that wasn't surrounded by rattles and blocks; Michael's books were now firmly piled, in an order only he could penetrate, in the last room, overlooking the street; and that's how I came to have the most beautiful room in the apartment. It lay on a side street in the center of town.

It's half an hour's ride from Kreuzberg, but the mood was another entirely. Charlottenburg's noises were different: shoppers pushing in the bleak and crowded Wilmersdorferstrasse; street musicians who play in the hope of receiving change; barking dogs, and motorcycles on the Bismarckstrasse; the

Berlin beau monde, weaving from kneipe to kneipe round Savignyplatz; on warm nights, the men's chorus which meets in the church hall to sing patriotic hymns. The Wall was invisible, the Turks were subdued. The occupied house in the Schillerstrasse was a neatly painted artists' cooperative, supported by the Senate through the personal intervention of Joseph Beuys. Kreuzberg was rawer, on the edge, at the border, and every time I found a reason to go back there I felt wistful. But there was really no question, once we decided to move in together: Michael paid the same rent for three and a half rooms that I was paying for one; it was an unrenovated building, without central heating or hot water. Besides, he had, very nearly, made the neighborhood his own.

* * *

Alarm-Evchen leaned from her window when she saw him go by. "Hallo, sweetie!" she would shout, pointing to her breasts. "How do you like my onion sacks?" Alarm-Evchen lived with her mother, Uschi, and their cat, whose name was Mouse. The moldings in their apartment were painted pink; a collection of enamel plates hung on the gaudy wallpaper. Sometimes Evchen's son came by to ask for money. He was twenty-one, unemployed, and had the shiftiest eyes I ever saw. When he bullied her, Evchen would cry on the street. "It's the worst thing there is," she said, laying an arm on my shoulder in tentative despair. "You love your children more than anything in the world, and then..." But mostly she walked with short steps and proud shoulders, smoothing her tight skirt over plump hips with careful hands. Evchen worked nights at the cafeteria in the opera house. She had a strong, husky voice, she might have been a chanteuse. One night we sang "Tom Dooley" in harmony; it was the only song she knew in English, and Evchen insisted on repeating it for hours.

Evchen grew up playing in the ruins with Eddy, who lived forty-six years in the house next door. Eddy's face was helpless, soft like a girl's, and his unwashed hair hung stringy and straight on his neck. His father never left the apartment. After he died the landlord gave Eddy three months to get out of the building. "Leave me alone," Eddy said when Michael offered to find a lawyer, or fill out welfare applications, but he'd accepted help cleaning out the stinking apartment. The floor was covered with bottles left standing up so long they had started to sprout; a narrow corridor between them allowed one to pass from room to room. Under his father's mattress were twenty thousand marks. Eddy brought them to Bauernstübl for safekeeping, but they didn't last very long. The management may have cheated him out of a thousand or two, but Eddy drank day and night, and was generous in buying rounds for the rest of us. After a couple of months the bartender told him that his credit was used up, and called the fire department to take him to the detox ward.

There are hundreds of kneipen that looked like it, dozens with an identical name. Bauernstübl contained a jukebox, a pinball machine and two round tables covered with flowered cloth. Conversation stopped when a stranger entered the room and the mood was threatening, sometimes openly so, if he tried to take a place at the bar which belonged to one of the regulars. The door key was lost long ago but it didn't matter: Bauernstübl was open twenty-four hours a day. For all the light that penetrated the checkered curtains it might as well be, permanently, four o'clock in the morning.

The night that we met Michael took me to Bauernstübl and warned me that it could get rough, sometimes. I found his solicitude funny, for I'd seen all at once that this was a place where I could let go. Who came to Bauernstübl? It was a neighborhood kneipe, and except for an occasional actor or a lonely schizophrenic, we were the only customers without working-class origins. The price of the humanity we found there was a great deal of beer; the wine was undrinkable, and nobody left Bauernstübl sober. Luck, or success, were out of place there. People who'd had them spent their nights somewhere else.

If you're hoping for a remnant of the proletarian spirit of the twenties, you'll be disappointed: Bauernstübl wasn't that kind of haven. Evchen and Wolfgang stared suspiciously when Michael brought in the remainder of a quiche he had baked. "What's that— pizza?" "Try it," he said. "It comes from the Elsass," giving Alsace-Lorraine the name it bore when it was a German province. "*Ach* so," said Evchen, guardedly accepting her first piece of quiche lorraine. Eddy giggled when three young Africans found their way into Bauernstübl one night. "Look at the tar paper!"

Still Michael was at ease in Bauernstübl: where everything was in the open, you knew what you were up against. He had learned to distrust swanky liberal circles, where bursts of nationalism erupt suddenly behind predictable polite self-deprecating murmurs. After years of rambling in the sleek rooms surrounding Savignyplatz, he set out to possess, in Bauernstübl, something like truth.

They'd accepted Michael, and they took to me. The day we got married, the people at Bauernstübl sent us a card, special delivery, printed with chirping bluebirds. Later they collected money and presented a bag of brand-new baby clothes. Fat Elke, the teetotaling bartender, contributed a handmade coverlet. The men hailed me with wet kisses, the women talked of tired loves.

* * *

He'd directed theater, been a carpenter, an architect, a historian. When I met him Michael was spending most of his time writing poetry on the backs of beer coasters. His unemployment checks were supplemented by gifts from a series of fashionable women who loathed one another. He gave forth an air of permanent melancholy, and he was the funniest person I'd ever known.

We met by accident.

The telephone rang one day in October. The voice on the line belonged to a friend of Lutz, one of the people whose names I'd been given upon coming to Berlin. I had met Lutz briefly the week before. Perhaps a friendship, or at least a contact, was about to ensue?

"Lutz gave me your telephone number because I'm looking for someone who can tell me the Hebrew word for 'admiral.'"

"Oh." Disappointment and annoyance replaced initial pleasure. I had begun to tire of playing the local Jew, and was in no mood for another ignorant German who supposed that all the remaining Jews he might encounter spoke fluent Hebrew. I answered the caller icily. "I am indeed Jewish, but I don't know a word of Hebrew."

"My mother was Jewish, and I don't know a word of Hebrew either," said Michael.

The ice melted slightly; I was curious. We asked each other questions about work. He was writing about Berlin street names. Investigating the history of Admiral Street he had discovered that the word for 'admiral' was the same in every Mediterranean language he knew. I listened. He might have been loony, he might be a pedant. There were other possibilities, there was no way to know. We agreed, quite casually, to get together sometime.

What happened when we met two months later couldn't quite be called love at first sight. It was more of an awful certainty that almost nothing could keep us apart.

"The worst of it," says Michael when he's feeling provocative, "is that I knew three Israelis who could have helped me with the Hebrew. What fluke stopped me from thinking of them?"

* * *

Professors get nervous—first enchanted, then nervous—when Michael, oblivious to the rip in his jacket, tells, exhilarated, of a recent discovery. For he embodies what I'd like to call the innocence of thought. He's the one who looks up all the references, scanning pictures, texts and public files, stopping only when a trail has come to an end. A boiling kettle, a crying baby, a ringing telephone may interrupt him, but nothing (like a life plan) less immediate than those. It is all free play here, a refusal to pragmatize. Yet there's nothing about him that smacks of the *Luftmensch*: he can build stairways, kill chickens, console a frightened child. All that he learned in the village near the Baltic where he spent his childhood. Its bucolic vistas seem an unlikely setting for someone once dubbed the only New Yorker in Berlin, and Michael was conceived there by accident. The village was near the POW camp where his mother located his father after two years of searching: by the time she found him, their hometown was part of the Russian zone. They settled down to raise five children in a silence broken only by severe strains of classical music. It wasn't reticence in regard to the war years which set them apart: nobody in those days inclined much to talk. I sometimes think it must have been shame. On his father's part: helpless, unyielding, for a war he could neither support nor lose. On his mother's: diffident daughter of a brewer whose ties to the Jewish community would have been forgotten had the Nazis remained on the fringe. Married to an Aryan, her survival was merely an inconvenience; somehow she shepherded two babies through the years when her man was off at the front. Ironing in the kitchen, she told her son about Kafka, and when she tired of life, she left it. Michael wishes he'd asked her much more.

The Ost Holstein coast recalls that of New England: stark and stony, with resonant light. In May the land rolls golden with acres of rape fields, and the forests behind them still teem with soft deer. But everything made by human hand is jarring, a blight: grim and heavy, at wrong angles. Even a cottage here looks like a fortress. As soon as he was old enough to find a plausible excuse, Michael left for the city.

* * *

We had little money. It mattered, and it didn't. We could squander unexpected checks eating blini and caviar at a mournful restaurant in the Kantstrasse, thinking of the twenties, when three hundred thousand Russians lived in Berlin. If anything is a sin there it is nostalgia and I learned to suppress it: where everything tells you the Old World is gone. Where money doesn't matter: you can even travel without much of it, if you ask around long enough you're sure to find an empty house in Andalusia or an extra room in Paris. There is more time, always; even the unemployed are allotted a three-week vacation, funded by the state. Where money matters, of course: winter is long, six months of black dust under short fingernails, tired arms trembling lightly hauling buckets of coal. Cold running water. Weeks of potatoes. Holes in the shoes. We were no longer very young.

The people we knew there lived the same way. They'd sell a painting, get a grant, write a piece for the radio. When nothing else came they would translate their native languages, or teach them. Spanish and English, Croatian and Greek. Our friends, for the most part, were foreigners. It seems artificial, this frozen impermanence. Nobody came here intending to stay. Yet children were raised, and heads have gone gray now, in the steady uncertainty of this day-after-day. Sometimes I want to call it a world.

Hands in the pockets, or pushing a stroller. Streets full of dreams. "That plumber hid Jews for years," said Michael as we passed a shop in the Pestalozzistrasse. Sometimes we sought the dead: steps to an apartment where Walter Benjamin once lived; a forgotten cemetery on the edge of the Grunewald. "Look," I said, "the Germans even put 'Dr.' on their tombstones." The others smiled at my surprise. "Here's something funnier," said Irena, pointing to an inscription: THE BEST DIE YOUNG. Then the dates on the tombstone of a man who had lived to become eighty-nine.

The dead, a mother, the past, a spring.

* * *

Michael at the market, pockets turned inside out, in the rain. "Can you lend me ten marks?" he says, looking black. I reach for my wallet sullen, eyes heavy with the tears of a fight till the dawn. Everybody warned me: it wouldn't be easy. Stare at a girl kicking holes in the mud.

He returns with a bunch of pale roses, bought with the borrowed bill. "Wait," he says gruffly before thrusting them into my hand. He counts the roses and tosses one away. "Twenty's a lousy number," he insists. Nineteen is his favorite.

His face unshaven; all our eyes are red. A figure returning. And still there are glances that go to the soul.

* * *

A figure returning.

This is just to suggest there were no happy endings, though I couldn't help but seek one. ("Pitiless optimist," he could roar, "so fucking American!") I wouldn't forget the nights (always nights) of locked doors, tearstained voices, 4 A.M. taxis when the subway shut down. Couldn't forget them, but I sought to find them a place. Lovers always quarrel. Yet often it was that which first brought us together which threatened to tear us apart.

"I'm a bastard," he'd say angrily. For his loneliness was clearest at the point where he hit the streets and succeeded, for a moment, in creating a world. From his father, deaf and dying, came still accusation. For assimilated German families, Jewish roots had been but a source of suffering. One who tried to uncover them could only seem perverse. It mattered little whether the family had been gutted by history or by more common troubles. Sense lay in persevering, meeting life's edges with the north German obduracy Michael despised.

I sought clarity. He called it kitsch. And just when he'd seemed to have turned an ordinary Berlin street block into a fair approximation of the shtetl, he'd insist on the madness of seeking a home. We might marry under a chuppah, raise children who would sleep to the soft sad strains of Yiddish lullabies. What we sought had been shattered. The music had to be learned from a record; everything else could be looked up in books. Or could it? Nothing's less natural than raising the dead.

* * *

Later on we spent hours, looking out the window. From my room, leaning downward, to see if the landlord was in the courtyard; from the balcony, in the front rooms, to see if he was on the street. If he was around we would stare, with fascinated hatred, and put off leaving the house. If he wasn't, we were lighter, gazing toward the stones again as if we still belonged there.

Michael spent more time at this than I did, but then Michael always looked out the window anyway. Sometimes he called me to watch birds circling a point where the light scattered clouds, or to hear someone break the ordinary passing of time on the street. Once it was Bruno S., catapulted to brief fame in Herzog's films and now left to play chimes for pennies in the *Hinterhof.* Once it was a traveler carrying a walking stick and shouting, "We've had enough of the Third Reich! We don't want no more mass-murder weapons, no atomic weapons and nothing at all!"

Michael looked out the window.

* * *

I didn't see the danger; it was a while before the pigeons came into the hallway to die. When the building changed hands we were full of love and wonder, blessed with a baby and no sense of time. The old landlord had often called Michael a scoundrel; they exchanged dry witty letters when the rent was overdue. The new owner was rumored to be his favorite call girl, the house a gift for services rendered. Once she had the papers in hand, she kissed the old man good-bye and left the house to her lover and pimp, a young man called Borchert. The crushed old man could be seen prowling in the courtyard till he died, two months later, of a sudden stroke. Michael cut the death notice from the newspaper and taped it to the building door.

Still there were no signs. "We mustn't romanticize," I said in the glare of the naked light bulb which graced the kitchen table. "It wasn't the Garden of Eden, before." It wasn't; just a home. The neighbors paid calls to admire the new baby, dressed in stiff clothing, orchids in hand. Benjamin slept in kitchen corners or gallery openings amid smoke and laughter. Michael wrote radio plays. I picked up my thesis again. When spring came we visited Spyros in Crete, picking wild thyme and lemon flower; during a layover in Athens, Michael carried the disinterested baby all the way up the Acropolis.

One morning I discovered the mezuzah was gone. It had belonged to my grandmother, and the loss left us sad. Michael suspected his old friend the drunken actor, who threatened to stab him with broken bottles in moments of rage. I suggested the new landlord, clean-shaven and thuggish, who appeared in the house at odd moments. But why would any of them steal a mezuzah? As we would learn, no one in Berlin knew what a mezuzah *is*. Seeing the empty space in the doorway, we were rueful for a number of days; then we gave in to petty mystery, and forgot.

The disaster at Chernobyl brought the world to our door. The news hit Berlin on a day of unearthly beauty, and for weeks thereafter conventional assumptions were turned on their head. Waiters assured anxious customers that their food wasn't fresh. People who normally refused to eat South African produce now sought to buy anything from the ends of the earth. Children were ordered to play on the asphalt, away from the grass. I scoured the markets for powdered milk and canned baby food, the suddenly popular Chilean grapes. And still we were safe.

* * *

Bauernstübl was nearly empty, and Elke was upset. Pietro had come to take money for cigarettes, and to say he was in love with the Polish woman upstairs.

"He wouldn't even eat what I brought him tonight. Said he could get something later from Fritz. But what's wrong with my food?" cried Elke, emptying a shopping bag onto the bar. Out tumbled single servings of margarine and jam, gleaned from a cafeteria; Velveeta cheese, wrapped in paper; two packages of instant coffee. "And good sausage," she said, pointing to the depths of the bag. "What's wrong with all that?"

"Elke," I told her, "you've been running after him. He may get interested again if you leave him alone."

"Service, please! Service, please!" It was Jochen's voice, calling from a bench in the dark of the back room. Elke sighed, washed a glass and tapped a beer. Jochen's age was hard to guess. His beard was white, he had a face like a sailor. He'd been living on the bench for five or six weeks now; for the last four he'd said nothing but "Service, please!" or sometimes "Mr. Waiter?"

"He's gonna die soon if he keeps up like this," said Elke, but Jochen didn't die; one day he stood up as suddenly as he'd sat down, stopped drinking and began to tend bar.

The girl by the jukebox was flirting with the fireman when Plumber-Manny entered the room. Sliding into middle age, he was not very tall but his arms were strong. His eyes were set deep and flaring, that night, at his faithless girl.

"I was waiting for you," she protested. "You can ask the others. We were just chatting. He bought me a beer."

"They weren't up to anything, Manny, they really weren't." A bartender at Bauernstübl has to know how to becalm, and to distract Manny, Elke began to tell a string of dirty jokes. On the street, a distant siren. The jukebox played James Brown.

"I've got a joke too," said Plumber-Manny. "Old Adolf—you know who I mean?" Michael nodded. All of my muscles got tense, at once. "Old Adolf is sitting up in heaven, on cloud twenty-seven, and Saint Peter gives him two weeks' vacation. To take care of the Turks. Two weeks are up, he hasn't returned. Three, four weeks go by. Finally he shows up. Saint Peter is mad. 'What took so long? I said you could have two weeks!' So Adolf says, 'The Turks were no problem. But the Jews, the Jews are still there!'"

"What do you think is funny about that?" I asked, hearing my voice come from a very distant place.

"It gets the point," said Manny. "The Jews still run the world. Adolf didn't finish his job."

"Do you know any Jews?" asked Michael.

"If you knew what I've suffered, because of the Itzigs. They swipe whatever they can get their hands on. Look, they even stole the land from the Palestinians."

I began to scream. "Where else could they go, after they'd been murdered in Europe?"

"In the sea, for all I care," said Plumber-Manny. "Taxes are getting higher all the time, and it's still not enough for the Itzigs."

"Nazi crap!" I shouted.

"I'm not a Nazi," said Plumber-Manny.

"Come, Susan," said Elke. "You pay too many taxes, too."

"But not because of six million people who were murdered!"

Michael's arm on my shoulder offered solace or calm. It had all gone too far.

"Shut up," I said to Plumber-Manny. "Just shut your dirty mouth. You could get taken to court for saying that kind of trash."

"There's the telephone," he baited. "Call the cops if you want." He'd realized, finally, with whom he was talking. "The Germans have been suffering for forty years, and you're still trying to say it's our fault! Who started the war then, we or you?"

"Everybody should just stop shouting," said Elke. "I don't understand any of this. I was born after the war. I don't know any Jews."

"Hey," said the girl by the jukebox, "pay attention to me. I thought you were jealous."

"I'm going," I said. "I've heard enough shit for one night."

"Go," said Plumber-Manny. "Go back to Tel Aviv. Buy yourself a one-way ticket."

"I live here," I answered. "And I'm staying here."

"Where do you live?" he asked.

"Next door," I answered. Not without fear.

"Go back to wherever you came from."

"And where should I go?" asked Michael.

"*Tja*," said Plumber-Manny. "Follow her, if you're one of them."

"I was born in Ost Holstein," said Michael. "My father fought in the Wehrmacht."

"That's your problem," said Plumber-Manny.

Elke offered me a shot of vodka. "Politics in the kneipe is always a mistake," she said.

On the sidewalk I gave in to the tears I'd held back. "Don't you know it can get like this?" asked Michael, holding me.

"But I felt at *home* in Bauernstübl."

"Don't mythologize," said Michael. "It's a place like any other. And none of the regulars were there tonight."

Wolfgang told Plumber-Manny he'd knock him through the window if he bothered us again. "I got nothing against Jews," said Wolfgang. "They're just human beings like everybody else." Alarm-Evchen declared she had never been able to stand the sight of him anyway. "Ugly old toad, and a dope of a girlfriend." Plumber-Manny kept out of Bauernstübl for a couple of months; when he returned he was wary, tamed.

Portraits at Random: Jews in Berlin

R*abbi S.'s advice to go back to America was my first introduction to the Jewish Community of West Berlin.

My second was his visit to the maternity ward where I was a stop on his round of duties some six months later.

"Mazel tov," said the rabbi. "What a beautiful boy." He had already made the arrangements for the bris with my husband. There remained only the question of the baby's Hebrew name.

"Benjamin Chajim ben-Michael," I said.

"The case isn't settled," he said with a cough. "Michael isn't yet a member of the Community."

"Rabbi," I answered, "we've discussed this before. You agreed it was complicated."

"There's no problem about whether the *baby* is Jewish, since that goes through the mother and there's no question about you."

"If it goes through the mother then Michael is Jewish too."

It happens rather often. Children of assimilated Jews who survived the war one way or another are astonished to discover that their decision to join their forefathers' Community is greeted with something less than enthusiasm. The Community, first, demands proof of their claims. But birth or marriage certificates were lost even easier than lives in the war, especially when those concerned were desperate to conceal any document which contained the word "Jew." And even written proof won't suffice to allay Rabbi S.'s misgivings. He emphasizes the importance of a Jewish education; otherwise Judaism is merely a racial concept, perilously close to the Nazis' own views. But these children were raised without ties to Jewish tradition; those who didn't grow up in an orphanage lived in the shadow of fearful mothers who remained, metaphorically, in hiding. Rabbi S.'s usual solution is to send them to the class in Hebrew and history for prospective converts. If they endure that for a year, they are examined and admitted to the Community. Rabbi S. lets his nose for Yiddishkeit determine whether to write "Converted" or "Returned" on their certificates of admission.

Although the more Orthodox of the two West Berliner rabbis, Rabbi W. is less severe than Rabbi S. in this matter. With the right sort of aura he's been known to accept people whose grandparents had converted to Christianity. Halakhah, he says, doesn't recognize conversions; there's no escape from being a Jew.

"And for a significant sum, he asks no questions at all," said Rabbi S. darkly. "Besides, he doesn't get the kind of cases I do."

"Cases?"

"Guilt-ridden young Germans wanting to solve their problems by inventing a Jewish grandmother. Older people too, with who knows what on their conscience. Seeking redemption by sacrificing a piece of foreskin." The rabbi snorted and sighed. "And just plain nuts sometimes. You wouldn't believe the people who call here."

All this hovered over a newborn head.

"Look," said Rabbi S., "there's a lovely old Sephardic tradition of naming the baby after the mother's family, since that's the side that counts anyway, according to Halakhah. Perhaps there's a deceased grandfather you particularly cherished?"

"We're Ashkenazim," I answered, "and I loved my grandfather dearly, but this baby is going to be named after his father."

I looked at the rabbi. The rabbi looked at me.

"Alright already," he said hastily, rising. "Benjamin Chajim ben-Michael. If anybody asks me, I can say it was an uncle."

* * *

One week later Michael and I were making potato salad in our kitchen when the doorbell rang.

"Nothing's *ready*," we groaned. "Who the hell comes to a bris an hour early?"

"Mendel Leisner," said Mendel Leisner as Michael reluctantly opened the door. I offered my hand in welcome.

The elderly man shook his head kindly, with apologetic eyes. Was I the mother? Then I had to forgive him, but he couldn't shake my hand until I'd been to the *mikveh*, and that would be thirty days after the birth.

My unclean hands shot behind my back. "You must be a friend of Jacob Taubes," I said. When he wasn't teaching philosophy or Judaica at the university, Jacob Taubes could be found in the worldweary Paris Bar, clad in cape and beret. "I'm a sinner," he'd say, "but an *Orthodox* one." We had asked him to be our son's godfather and he'd called, innocently enough, to request permission to bring along "a few *frumm* Jews."

"A friend of whose?" asked Mendel Leisner.

"Professor Taubes?" I repeated uncertainly.

"Don't believe I know him," said the guest. "There was a sign with your address on it in the Joachimstalerstrasse Synagogue. It's a *mitzvah*, you know, to celebrate a B'rit Milan."

Michael and I exchanged glances.

"But let me help you," said Mendel Leisner. "There isn't much time, and you're hardly prepared." He took instant authority, issuing commands: the table must be set this way, the light must be there, and was that a *cat* in the corner? Michael was still unshaven but the room was in order when we opened the door at two.

At the head of the *minyan* was Jacob Taubes, looking majestic, without a trace of his usual irony. He had exchanged his cape and beret for a magnificent set of white satin robes. The others were bearded and dressed in black. We recognized the owner of Berlin's kosher store. None of the others introduced themselves, but proceeded to occupy all the seats around the festival table. Baffled, uncertain, we rushed between doorbell and kitchen. The telephone rang constantly: the half-Jewish surgeon who serves as the *mohel* had been held up at the hospital. The room was already brimming with impatience when Rabbi S. arrived.

He was so surprised by the scene which awaited him that he nearly dropped the gift he'd brought: a yellow plastic baby bib emblazoned with a picture of Donald Duck.

"Come here," he said furiously, and shepherded us into the empty bedroom. "What are those *fanatics* doing in your house?"

To Jacob we'd said: the more the merrier. We didn't know that one of the minyan was Rabbi W., and we didn't know that neither Rabbi S. nor Rabbi W. acknowledges the other's existence.

"Get me Jacob Taubes this instant," said Rabbi S.

Jacob entered the bedroom with regal disdain. *His* gift for the baby, an antique tallis bought in Jerusalem that summer just in case it was a boy, with a letter to be opened at the newborn's bar mitzvah, already lay on the dressing table.

"Did you arrange this performance?" shouted Rabbi S.

Jacob answered coolly. It was his responsibility as godfather to see that the baby was given a *proper* bris. There was hardly a law he didn't break, and his lectures on early Christianity brought him to the border of heresy. But when it came to rites of passage he returned to purest form: scion of twenty-four generations of rabbis, Jacob viewed Rabbi S. as an illiterate yokel.

"Come off it," said Rabbi S. "You know as well as I do who these people are. They're not only not Orthodox; it's not even clear how the baby should be named!"

"Benjamin Chajim ben-Michael," said Jacob simply, and pointed to Michael. "You're not going to look at *him* and tell me he isn't Jewish?"

Rabbi S. fumed. He refused to enter the room unless Rabbi W. and his followers left it. Michael and I stood speechless. The baby began to cry.

"Time is wasting," said Jacob. "We are committing a sin every minute this baby remains uncircumcised." Seeing his triumph, he softened. "So you don't perform the ceremony," he said to Rabbi S. "Won't you join us and celebrate as one Yid among others?"

Rabbi S. would not, and he was only the first person that day to leave the house in a rage. Spyros, son of a Greek priest, walked out when one of the *minyan* yelled at him for entering the room without a yarmulke. Claudio left after the sardonic Israeli atheist pulled the yarmulke off his head. Alexandra heard the baby crying and retreated outraged at his subjection to a dim barbaric rite. Only the *minyan* left satisfied, having performed their ceremony in strictest style. They declined to touch the herring and potato salad we'd prepared on paper plates, but helped themselves, singing, to the kosher wine.

Hours later Michael and I were finally alone. We sat very weak, searching for joy and finding helpless black laughter instead.

* * *

In the small West Berlin Jewish Community, the political implications of Benjamin's bris provided months of discussion. The tiny contingent of Orthodox believers vaunted their victory over the miserable heretic posing as a rabbi. The larger contingent of Reform Jews rankled at the surprise attack by the forces of darkness.

Several months later we received a note from Mendel Leisner: Did we remember how he'd helped at our dear son's bris? How fortunate that he'd been visiting Berlin that week; he normally resided in Hannover. Perhaps we could send a picture of the baby?

Mendel Leisner sent presents on Benjamin's birthday. One year it was a pair of red shoes; the next, a little blue velvet yarmulke with gold trim. The gifts were accompanied by letters expressing wishes: that Benjamin may grow to be a good person in the sense of the Torah; that G-d's blessing would rule over our house.

We never read them without a tear, at least.

* * *

Brises are rare, as you might expect; few Jewish babies are born in Berlin. With 6,700 members West Berlin's is the largest West German Jewish Community, which includes some 30,000 souls. Why are they here? Some never left. Those who survived the war in hiding could not have done so without the help of non-Jews who sheltered and fed them at risk to their own lives. They are, therefore, less inclined to flee the Germans as such. Others came back: too broken or weary after surviving the camps to start over somewhere else, or disillusioned with exile in Israel or America. There are several thousand Russians who left the Soviet Union in the seventies; they're said to find the German welfare state more congenial than the social arrangements in the high-capitalist West. There are some like Michael, born after the war, who join the Community to keep faith with a mother's history, a child's future. There are a few who convert, without ties to the past.

But 30,000 reflects only the number of Jews who go through the formal procedure of joining the Community. Official sources concede that at least twice this number live on West German soil. They refrain from joining the Community for the same reasons which keep many Jews anywhere from joining a synagogue, or because the frightened conservatism of the Community's policies revolts them.

It needn't be anything as disturbing as Heinz Galinski's inviting German dignitaries to preside over the ceremonies for the fiftieth anniversary of Kristallnacht just after they'd passed a bill regulating political asylum which was reminiscent of the Nürnberg Laws; or the news that Werner Nachmann, head of the Jewish Community of West Germany, had funneled 33 million marks of interest on the reparations paid to concentration-camp survivors into his failing businesses. The German Jewish Community played a remarkable role in the history of the Federal Republic. The government needs them. Their protected existence serves to belie continuity between the postwar government and the Third Reich. Nazism was thereby cleansed of broader political implications and reduced to the crudest sort of anti-Semitism. Where this is absent, one can claim there is no more need for vergangenheitsverarbeitung. So it happened that prominent right-wingers like Axel Springer, owner of Germany's largest and most virulent press, were the loudest supporters of the State of Israel.

You might express it as a syllogism:

Premise 1 Where Jews are permitted to live in peace and prosperity, there can't be any Nazis—at least of significance.
Premise 2 In the Federal Republic of Germany, Jews are permitted to live in peace and prosperity.
Ergo In the Federal Republic of Germany there can't be any Nazis—at least of significance.

Classical logic won't show you the fallacy.

***

*T*hough his brother was deported and murdered, Hans Rosenthal survived the war hiding in a hut in southwest Berlin. The day after the liberation he found himself surrounded by Russian troops with machine guns. Trying to smile, he pointed to the yellow star he'd resewn to his jacket, but they pushed him to the wall. Hans Rosenthal was lucky; at that moment a Jewish officer of the Red Army passed by. "Can you say the Sh'ma?" he asked. Hans Rosenthal could. "The officer released him and warned him to take off the star. The division had liberated Maidanek, where the SS officers tried to save themselves by putting on prisoners' clothing. After that it was ordered that everyone wearing yellow stars was to be shot on sight.

It was the seventh time he'd escaped from nearly certain death. Experiences like these taught Hans Rosenthal never to give up hope: there's always light at the end of the tunnel. His postwar rise to fame and fortune as Germany's favorite TV star paralleled the German road from the deepest darkness of the Third Reich to the bright sunny security of the Federal Republic. That's what he wrote in his autobiography, and that's what he imparted to 15 million regular viewers every Tuesday evening.

Hans Rosenthal was small and wiry. His trademark was a high spring in the air accompanied by the gleeful cry "That's the tops!" He didn't sing or dance on his show, but he changed costumes: as a postman, train conductor, or eighteenth-century soldier, he interviewed persons of general interest, told mild-mannered jokes and directed quiz games. Outside the show Hans Rosenthal could be found making appeals for good works: donating blood, playing soccer, or contributing to a children's charity. More discreetly, he served on the board of directors of the Jewish Community of Berlin.

His sixtieth birthday occasioned a two-hour program on the radio station where his career began. The giants of the German entertainment industry paid tribute, as did the president of the Federal Republic and the mayor of West Berlin. The success of postwar German democracy, said the former, is proved by the fact that despite the ... events of past history, Hans Rosenthal is simply "our Hansie" for millions of Germans. "He's just a regular guy," said a famous pop singer, "a friend like any other." Heinz Galinski was on the air as well, praising

Hans Rosenthal for the fact that he'd never denied his Jewishness, praising the German nation for the fact that they loved him nonetheless. Nonetheless? But that was the very point! A Jew who appeared on television once a week to show the German nation he was always happy, never bitter, the Germans have changed and even the ones back then weren't all that bad— "truly a gift from heaven," as Mayor Eberhard Diepgen intoned.

Yet all that was nothing compared to the uproar surrounding his death in 1987. It was front-page news for five days running. Axel Springer's tabloids went to town, with headlines like "Adieu, Hansie!"; "Germany Mourns a Great Berliner"; and "This Man Was a Great Example for All of Us." The press may have amplified, but the feeling was genuine: thousands of simple folk came to pay their respects at the public wake. "He was so cheerful, after the war he let us forget all the horrors," said one old woman who'd come to leave a rose. Hundreds more waited in the rain outside the studio where a memorial service was held. "Even the heavens are crying!" wrote the editors of the *Berliner Zeitung.*

"It's a shame about Hans Rosenthal," said the elderly baker. "Such a young man. And he didn't have it easy either. You know, don't you, that he was a Jew?"

Germany's highest officials avoided mentioning this fact directly. Instead they kept to discreet references like "his difficult fate." The press seized the opportunity to arouse curiosity about Jewish burial customs and beliefs concerning the afterlife, and interviewed both Berliner rabbis. "Red Roses and Holy Earth from Israel, On the Mountain Where Jesus Met the Apostles for the Last Supper!" In the end it was yellow roses, a thousand of them flown direct from Tel Aviv, although flowers play no role whatsoever in a traditional Jewish funeral. "600 Invited Guests—And the Son Who Will Say the Prayer That Can Only Be Spoken By Men!" Now the family was hardly Orthodox; Mrs. Rosenthal wasn't even a Jew. But for Hans Rosenthal the Jewish Community ignored its usually strict rejection of mixed marriages, so that his son could not only say Kaddish but be groomed to assume official functions upon his father's death.

A police convoy escorted the hearse to the cemetery; the traffic lights were shut off as a convoy of buses full of mourners rolled through the city. I'd never seen them at the synagogue before, but the funeral took place on a Friday afternoon, so it was only natural that the Rosenthals should go from the cemetery to Shabbos services. Not even on Yom Kippur is the synagogue so full. True, most of the men wore no yarmulkes, many of the women carried cameras—but hadn't they a right to participate too? For reparations had been paid before, but Hans Rosenthal's funeral was Germany's big chance—to make up for six million funerals that never took place.

Adieu, Hansie. I have to confess that I liked you myself. The Germans have no term for "Uncle Tom," but it wasn't your fault that the part fell to you. And for all that you played it, there was something about you that remained refreshingly humble, never wholly servile. Maybe it got to be too much for you too. Who knows why sixty-one-year-old men die of stomach cancer?

* * *

Four synagogues and a cemetery serve the Jewish population of West Berlin. The Community also runs a kindergarten, a home for the elderly, a kosher restaurant and an adult education program offering courses in Hebrew and Yiddish as well as lectures on a variety of Jewish topics. In addition, it provides what might be known as public-outreach work.

The Jewish year is shaped by a series of holidays, marking and shaping time. In addition to the sequence which begins with Rosh Hashanah and ends with Tisha b'Av, another has been added in Berlin. It follows the secular calendar, not the Jewish one, and the dates are draped in black. The Wannsee Conference, the Nazi Takeover, the Liberation of Auschwitz, the Warsaw Ghetto Uprising, the Liberation, Kristallnacht. Unlike the Jewish holidays, they are virtually indistinguishable. The rites are reminiscent of a high-school assembly: they are always the same, and nobody wants to be there. One description may serve for them all.

In the lobby of the Jewish Community Center, a small group formed around Heinz Galinski, the head of the Jewish Community, and Eberhard Diepgen, the mayor of Berlin. They shook hands several times for the photographers before climbing the stairs to the auditorium. The stage was draped with flags representing the Federal Republic, the State of Israel and the city of Berlin. The black bear on the Berlin flag leaned toward the center, as if he were about to eat the others. Giora Feldmann played his melancholy clarinet to open the ceremonies. Applause was out of place. Galinski stepped to the podium.

"Honored members of the Jewish Community, honored fellow citizens of Berlin, honored representatives of the Protectoral Powers." He gave a nod to the officers of the French, English and American commands. "The Twentieth of January, the Twentieth of February, the Twenty-sixth of April, the Eighth of May, the Ninth of November. So many days of the year give occasion for thought. We are gathered here to commemorate the last chapter of Polish-Jewish history. The destruction of the Warsaw Ghetto marked not only the end of a great literary and scholarly tradition, but—with a community of three and a half million Polish Jews—the end of a natural Jewish way of life." Galinski was visibly weary. He said there are two things we must never forget: the great contributions of the Jewish spirit to Western culture, and the terrible suffering that was brought upon us. He mentioned current events: the history teacher who told his classes that the Jews provoked Nazi anti-Semitism; the bishop who said that Edith Stein died for the sins of the unbelieving Jews. "Events like these suggest the danger that the history which has not been worked through, but merely repressed, will repeat itself. We must never forget the past, so there will be no occasion in the future which calls for new memorial days...."

Eberhard Diepgen was a better showman than Heinz Galinski, who hadn't even bothered to try to look moved. But then Diepgen was a dynamic young lawyer before becoming mayor. Unlike Galinski, he has a full head of sand-brown hair; unlike Galinski, he lost no family at Auschwitz. His speechwriter picked up the themes which Galinski began.

"The Jews are a part of the history of this city, a part of the history of Germany. And there can only be friendship between us when we all begin to feel the unspeakable burden of this history. The Holocaust was unique and without historical precedent." This was Diepgen's contribution to the currently raging *Historikerstreit*, in which conservative historians attempted to excuse the concentration camps by reference to Stalinist gulags. "What was done to this people, to whom our own culture is so deeply indebted?" Diepgen's voice quivered gently, then continued in rhythm. He quoted Gershom Scholem, then nodded to his host. "If I understand Herr Galinski correctly, he insists that the Jewish Community is a part of the community of Berlin. Now I'd like to read you a letter I received from one of our Jewish fellow citizens whose father, like many others, was decorated in the First World War. He wrote: 'My personal problem is—am I a German Jew, or a Jew in Germany?' " Diepgen paused for emphasis. "We non-Jewish Germans cannot decide this personal question. We can only do one thing: be glad about everyone who feels himself to be a German Jew but respect everyone who, in the face of our history, feels himself to be a Jew in Germany."

It was hard to imagine a real Jew writing to the mayor with such a quandary; silence before the goyim is assumed in Berlin. Whatever its origin, the story of the letter concluded Diepgen's speech. He left the stage to cantor Estrongo Nachama, who excused himself in advance: having a cold, he was not up to form. Then he took a deep breath and sang a mournful chant to close the ceremony. The audience filed downstairs to the monument listing the names of all the death camps; before it wafted a flame creating real smoke. Heads were covered while Rabbi W. said Kaddish. Rabbi S. was nowhere to be seen, but presumably a neutral party arranges these matters so as to avoid embarrassment to the Community. (I'll do the Warsaw Ghetto, you take Kristallnacht?)

In the crowded lobby after the service Diepgen removed the black yarmulke from his head and folded it gently into his pocket. I wondered whether he had his own, for such occasions, or had it been discreetly handed to him earlier that morning? The American commander tucked his officer's hat under his arm.

"The fighters in the ghetto deserved something better," I muttered in English, catching the attention of an elderly couple before me.

"Is it always like this?" asked the woman. "We're just visiting from London."

I shrugged my shoulders.

"We thought it would be something religious. Not such a political forum."

"The clarinet was good," said her husband.

"The clarinet was good," I agreed.

* * *

"It was one memorial day or another. The sun shone in the Fasanenstrasse, where a couple of hundred people stood behind the guarded gates of the Jewish Community Center. There were the usual speeches, and representatives of the Jewish Community shook hands with representatives of the city of West Berlin while the cameras rolled. The past had been resurrected and buried again; we turned to go. Suddenly a German official announced, 'And now you're all going to be deported.' In the shocked silence of the first seconds we thought it was simply a very bad joke. When the policemen who are posted to protect all Jewish institutions in Berlin turned around to line us up, we knew it was for real."

"*Tja*," said Alexandra. "I don't dream about deportations anymore. I'm always in the camps already." She bent toward the table to pour coffee into a porcelain cup. Everything in Alex's house was carefully chosen. Her daughter's toys were made of polished wood; there was always a bunch of exquisite flowers on the counter.

"But the worst part was this," I told her. "They didn't take us straight to the trains. They let us go home to get our bags, and we just waited. All I could think to do was to leave a note for the American consulate. This though we didn't know whether we were being sent straight to a death camp!"

Alexandra shook her head with a bitter smile.

"When I woke," I continued, "I wondered why we hadn't gone underground. And I couldn't get back to sleep, because I couldn't be certain that any of our German friends would have hidden us."

"I pick my friends," said Alex, "according to whether they would hide me or not."

"Who would hide you, then?"

"Andreas, for sure. And Louise." She paused. "Although I'm not certain about Walther, for example. I rather doubt it."

"But you lived with him for years."

"Contradictions."

It's a funny kind of comfort I got from Alex. Our children played together. We had the same kind of nightmares. She wasn't very happy but I could count on her to react to the world with a biting sort of irony that always made me smile.

She edited a small magazine for belles-lettres, but her real dream was to direct a production of *Tristan und Isolde* someday. "Or the *Ring*," she added when I teased her about this. That's not the only reason why I called Alexandra the last genuine German Jew. Nor was it the way she looked down her nose at the East European dishes in the Russian restaurant where we spent last Rosh Hashanah; nor the fact that she considered it just short of scandalous to raise a child in a home like ours, without hot running water or an automobile. Unlike the great cultivated German Jews of the years before the war, Alexandra knew she was stuck. The books and music which filled her living room were already tainted when she began to love them; but what could be put in their place? What was Jewish in her parents' home was a certain network of guilt-laced interaction. Everything else they had managed to hide.

"My mother's biggest problem," said Alex, "was that *her* domineering mother's deportation to Theresienstadt was a relief at the time. It was her first real chance to break away from home. She's had to live with that for forty years. So I feel for her, right? But someday we have to stop blaming our neuroses on this goddamned history."

Had things worked out differently, Alex and her family could have paid large sums of money to have their neuroses treated as purely private problems. But Alex's father had been in a Nazi prison before he went into hiding, and American immigration authorities denied them a visa after the war. They might have appealed the decision, but Alex's parents were weary. They unpacked their bags, changed their very Jewish name to something inconspicuous and built up a flourishing little business in the suburbs of Berlin. Alex was twelve when she heard from an unexpected relative that she was Jewish.

"But I'm not Jewish either. My parents did everything they could to deny it. I don't know the difference between Hanukkah and—what's that other holiday, with the unleavened bread?"

Alex often proposed to take the kids to the synagogue, only to call up on Friday with a splitting headache or a suddenly remembered urgent errand. When she did accompany us to a holiday service, she regretted it the next day.

"I can't help it. When Mimi talks about the chocolate she got in the synagogue and everyone in the supermarket turns to look at her, I get chills down my spine. And it will be harder as she gets older. I'm not taking her again."

"Then you're just repeating what your parents did with you."

"So she can hate me for it when she grows up too, if she wants. What else should I do? I can't give her anything of the Jewish tradition; I don't know it myself."

"You named her Miriam."

"Miriam Esther. My parents were appalled."

"So why don't you—"

"I'm not in your situation! You've got it easy! Although," she remembered, "there's a new series in *Der Spiegel* about anti-Semitism in America." With the knowledge that I was leaving, Alex had taken to deprecating America with particular fury. "I don't believe it's really any different there at all. But Amis are optimistic. Keep smiling, and maybe it'll all go away."

"There is anti-Semitism in America, but it's different—"

"You have to go all the way to America to find a different kind of anti-Semitism? And that where your salary isn't enough to support a family? I still don't understand it, where college students have to pay all that tuition. But what can one expect in a country which has never valued the intellect? Movie stars they like."

Still Alex asked me to take her to the synagogue again; sometimes we would go. She passed the elegant clothing which no longer fit her child on to mine. We could argue and confide. For we had the same sense of humor, and the same kinds of nightmares.

* * *

No laughter, no tears.

Live broadcast from Munich. A roundtable discussion was devoted to interviewing young Jews in the Federal Republic. The twenty-two-year-old moderator beamed chic sunny spirits, her bobbed head breezy with the first question: "The Jews must feel really safe in the Federal Republic. Their schools are guarded by the police, their synagogues are guarded by the police, even this program is being guarded by the police. Tell me, do you feel safe?"

No tears, no laughter.

The fragility of it all was overpowering. Being Jewish in Berlin is something precious and secret, to be shared, alone, with someone you trust. The lowered voice, the searching eye. We were on the lookout, always, for others.

* * *

"I haven't seen you in ages," said Frau Kalish reproachfully. "Round about a year."

"I must have been here at Pesach," I replied. "Yes, of course I was here at Pesach."

"Pesach is half a year ago already. A year, half a year ... he's grown. Good-looking, too. Quite a big boy."

Benjamin regarded her with the slightly irritated gaze of any child hearing this information. I asked after her granddaughter in Los Angeles. She dug into her apron pocket for photos.

"Well," said Frau Kalish to Benjamin, "isn't it about time for you to be getting a sister?"

"I want a sister and a brother," said my son.

"Your mama will never manage that," said Frau Kalish, "not with those little hips."

"They're not so little," I answered, "but I have to work."

"My mother had four children and she ran the store," said Frau Kalish. "In Czechoslovakia."

"I've read about them," I said, "but I don't know how those Jewish mothers did it. Raised the kids and supported the family, while their husbands sat in the *schul*."

"Men never work," said Frau Kalish.

"Perhaps they were all old at fifty?" I wondered.

"My grandmother was ninety-four and she could see straight as an arrow," said Frau Kalish. "Would have lived longer, but for the Nazis."

She turned, unhurried, to serve the other customers who entered. The gentle melancholy of the room draws unlikely faces. A Japanese father and son order candy and soda, three watchmen who work on the corner drink beer from the bottle. Shalom is the only Jewish store in Berlin. You go there if you need matzah, kosher wine, yarmulkes, mezuzahs, Manischewitz gefilte fish or records of Estrongo Nachama the cantor who sang in *Cabaret*. Frau Kalish supplements this with a little business in falafel-and-hummus sandwiches; her husband comes in occasionally to look at the stock. They are said to be wealthy. Frau Kalish always wears the same spotted apron and gives nothing away.

Once the store stood in a main street, with a sign reading SHALOM in big letters. After it was bombed in 1977, they moved to a side street and left the word SHALOM on a printed square of paper at the bottom of the window. The sign on the door says ORIENTAL SPECIALITIES; you might pass it often without a clue.

There's a kosher butcher around the corner who does business twice a week. The rest of the time his blinds are closed. When they're open, you can see a large signboard reading KOSHER MEAT AND SAUSAGE PRODUCTS, but only if you know it is there. For the sign is posted backward, designed to be read only by those who are already inside. One corner of the window shows a crack in the glass. I no longer asked questions. Berlin taught me silence.

The bell on the door jangles softly whenever a newcomer enters the store. Frau Kalish moves slowly, barely turning her head, but nothing in the little room escapes her. Though she is anything but sentimental, I like to think that her heart has a place for us. Michael ate her falafel for fifteen years, and her husband was part of the *minyan* at Benjamin's bris. We never discussed religion.

"Still waiting for the shipment," said Frau Kalish to the elderly lady who'd entered the door.

"Ay," sighed the lady, settling herself onto the stool by the counter where Frau Kalish dispenses samples of wine. "So what's the *good* news?"

"You can make them yourself," said Frau Kalish.

"I like them in jars," said the lady. "I haven't made kneydlakh in years."

"You take an egg," said Frau Kalish.

"And if one, why not two?" said the lady.

At the bare table in the background, the three watchmen stirred. They knew that the store closes early on Fridays. The elderly lady whispered fretfully across the counter. Frau Kalish interrupted her to give Benjamin a napkin for the sticky hands he'd been about to smear on her glass.

"Italians," said Frau Kalish, tapping a finger to her forehead as soon as the lady withdrew from the room. Her eyes rolled to heaven, and followed the customer as she disappeared into the street. Then she glanced at the sky and began to wipe the counter.

"Good Shabbos," I said, departing.

"Good Shabbos," said Frau Kalish.

* * *

*J*ewish holidays in Berlin remained outlined in poignant impotence. We knew both too much and too little for joy. There was the seder where half the guests were ill and the others offended, interrupting the service with a series of dramatic exits; the kneydlakh dissolved in the chicken soup. There was the Rosh Hashanah dinner when the Russians never came, the children danced on the table and I sang Dylan songs with Claudio at the piano. However we tried, something crucial failed.

Before Simchat Torah services, policemen cleared cars from the block. "For your own good!" they insisted to worshipers frantically looking for parking space. "Police!" shouted Benjamin, still shaken by the police occupation of the city during the World Bank Conference the previous week. "This time they're protecting us, honey," I quieted him uncertainly.

Bright confusion mastered the synagogue. Alexandra and I hesitated before the seats in the main room usually reserved for men. Seeing an elderly woman with a video camera, I moved to join husband and son, but a furious look from the cantor and a word from the shammas sent us back to stand in the last row. "I'll never set foot here again," said Alex. "Not even a bus driver would dare speak to me that way." "Then you can forget about going to synagogue in Berlin," I replied. "They all have this medieval seating policy." "'Medieval' isn't the word for it," said Alex. "It wasn't a happy beginning," I tried to appease.

But the festival started, bursting with delight: the Orthodox celebrate this holiday with a wild rapture missing in other congregations I'd known. What joy on the face of the usually taciturn shammas throwing the Torah in the air, dancing through the room. Children scrambled to collect the showers of candy thrown from the balcony. "The women are requested not to shoot candy at the men's yarmulkes!" called the chazzan, laughing. "Are we in Spain?" asked Michael happily, but declined to carry a Torah.

Alex allayed her discomfort with a dryness I had no taste for that night. "This is just like my family: everybody does what he likes and forgets all the others."

"Can't you relax and enjoy it?"

"What's to enjoy? When we visit America you'll take us to an orderly synagogue, where everybody listens."

Michael, divided, joined her in scoffing. Ancient melody too remote from a West German childhood; nothing rang in their ears. I sang to the songs I knew, clapped to the ones I didn't. But the proud ease of the Orthodox eluded me, and sardonic glances burned behind.

After the service, people pushed to the adjoining room, where a white table groaned with wine and vodka, lox and herring, cake and fruit. Alex looked aghast at the crowded chaos. "Wouldn't we rather go to a kneipe?" she pleaded. A children's band began to play off-key. To please me Michael sang along to "Tumbalalaika," then he drank too much vodka and started to cry. "I can't stand to see any more numbers on people's arms—"

"Who?" I asked him.

"Ah, you're curious. The woman on my right. No, not that one." Tears shone on his face. "Do you know how desperately I need to leave this country?"

At the head of the table the cantor intoned, but the loud lusty voices I'd expected remained still. In their place were the sounds of scraping chairs and elderly people rising to go.

"Why is everyone leaving?" called Michael, momentarily buoyed by another shot of vodka. "It's time for the celebration to *begin!*"

"The police want to go home," said the woman beside him. "They've had a long day."

* * *

"Michael," said Jochen, "I have to tell you something." They had met on the corner in passing; Jochen always looked smaller in broad daylight. "Actually I've wanted to say it for a long time, but I haven't had the nerve."

"Don't say it, then," said Michael.

"No," said Jochen, "I have to tell you. I wish I could make it go away. I wish I could buy you a beer and talk about something else." He nodded uncertainly toward the music hammering from the Bauernstübl door. "But last night, when I saw the three of you, I knew I had to say it sometime."

We had stopped at Bauernstübl on the way home from the synagogue, lost as we were after every holiday. Benjamin still carried the blue and white flag he'd been given to wave. Michael bought a desultory round of vodka and we stood chatting vainly, expecting no more.

Now Jochen began to cry. Not stray tears, he was really sobbing, at three o'clock in the afternoon on the Sesenheimer street corner.

"What's the matter?" asked Michael, but it would be minutes before words could come. When Jochen spoke, he still choked with weeping.

"I can't help thinking," he said. "I can't help thinking that it's *you* they deported. You and Susan and the baby. That's who they mean when they talk about Jews. And I don't understand it. I don't understand how they could do that to you. And the worst is"—Jochen faltered, caught by tears—"the worst is that the people who did it are still around. Doing fine."

Michael laid an arm on Jochen's shoulder.

* * *

***"A**re we having a state visit?" asked Michael. "You don't usually clean the floor when guests come for dinner."

"Lay off it," I answered. "I told you how lovely she was when I dropped in unexpectedly. I want to return the hospitality."

"That's not it," he said. "You're much too excited."

"Well," I conceded, "they are sort of special."

"Why special?"

"They're eighty years old. They're rather well known. They've been all over the world."

"Including Auschwitz. Not just any old concentration camp, but Auschwitz itself."

"Auschwitz itself. But that's not the reason—"

"It's not?"

"Well," I wavered, "because she was in Auschwitz and remained such a mensch."

The dinner invitation to Lilli Segal and her husband Jascha fell on a Friday. All the better, I'd thought, and proceeded to prepare the finest East European dishes I could muster. The recipes came from a cookbook; my grandmother, a lawyer who defended the poor, had no particular inclination to cook, traditionally or otherwise. Nor was the Sabbath of my childhood very strict or very grand. Yet after my son was born in Berlin, I began to try to observe it. Tentatively, ignorantly, but certain of one thing: being Jewish was not to be reduced to being a possible victim of anti-Semitism. I balked at Sartre's dictum: a Jew is one who is regarded as a Jew by the Other. It seemed the final fascist triumph. Preserving and renewing Jewish tradition was a matter of taking my life in my hands. And something within me had begun to believe.

Everything seemed to go wrong that night. Gathered round the table, I removed the challah from Benjamin's reach. "Wait till we say the blessings, honey." Lilli and Jascha stared as if suddenly learning they'd arrived in a jungle. East-West visits had their own uneasy logic, but the white-bedecked table, the candles in brass might have been a simple tribute to an elder honored guest. Now they wondered, in disbelief and scorn: were we seriously about to celebrate the Sabbath?

"Your wife seemed to be such a reasonable person," muttered Lilli to Michael, who was distributing yarmulkes over her mocking protests: so where were the women's *shekels*? If we subscribed to this nonsense, why stop halfway?

Restless and fitful, I tried to explain in terms we could share. The Sabbath marked a wonder which we needed more than ever. One day in every seven, free from commerce and consumption—

"Rubbish," said Jascha. "You're just sentimental." In the shtetl, he told us, it all looked quite different: commerce proceeded, touched merely by form. "'If it weren't Shabbos, I would offer you ten bales at seven rubles.' 'And if it weren't

Shabbos, I would tell you to take your seven rubles to the devil.'" Legalistic convention: was that the tradition we wished to revive?

Of course not, I answered, as yet undeterred. The old man demurred when asked to say Kiddush, then gave in and mumbled at horrified speed. Things only got worse. Nervous and distracted, I forgot to serve the Soviet champagne they had brought from East Berlin. Even the beef with plum sauce tasted unsavory. Slowly I began to curse my obtuseness. Vaguely and dimly, I'd supposed it might please: food from his childhood, rituals shared. From Lilli's book I'd learned that Jascha came from a large, traditional Litvak family. Yet the book also told me that his large, traditional Litvak family was murdered. Why ever had I dreamt he might want to recall?

"In the camps," said Lilli, "the believers were lost." A few had survived, but they couldn't resist; she had seen them suffer helpless, defenseless, alone. Her comrades, by contrast, could organize even there: it was politics, not prayer, which had helped them endure. Once four of them hid a pregnant woman at Auschwitz—delivered the baby, saved the mother's life. Faith hadn't done it, but plotting, discipline, contacts and nerve.

Still I resisted. For what I wanted to revive was not classical Orthodoxy, but the spirit of Judaism, and that was compatible with internationalist political commitment—

"*Ach*, the Bund," said Lilli dismissively. Nor was she wrong: the Bund's attempt to uphold elements of Jewish tradition while participating in a larger socialist movement deeply appealed to me. Born earlier, in another country, it was the group I'd probably have joined. Waking wretched next morning, I had to reflect: it wasn't only human souls but ideas whose lives were staked. So many had flourished in Eastern Europe. Zionism, communism, Orthodox Judaism all survived the war; only the Bund was completely destroyed.

Cold plum sauce and onions shimmered on plates. Michael rose to take the baby to bed.

"Should there *be* a God," said Jascha, "who saw and permitted ... all that—then I don't want Him."

Does the Shoah demand more than God's answer to Job? A world of theologians may toil as they will: there is no response to a statement like that. "I don't want Him" is irrefutable.

Stupefied, despairing, I walked the guests to the subway.

* * *

He arrived bearing a slice of apple cake loosely wrapped in a napkin. It was untouched, he assured me, left over from lunch at the Community's kosher restaurant; perhaps my little one would like a piece? Mendel Leisner's sister died in Israel; he had come to Berlin to sit *shiva*. The synagogue in Hannover was only open for Shabbos, and as for a *minyan*...

I never would have asked him, but he wanted to tell his story. Sitting at my window in the sunlight, near the tree. Mendel Leisner and his family spent the war hiding in Belgium. When it was over they went to Palestine. There they lived for ten years, but there was a problem. It had to do with his son. "He's..." Mendel Leisner waved his hands helplessly, then pointed to his head. "Meshugge because of the Holocaust. All those years in hiding, he was only a boy. We can't keep him at home." Now came the hitch. His son's illness wasn't covered by Israeli insurance policies, which only paid for damages caused directly to older survivors. Mendel Leisner couldn't afford the costs of permanent hospitalization. He left the Holy Land to travel through Europe seeking a place for his son. The only institution providing care he could afford turned out to be located in a little town in northern Germany.

I persuaded Mendel Leisner to accept a glass of water.

The Almighty had been good to him, he continued; blessed with a wonderful wife, Mendel Leisner had had no thoughts of other women in the more than fifty years they'd been granted together. Speaking of her, Mendel Leisner's face glowed. He had only one worry. He wasn't getting any younger, his dear wife was nearly eighty. They lived near the hospital, so their son could come home every Shabbos. But what would become of him after they were gone? There was a daughter in Tel Aviv; she had her own family, and troubles now. She had turned away from the Torah. She no longer really cared.

"Good people," said Mendel Leisner, "are usually *frumm.* It's easier to do the right thing when you live by the Torah. You'll think of that, won't you, when you're raising your son?"

I assured Mendel Leisner I would.

After his departure we stood staring at the door. Michael and I tried to unravel the story. Was the son schizophrenic? Autistic? Paranoid? We gave up in a hurry: all our speculation useless, all the categories wrong.

"Meshugge because of the Holocaust," we concluded, with very frail laughter.

The Rose Sellers

Children ask questions before they can talk. It seemed to be names my son wanted to know. Pointing to an object, he would demand "There?" and was satisfied when I told him "That's a streetcar" or "Those are pigeons in the tree." Searching to know him I wished terribly that he could tell me what he was seeing before I taught him the words to do so. When I told him that's the crane loading coal onto a barge, was he watching a religious ceremony? A law of nature? The wish was as useless as any mother's, as useless as the wish, today, to see his world with his eyes.

He was born in a country with castles, he fed his first ducks in the shadow of the graceful yellow Schloss Charlottenburg, treading on formal beds of flowers. He took his first steps near a ruined Moorish fortress on the Spanish coast where we spent six weeks in a borrowed cottage. There was no plumbing and we huddled, freezing, when the sun went down. Antonio, who owned the bar where we gambled in broken Spanish, brought fresh guavas from his garden; a pack of little girls came giggling every morning and drew chalk hearts on the pavement before our door. In a rough crammed hall Benjamin clapped to Flamenco dancers till three in the morning. When we returned to Berlin, he toddled to the guitar and sang with expression that is only Andalusian. Of all of this he will remember next to nothing.

For his world was also bounded by two blocks we traversed daily. Its farthest point was the Turkish café in the Krummestrasse. The sulky Anatolian who owned the place liked children, and kept a carton full of building blocks under the chess set on the wall. Benjamin was at home in other kneipen as well. At Bauernstübl he was allowed a sip of Coke and a turn at the jukebox; at Kabale he watched pool games and climbed on the overturned bicycle rack which served as a train.

There were the chimes that rang in twilight from the church tower, the block where he raced autos with the other children after kindergarten. There was the cobbler from Odessa nodding warily before his shop, the Greek tailor next door who greeted him with overflowing smiles, the old man playing off-key violin in the Wilmersdorferstrasse, empty hat before him; everyone but Benjamin passed him by.

There were, most notably, the playgrounds. Three of them within a five-minutes walk from our door. They were spacious and inventive, with vast piles of sand and fresh equipment, and benches for parents under broad new trees. Berlin's playgrounds may be the best in the world; they are surely the most numerous. Every innercity neighborhood has scads of them. This was, in its way, a gift of the Allies. For the playgrounds were built in the spaces where the bombs had left nothing but ruins.

* * *

*A*cts of friendship; and faith. Not just the way Claudio, Ingrid and their two teenagers spent a weekend cleaning our apartment when the prospect of a wedding journey left us flailing in inaction. Or the time I was ready to succumb to a publisher's rejection and Irena dropped everything to sit down with a dictionary and edit my manuscript. What I most remember wasn't out of the way. Claudio's guitar; singing in the kitchen. The sharp probing silence when new work was read. How often a traveler would stop for the night, bringing tales of old cities, new tongues. Michael says there were no forecasts, people simply dropped by, but I think he's mistaken: most often there was at least a phone call, and some gatherings were planned. What he misses is the way we plunged into each other's lives. Anything could belong to the public domain. An unpaid bill, a set of paintings, a visiting mother, an injured child. It subverted the space between ordinary, and art. Not that there was anything like an arrangement. To get by in Berlin you had to laugh a great deal. And lie, says Irena. So we did some of each. The days often rose and veered into jubilation.

* * *

*T*here were rituals, institutions, days of ease if not rest. Saturday mornings we went to the open-air market and then to the Turkish café, where friends in the neighborhood were likely to be.

"I hear you're writing a novel?" asked Filippo.

"It's not really a novel," I answered, looking over my shoulder for Benjamin. He was standing in the doorway, spitting cherry pits onto the sidewalk; the neighbor's nine-month-old daughter beamed at him, entranced. "It's a description of things I've experienced here. Under the rubric vergangenheitsverarbeitung."

"More cherries!" said Benjamin, returning to the table. Standing up to search through the paper bags we'd left in the corner, I collided with Murad, carrying a platter full of Turkish tea. He grunted at me, as always, put down the platter and threw Benjamin in the air.

"You said description?" asked Filippo, when I'd sat down again.

"There are philosophical allusions here and there, where I can't help it. See, I came to Berlin to write a dissertation about the concept of reason."

Filippo found this very funny. After he'd stopped laughing, he reflected: "When I first started writing, I wrote out of rage." His dark summer skin provoked threats, prohibitions. Even worse were the occasional apologies, when Berliners learned that he wasn't a Moslem, but fled to these parts after the putsch in Chile. That's something else, they would tell him: the Chileans are the Prussians of South America! "The problem," said Filippo, "is that rage produces bad literature."

"I know," I answered. "I'm not writing from rage."

"Mama," asked Benjamin, "where's Oliver today?"

Chimes sounded the hour; the church clock was repaired. Benjamin and Oliver took turns jumping down the café stairs. Sofia, from Iceland, beamed quiet grace. She was expecting Filippo's child, of late he too was radiant. Softened and lazy, we ordered another round. The lull of the private held sway.

"Oh look," called Benjamin. "Here comes Benno and Irena!" He ran out to greet them, there were kisses all around. For a world, it wasn't bad.

* * *

*Y*et it is only amnesia which sustains an illusion of childhood's simplicity. If I hadn't learned this from Freud, I'd have learned it from my son. My tears, Michael's depressions, slammed doors, broken glass. They too have made up his planet from the very beginning, he's made sense of them as he can. And the incomprehensible prohibitions. Ovens are hot, and streets contain cars, but why did I seldom let him linger in the courtyard, collecting fallen chestnuts? Why did I start on the staircase, urging him to hurry at an open door?

"Borchert is an idiot," said Benjamin at dinner.

"Borchert is an idiot," Michael agreed.

"Borchert is a big idiot," said Benjamin. "Papa, may I spit at him?"

"Yes," said Michael. "At Borchert you may spit."

"*Michael*," I countered, "the man is *dangerous.*"

"Stop it," said Michael. "He wouldn't dare."

"We don't *know* what he'd dare. The last time—"

"The last time was different."

We were at it again.

* * *

*T*he eviction notice came the day I finished my thesis. That seemed rotten luck, but we weren't really worried. The landlord had no reason to like us; Michael had helped two elderly tenants to write letters demanding some long-due repair. But the notice was only valid if Borchert could prove he needed our apartment himself, and we knew he had two other addresses. The lawyer we consulted advised photographing the name-plates on all the landlord's residences, which is how Michael came to be standing in a hallway in the Sigmaringerstrasse, suddenly weak at the knees.

He was looking at our mezuzah, not on a doorframe, as it's meant to be hung, but nailed right to the middle of the landlord's door.

Michael left the building. He reentered the building and took photographs. He left the building again and called Claudio, who came at once to witness, advise. They took the mezuzah from the door. It had, after all, belonged to my grandmother.

We were, quite simply, confounded.

"He wants you out of his house, and he puts your mezuzah on his door," said Claudio. "It's hard to call it anti-Semitic—"

"Perhaps it's Homeric," I ventured. "Hanging the arms of the enemy over your hearth."

"And maybe he just thought it was a classy good-luck charm," wondered Michael.

The perplexed young lawyer advised discretion. Nothing about mezuzahs, stolen or otherwise, stood in any of his casebooks. The eviction case, on the other hand, could be won on its merits. The lawyer kept his promise: a few months later, the court ruled in our favor. The landlord appealed. The appeal was overturned.

* * *

Most of his friends were skeptical and indifferent when Michael first introduced me. The last time it had been a German pop star, then briefly, a Spanish gypsy; an American philosopher seemed another careless piece of exotica. Benno was aloof and Irena just slightly cutting when we met unavoidably at large gatherings in Claudio's kitchen. For years we resisted any chance to get closer; then it was sudden, unfathomed.

Irena brought Benno to write again after a decade of silence, and initially, she overshadows him. Benno's pale blue eyes often hover on the verge of apology, for no obvious reason. He was born near Berlin in 1928. This made him too young, by a shade, to be called up to the Front; and too young to have childhood's worldview formed by anything preceding the Nazi period. When he started school, they were firmly in power. As I asked about residues, Benno turned shy. Once he said it was peculiar growing up with no Russians: could I imagine a *writer* whose adolescence went by without Tolstoy or Dostoevsky? I could not; there we meet. Benno never complains, and composes beautiful letters in the spare prose which has won enough prizes to make him count as part of the lower-key literary establishment.

He writes next to the room where his parents were found. Dead, double suicide. His father was a journalist for the Nazi papers. For two years after the war's end he scoured the country looking for work of any kind. The mother went crazy, speaking in tongues. Unable to bear the thought of a public asylum, where patients were chained to the corridor beds, Benno's father spent his last coins on a handful of cyanide.

Still it's easy to see why he kept the apartment. Four attic rooms looking out to the heavens. Sloping walls covered with paintings, mostly gifts from old friends. The books are well chosen. At sixty-two, Benno had never used a library or been on an airplane. Entering their dwelling you must feel that something's been preserved.

It's too hot in the summer, and cold in the winter, but not nearly as bad as the two rooms they keep in Zagreb, where Irena was born. For twenty years they have shuttled between West Berlin and Yugoslavia, depending on the seasons. Recently she wrote: "I'll tell no one more: I have no time." Somehow she always finds it; to translate a poem, bed down a friend's wayward children, hear a story about broken plumbing or a threatened suicide. She listens carefully, asking all the right questions, and gives advice, just often enough. Sometimes she turns it into literature, but always discreetly. One feels flattered upon recognizing a confided incident in Irena's latest book.

Her great dark eyes are stunning, disarming. During the summer, light disfigures her skin. Her books get darker all the time. She dismisses the doubts that lead to inertia: the question "Why write?" is as unanswerable as "Why live?"

I think she believes that both are quite senseless. Still she writes every morning. Occasionally, trying not to boast, she will translate a Yugoslavian review of her work. She is big-time there, the national prizewinner. Here she rises obscurely, and goes for a walk. Buys fresh rolls for breakfast before approaching her desk. There she writes poetry, plans theater, types Benno's scrawling pages. Then she cooks a pot of soup, never very fancy, and listens to the troubles of a Yugoslavian immigrant who got hold of her name from a cellar in Kreuzberg. Or hears the latest news from Belgrade, with tightened somber lips. "There is nothing but fragments: forget about the whole." She is speaking of contemporary literature but I think of all that's been shattered, here. It is now all a matter of just getting by. Still Irena will warn that it's comedy which is easiest forgotten.

***

*D*ownstairs, the Bulgarians practicing, and the still sweeter sound of the typewriter in the next room. After weeks of blocking, Michael had started to write again. "In my next life," he said, "I'll be reborn as an ant. Diligent, undeviating, single-minded..." Working, he listens to Dvorak's *New World* Symphony. When we'd first met he called once late at night to play me the entire symphony over the telephone.

Knots of sunlight reflected through leaves spattered the afternoon wall. "Look at the light here!" he exclaimed. "This is one of the most beautiful rooms in the *world!*" At my desk, I nodded. He'd come to bring me an interview with Berlin's oldest puppet-maker, dedicated to his trade. After the war there was a paper shortage; supplies for making papier-mâché Punch-and-Judy heads were very low priority. But the puppet-maker had found a solution. He scouted bombed-out homes for copies of *Mein Kampf.* It didn't count as stealing; nobody wanted them anymore. Dismantling the books left him plenty of paper, so the Punch-and-Judy shows could begin again.

***

*F*rom the window you could see that the neighborhood was changing. Porsches and Mercedes were parked in the street. The room where the drunken Welshman used to give guitar lessons was now a shop for water beds; an overpriced boutique was now housed in the paper shop that had been empty since its owners were deported. Borchert shouted, "You old tramp, d'you think you're in Kreuzberg?" when Alarm-Evchen stepped to the balcony in her bathrobe. For some, Berlin was prospering.

But pieces of the old neighborhood obtruded now and then, and with them questions that had to be considered. How much do you help your neighbor? How much do you help your neighbor if you know that she was a Nazi? How much do you help your neighbor if you know that she was a Nazi and would be one again tomorrow if the times were right?

Rennie had called, frantic and tearful. Would I please come downstairs, just for ten minutes or so? Was the little one there? No problem at all, I could bring him along. It wasn't the first time; laid up for months with a broken leg she had called, several evenings, and begged me to fetch her a six-pack of beer. I did so, unwillingly, but Rennie never noticed my coolness. I was always polite, and thanked her for the little packets she offered in return; shades of expression and tone had no place in Rennie's world.

"I'm kind of busy at the moment..."

"Just for ten minutes, please! I got a letter from the landlord—or the court, I'm not sure—I'm so shook up I can feel my heart all thumping! And the lawyer's on vacation, so I thought, you understand about those things, don't you?"

Rennie's was the thinness of long uncertain illness; her short brown hair was pushed back from a horselike face. Her husband was the *Blockwart*, in the old days; his job was to denounce everyone in the street whom he suspected of opposing the Nazis. I learned this from Alarm-Evchen and Uschi. Rennie herself, on the other hand, may be one of the few who can truly claim not to have known anything at all about what was going on with the Jews; she is the very stupidest person I ever met. With only a shortened sigh I collected my son, took my keys and went downstairs to Rennie's apartment.

Legal German is hard to decipher, but the letter wasn't complicated; the landlord was taking her to court for refusing to pay a rent increase. Rennie's hysterics seemed to be caused by the court's request for information.

"What does my husband have to do with it? We've been divorced for ten years!"

"He's listed on the lease, Rennie, and the court wants to know why he isn't named in the case."

"But he doesn't live here!"

"But the court doesn't know that, Rennie. That's just what they're asking."

"We've been divorced since 'seventy-nine. He has a girlfriend—"

"Rennie. They just see the lease. Your ex-husband's name is on it. They have no other source of information. They want to know why he hasn't been named in the case."

"But what does he have to do with it at all?"

Every conversation with Rennie was like this, not merely the excited ones. It was frustration and boredom, not uneasiness and fear, which kept my encounters with her to a minimum. I wasn't sure she understood my explanation, but she was calmer, at least, when she bade us good-bye, laden with gifts I could not refuse. There were teeth-rotting candies for Benjamin.

"Take two," I told him.

"He can have the whole bag," said Rennie.

"No, thank you, Rennie, that's very kind—"

"It's alright," she said. "I always had a heart for kids—"

"Mama, she says I can have the whole bag!"

"He sure is talking a lot these days," said Rennie. "Do you speak Israeli with him too?"

"No," I said, "I'm American. I speak English with him sometimes."

Rennie looked puzzled. "But Frau Tobien said—or was it Herr Winkler—that you all were Israelis?"

"We're Jewish," I answered, "but I come from America."

"Oh," said Rennie, "I thought you had something to do with Israel." She offered me a white vase she had stolen from a bar. Inside were plastic ferns, and chocolates wrapped in red paper to form the petals of a wilted flower. "But don't eat the chocolates," she said. "I bet they've gone bad by now."

"That's awfully kind," I returned, "but don't you want to keep it yourself?"

"Just look!" she said, pointing. "I got so many pretty things here. Every time a friend comes they bring something new for me. I've hardly got room for what I have now." It was true. Her dim green apartment was crammed full of the ugliest imaginable bric-a-brac: garish dolls sitting in the armchairs, plastic flowers in crude painted porcelain waiting on every ledge.

I tried again: "I'm afraid Benjamin may break the vase—"

"Just put it where he can't reach it. I swiped it last Sunday, after I'd put five marks in the slot machine and didn't win a penny. Nice vase, don't you think?" She pressed a box of cookies and a Jack Daniels whiskey glass in my hands. "I know you all don't have a lot of money." With relief I watched my son refuse a giant moldy teddy bear with joggling eyes.

* * *

***"T**urks,"* he said. One eyebrow was raised. "Part of their ... culture, I suppose."

"*Ach* so," she answered.

"A jealousy drama. She had left him for another, a week or so before. So he came with a bread knife to the greengrocer's where she worked. Kantstrasse, corner of Bleibtreu."

"Corner of Bleibtreu?" The name means "Stay faithful."

"You know the store. He tried to get away after stabbing her, but he ran into a shelf full of strawberries. He fell, she lay dying, and the Kantstrasse was covered with blood and strawberries. They closed it off for an hour."

"Blood and strawberries?"

"Said Laura. But she's a poet. I wasn't there."

* * *

***I**t* was general opinion that a heyday was over. Irena prophesied weekly the ending of Europe. On the verge of the millennium, an increase in everyday pessimism was easy to spur. Others said nonsense, the action had simply moved to Madrid. Berlin was losing its oddness, and with it, a vision. After twenty-six or twenty-seven years of near-isolation, the island had become the status quo. Nobody dreamed of return to the mainland, but gentrification was in process: no longer fearing imminent takeover by the Russians, conservative tradesmen began to invest. A motion was carried to abolish the rent control which allowed us to live as royal paupers. Those ceilings! That space! The developers would take them. Late at night, more than ever, conversations turned to casting around.

All over the city you could see signs of polish. Brawny men were employed to replace the old sidewalks, tenderly knocking large heaps of small stones into prosaic patterns. They used no cement, according to a seasoned system which accommodates the weather, leaving room to expand and contract with the cold. Passing by I would watch them knocking; for nothing else showed how directly Berlin is built upon sand.

The occupied houses were evacuated, or legally transferred. But the movement did not go out with a whimper. The last illegally occupied space in Berlin was a triangle of land facing the Tiergarten; though it belonged to the East, it had somehow eluded enclosure by the Wall. After years of negotiation Berlin-the-Capital-of-the-German-Democratic-Republic deeded the strip to its neighbor. Once in possession of the territory, West Berlin lost no time in sending nine hundred police troops to clear the two hundred squatters who'd been living for months in shacks and tents on the indeterminate ground. The troops arrived at five in the morning, but somebody must have been warned. Surrounded on three sides by West German police, the squatters turned and climbed up the Wall. There they were met by East German policemen, who helped them over the Wall and into trucks which drove them to a room where hot breakfast was waiting. How the Vopos must have cackled, beneath bland officers' gazes; it wasn't every day that two hundred young people, citing terror, fled from West to East. After breakfast the squatters were escorted to the border entry of their choosing and told they were welcome in East Berlin any time. For future visits, it was suggested, they might use one of the regular border crossings.

* * *

An old drunk bent over the street like a branch broken in two.

Michael asked him if he was looking for something.

"No," said the man, face contorted and scowling.

"Is this yours?" asked Michael, picking up a frayed leather belt from the sidewalk.

"Yes," said the man. "Now leave me alone. I can go by myself." He tottered, just missing a fall.

"You can't go two steps by yourself," said Michael. "Where are you headed?"

"Spandau," said the man. That's a very long way.

"How are you going to get there?" asked Michael. "Shall I call you a cab?"

"Leave me alone," said the man. "I'm a corpse-washer. I have to wash three corpses tomorrow."

A wind blew between us, there were no passersby.

"Were you in the war?" asked Michael.

"Yes," said the man.

"In Russia?" asked Michael.

"Three corpses," called the drunk, stumbling toward a stoop. "I have to wash three corpses."

"Usually," said Michael, "it's the ones who fought hardest in Russia who drink like that."

* * *

Had he really started shouting "Shit-Jews!" in the hallway?

Were we beginning to panic?

The fist on the stairway was no illusion. "You'll move out of this house if you know what's good for you," threatened Borchert as Michael returned from the market, child in his arms. The neighbors who saw rushed by with a shudder. They didn't want trouble. None of them did.

For days we stood at the window, leaving the house only when we saw the landlord's white Porsche depart. Borchert was twice as big as Michael, and if he really was a pimp he was probably armed.

We'd never defeat him with his weapons, but occasionally we could muster our own. One outspent evening we hit on the idea of writing a comedy about the house and laughed, sketching scenes far into the night. The thought sustained us when nothing else did.

"I will kill him," said Michael under the light bulb.

"The comedy, Michael. Sit down and write the comedy."

"This was my *home*. You know what this street meant to me."

"A black comedy. A very black comedy."

"I think I have to kill him."

* * *

At seven in the morning there was a knock on the door. Borchert entered with three workmen who proceeded to dismantle our stoves while we stood dazed in helpless protest.

"They tore down your stoves?!" In Berlin, where the means of keeping warm is a matter of daily discussion, it was an offense which bordered on scandal. "But why did you let them in?"

We'd been expecting the chimney sweep. The stoves had to be cleaned before they could be used. Glad, in the threat of winter, at the prospect of heating again, we reacted slow and stunned. Borchert smirked. He brought, as replacements, tiny tin stoves which were ugly, stinking and expensive to heat.

"*Allesbrenner!*" groaned the Berliners. "But you have to stoke them every two hours!"

- Gestapo tactics, coming at dawn.
- When people are defenseless—
- And taken unawares.
- Still you've got to be careful—
- It's just two old stoves—
- And not human beings they hauled off.
- But it's us he's out to get.
- Though he'd be happy to get rid of the rest of the tenants.
- So the rents would be higher.
- But not with such hatred.
- He saves that for us.
- So it is Gestapo tactics.
- How far can one go?

On the way back from the lawyer's office we stopped at Shalom to buy a mezuzah from Frau Kalish. Michael nailed it to the doorway; my grandmother's mezuzah lay safe in a drawer. The following week we were served notice: the landlord had brought charges against us for hanging a mezuzah in the house.

* * *

Sometimes you needed a foreigner's eye. "Two Germans can't simply call each other assholes," said Claudio. "They have to say, 'Your father was a Nazi.'"

Discussion of the "People-Counting" was so impassioned that it was years before I realized it was only a census. Planned for 1983, it was hurriedly canceled under threat of a massive boycott. Four years later both government and opposition began careful preparations for action. Life-size billboards and subway posters praised the civic virtues of compliance. Smaller printing presses turned out leaflets advising tactics for avoiding the census-takers. Both sides called out the ghosts. Chancellor Kohl reviled the boycott organizers: like the Nazis, they were unlawfully undermining the governing process. The boycott organizers reviled the government: like the Nazis, it was engaged in massive totalitarian surveillance. The twenty-eight questions seemed rather harmless, but this only evoked further suspicion. In consideration of special sensitivities concerning the abuses to which an earlier census had been put, the government offered Jewish citizens the option of not answering the question about religion. This didn't prevent a clamor within the Jewish community. Heinz Galinski urged his charges to demonstrate their loyalty by complying with the lawful and democratic Federal Republic. In the back room at Terzo Mondo, members of the oppositional Jewish Group fumed: they could hardly be expected to fill out a form of the kind which had enabled their grandparents' deportation. The law requiring all residents of Germany to register with the police every time they move seemed to me far more menacing, but mentioning this elicited blank response: the *Anmeldungsgesetze*, in force for more than a century, seemed as unlikely an object of protest as the weather.

Not trusting to carrots, the government exposed its stick. Large fines and prison terms awaited anyone refusing to participate. Census-takers were instructed in methods of obtaining entrance to obstinate residences and told to remain until the form was completed. Members of the opposition pooled money for constitutional lawyers, and disseminated imaginative speculation about indirect ways to resist. When the census week came, open defiance was less than expected. But the government's triumph lasted only until the processors began to read the returned forms.

"What is your primary profession?"

–Sorcery.

–Hunting elephants.

"What is your usual means of transportation?"

–Spaceship.

–Rickshaw.

So many responses were so blatantly false that the data which had cost millions to gather was virtually unusable.

* * *

Was it that kind of resistance which allowed us to dream?

One clear autumn evening we stopped for a glass of wine at the newly opened Russian restaurant on the corner. Michael began to chat with the owner, who'd arrived from Moscow two years before. From a niche behind the curtain she produced heavy volumes of color plates by Russian painters unknown in the West. Most pictures were portraits, astonishing and open; the owner grew ardent telling stories of the subjects' lives. Soon she lapsed into sighs. She was bored with her business, serving fat faceless clients on their way to the opera. We all began to imagine something better.

"A Jewish bookstore," said Michael.

"With readings," said I.

"And a gallery," said the owner. "I'll run the café."

The wine on the house now, our thoughts really soared. We'd build up a center, begin a restoration. In two years, at the outside, Berlin would have a focal point for the German-Jewish synthesis which had once distinguished her. (Even now there were traces. Remnants of Yiddish in the city slang. More telling, more cloudy: that wild steady laughter in the face of misfortune, so Berliner, so Jewish, unmistakably bound.) A publishing company could follow, in time...

The three of us embraced at the end of the evening, and our intoxication continued for days. Want of capital was no deterrent: we surely could borrow. Perhaps there was time to apply to the Senate, now dispensing funding for projects which would celebrate the city's status as "Cultural Capitol of Europe '88"? We sketched spaces, tallied budgets. Quite suddenly, it reeled to a halt.

"For whom?" asked Michael.

We could name most of the patrons; our friends would be there. The place would surely draw a Jew or two from some corner of the city we didn't know. Then would come the philo-Semitic Germans whose painstaking participation in groups like Sign of Atonement sent chills up my spine. The city fathers' blessing would lay upon it like dust in an eye. Only a merciless idealism could suppose that a world whose inhabitants were gone could be restored by creating a place.

"For whom?" he repeated.

"For whom?" I agreed.

* * *

Helga brought out clippings from the *Völkischer Beobachter*. That was the main Nazi paper, but Helga was a librarian with access to archives. Her children are grown but her hair is still blond and her face can bloom, on good days, with a biting Nordic beauty which is nearly faultless. After the death of her first husband she married an Italian who has a wonderful voice, remembers all the lyrics to songs in four languages and paints a sort of surrealistic realism which has proven rather successful. Aldo's canvases are large: a potato in outer space, a zebra in an endless subway. Helga is proud of his nationality; it set her apart from those Germans who wouldn't condescend to marry a foreigner, and it made her a part of the precarious circle of half-exiles to which we belong. She is proud of his paintings, toward which she takes an understandably proprietary air: she supported him for the seven years before he got successful and began to spend most of his time in Paris.

"Just look at Aldo's latest!" Helga pointed to a canvas by the doorway, showing a string quartet playing before the ruins of the Reichstag. "It isn't quite finished," she explained. "He still has to paint the faces. The players will be Hitler, Hess, Himmler and Goebbels. Aldo spent the whole week in the archives."

"You learn so much," said Aldo, "by going through those old photos. How pathetic they all looked."

Helga had thought the clippings might be useful for Michael's research; she read them aloud in melodious tones. Her poise isn't pretense, but there's something relentlessly classic about her. It might be her name, or the fact that her father fell at Stalingrad. Or the way she announced over dinner, apropos of absolutely nothing, "My grandfather did so much to help the Jews who emigrated in the thirties."

I couldn't help thinking that as a toll-collector, Helga's grandfather's help must have largely consisted of accepting bribes to allow escaping Jews to smuggle a few of their possessions out of the country. But that's one of those things that a guest doesn't say and I didn't really care. There were times when I wished for nothing more than an end to these endless discussions.

"But, Susan, you're not peeling your potatoes properly!" said Helga. "You're taking off half the potato with the skin!"

When I serve potatoes, I either wash them or peel them beforehand, but that's another of those things that a guest doesn't say. I smiled weakly and began to cut my peelings thinner.

"Is it true," asked Helga, "that fried potato peels are all the rage in New York?"

"I can't say," I answered. "Last time I was there it was goat cheese with figs."

"Because I find it rather ludicrous, if they are. Potato peels were what we ate when we didn't have anything else, after the war. I don't think I could ever eat another potato peel in my life! Whereby," she added, "we were lucky. There were some people who didn't even have potato peels. Can you imagine, in 1946, in a civilized part of the world, there were people who actually starved to death?"

I can imagine it, because I know of people in a civilized part of the world who died other deaths, deaths which weren't imaginable until 1941, but that's another of those things that polite guests don't—oh when did I learn to hold my tongue? It had nothing to do with courtesy, little with fear. I no longer knew how words get their sense.

"I have a wonderful grappa to go with the coffee. Shall we move to the living room?"

Helga is never empty-handed, she lives with an eye out for something to contribute: a Roman liqueur, a droll picture, a piquant anecdote. Once she brought Michael a packet of sugar with an emblem resembling a swastika which she'd found on a table in Spain. She gives with measured grace, as she does everything else.

"Michael," asked Helga, "you're our expert on names. Have you been following the debate about the Court Square?"

"What's that?" asked Aldo.

"They want to rename it," explained Helga in the soothing tone she used with her husband. "To 'Square of the Victims of Treblinka.'"

"Rubbish," said Michael. "I hope it gets blocked."

"But surely you're not on the side of the Christian Democrats?"

"I don't care who else is against it. If they call it Square of the Victims of Treblinka, it won't be two weeks before every bus driver is saying 'Next stop, Trebi!'"

"I see your point," said Helga. "But that is Berlin. I still find the absence of monuments to the victims of fascism scandalous."

"Monuments," I said, "are all over the place."

We talked of Aldo's film. Helga returned to the kitchen to fetch cookies.

"Did you hear what she said about the chairs?" Michael asked. "They come from the Reichskanzlei.'"

"What was the Reichskanzlei?" I asked him.

"Nazi headquarters."

"The chairs that we're sitting in?"

"The chairs that we're sitting in."

I looked more closely at the fat worn armchairs. "Did she mean these very chairs, or ones just like them?"

"I don't know. The point is that she *said* it."

Our eyes met with the bitter smile we smile too often.

* * *

*I*n between there was always food to be bought, coal to be carried, the hundred daily steps that ground a life. I clung to the little acts of decency which sometimes accompanied them. I liked watching the fish-seller weigh out the amount I'd asked for, ring up the price and then throw another piece on the pile with a smile and a wink. He confided one day that he never ate fish himself, but he always gave me an extra piece, for nothing.

I could be cheered by things that bring no advantage, like the delighted look on the face of the cheese-cutter one morning. The man in line before me had ordered two hundred grams of Emmenthaler, and she beamed when she weighed up the piece she had cut. "Just look at that!" she cried. "Two hundred grams exactly! That hardly ever happens. One hundred ninety grams, or two hundred seven, but not just exactly what they order!" The man's face stayed motionless, sunk in bleak reverie, but the thought of the cheese-cutter kept me going all morning.

Cheese and bread, fish and fruit. There were diapers to be changed and clothes to be washed. There were fires to be lit and bills to be paid. A world can be made out of much less than these. Would it help if I kept that in view?

The blond cashier at the supermarket was a small wonder. Surrounded by mechanized chaos, she held up the line to exchange a few words with steady customers, kept a store of candy for the kids and tried to remember all their names, gave a free bag or a little credit to the people she liked. Her laugh might seem raucous, where laughter is saved for seclusion or stupor, but it wasn't raucous, merely warm. She hadn't really wanted to be a cashier, she told me; once she'd dreamed of minding children, but her husband is ill and couldn't cope with a house full of kids. Occasionally I saw her looking restrained, but never anything but sweet-tempered. Seeing her pass on the street I wondered once if she believed in God.

There were days when I felt unable to meet the naturalness of this decency. Then I pushed my cart around the back of the store to sneak into the checkout line which was farthest from hers, hoping to avoid her detecting what seemed like betrayal.

Outside, in the middle of the pedestrian zone, an oversized stuffed parrot repeated a recorded message at odd intervals. "Hello. My name is Charley. Charley likes to eat coins. Hello. This is Charley. Charley likes children. Charley has presents for children too."

Wilmersdorferstrasse, gray gray gray.

* * *

*T*here were always the thin men who trudged silently through the kneipen holding bundles of roses. From Sri Lanka, or possibly Pakistan, they scouted smoky rooms for the right combination of customers. They never approached a table full of men, and only occasionally appealed to women sitting in pairs; the best bets were mixed. They offered old couples the chance to bring back romance for the price of a beer. With new couples the insistence was different: they were watching each other for the first time, and who knew what might be risked by saying no? Words were seldom exchanged, for everybody knew the routine; in most kneipen the waitress would bring an old bottle filled with water the next time she came around. It rarely helped. The roses, usually, were the worst you'd ever seen, refusing to open, exuding no smell. Perhaps the flowers were better at the start of the night when the rose sellers began; but I never saw them before midnight. Many were refugees awaiting unlikely political asylum in crammed wretched quarters; for these, even selling roses was illegal. Their gaze encompassed all that's worn and foreign, but that wasn't why I liked to see them come.

* * *

*T*he notice had come by registered mail. After two court sessions failed to settle the matter, the judge himself would be coming in person. His mission: to determine whether the landlord's right to control the destination of his property had precedence over our right to freedom of religious expression. Counting all the witnesses and lawyers for both parties, there were ten people gathered in our doorway to inspect the mezuzah.

It was a modest examplar, not much to show: a piece of white plastic just two inches long. In his last brief our lawyer had explained its function to the uninitiated, introducing as evidence long texts from tomes of Jewish law. Borchert's lawyer countered: the mezuzah damaged the doorframe. There were, moreover, all sorts of tenants in the building. Imagine the conflicts, if each began advertising for a religious sect!

"Would you care to take a seat?" Justice was objective; the judge declined to go further than the entryway door. His assistant accepted a chair to facilitate dictation, which she took with Prussian fastidiousness. "It has been ascertained that there are cracks in the paint on the right side of the doorframe of about six centimeters extending to the upper corner..." There were several brief questions. The door was tried a few times. One week later the judge ruled in our favor. His decision covered six single-spaced pages and suggested that the cracks in the doorframe had more likely been caused by a faulty door. The damage created by the two nails holding the mezuzah in place was not significant enough to override the fundamental right to religious freedom guaranteed by the constitution of the Federal Republic. This in particular because the mezuzah itself was inconspicuous; the defendants lived on the top floor, where none of the other tenants could be disturbed by its presence in passing.

Daughters and Sons

*I*n 1987 *Stern* magazine printed a series called "My Father the Nazi Murderer." The editorial office was nearly buried beneath a flood of letters. An outraged public held no crime to outweigh that of denouncing one's parents, and castigated *Stern* for printing the ravings of a perverted son.

The story didn't make for easy reading. Its author described how he'd spent the anniversaries of his father's execution masturbating to the vision of the old man climbing the steps to the gallows at Nürnberg. His only consolation for being the son of a war criminal was being the son of a war criminal too important to escape hanging. He pitied the childhood friends whose less prominent fathers got off with a year or two of prison, then came home to subject their children to rotten pantomimes of paternal authority. Dance on a father's grave? Nikolas Frank couldn't dance, but he could celebrate in public, forty years after the execution, with a stream of printed calumny for his own ruptured life.

"Without Dr. Hans Frank there might have been no State of Israel," said the director of the Charlottenburg Library, where Nikolas Frank was reading from his book during Berlin's annual Week of Brotherhood. Well: that's one way to see it. Hans Frank was the governor-general of Poland during the war, the murder of millions his private domain. His son was still haunted by childhood memories: how the SS guards tortured prisoners to give the boss's kids a treat, how he'd laughed and stuck his tongue out the window at a doomed Jewish child. Children of lesser Nazis had been sheltered, left at home while Papa was busy following orders behind the Front. Perhaps Nikolas Frank sought expiation for his boyhood presence at the scene of the crime. His book was forced to be crude, he said, for nothing else could break the silence still shared by the land.

With a monstrous face, eyes like a sow's, and even uglier hands, Nikolas Frank was the unsightliest man I ever saw. He seemed spit out, giving form to his land's horror; neither his father nor mother were particularly ill featured. Still he left no place for pity. "Confronting our history means confronting our fathers." For years well-meaning Germans clung to those words like an oath. Faced with an example of real confrontation, they were revolted; sickness and loathing exhausted response.

Frank Senior murdered other people's children. Frank Junior, impotent patricide, reviled his own parents. The father's behavior proved less shocking than that of the son. This may be no surprise: the world depends on our following in father's footsteps; understanding, at least, the paths which he took. The alternative is paralyzing.

Frank's book caused a scandal because it was an exception; few Nazis' children rejected their parents so completely. Frank's own sister, he said, still honored their father. "She now lives in South Africa—in keeping with her worldview." Some of those tried at Nürnberg had happier sons, like the young lawyer who defended his father before the tribunal. The elder von Weizsäcker served as foreign minister for the Nazis so as to be able to resist them covertly; besides he'd known nothing of what was being done to the Jews. One who can convince a jury to believe statements like these may well grow up to be president. It's clear, in any case, that he sleeps better at night than Nikolas Frank.

Most fathers were less guilty, most children less scarred. But I went to hear Frank in person because he seemed merely to magnify what I'd already seen.

* * *

There were no weddings. Funerals and births were secluded and small. At the time it seemed normal: I never met parents of German-born friends. Many, of course, were conveniently dead, but most were merely absent. This was, oddly, true for both Germans and Jews. Though Alex often agreed to introduce me to her mother, she made very sure that our paths never crossed.

At Bauernstübl I sometimes glimpsed the uneasy truces maintained in proletarian homes. They seemed the most intact. After two glasses of beer any elderly woman might begin to talk of hard times gone by. Jutta's husband fell in 1945.

"But he fell for the Nazis, Mother," reminded her son, whose own hair was growing thin over a faded collar. "He wasn't a resistance hero. If he'd fallen for the resistance I would still be cheering."

"But we weren't *really* Nazis, dearie. Heaven forbid! And I have nothing against Jews. There were thirteen Jews in my class at school. I could see well enough what was happening."

"Mommy has changed her views."

"What?"

"You changed your views, Mother. It's good that you could change your views."

"*Na*, back then it was all so confusing ..."

"I was born in 'thirty-six," said the son. "I was supposed to become a Nazi. But I didn't become a Nazi."

"Nowadays," said Jutta, "I'm rather left-wing. I'm not a right-winger. They want war."

"You've changed your views, Mommy."

"Thirteen Jews in my class, there were. The school was in West-end, but it's no longer standing. I was invited to the Cassirers' once."

"Which Cassirer?" asked Michael. "Bruno or Paul?"

"Bruno Cassirer, Paul Cassirer, it was so long ago. I was invited to the Cassirers!"

Barring desultory exceptions like these, I heard nothing but the children's side of the story.

* * *

I wasn't thinking of any of this the day I met the Hellers. It was simply pleasant to sit at a sidewalk table with parents who truly cared for their grown children.

Herbert was a retired baker from the Rhineland who viewed his daughter's rise to success in the swanky world of Berlin theater with amused pride. His wife Gitta was cooler, restrained, with a worn, pleasing face. The day was warm, the conversation gracious. But Herbert waited for his daughter to excuse herself for a studio appointment before beginning to disclose what was on his mind.

"Now, Frau Neiman, I'd like to know: why did you come to Germany, of all places?"

"One doesn't ask that," interrupted Gitta hastily.

"I'm writing a book about it," I said cautiously, evading.

"That would interest me very much," said Herbert. "For I'd really like to know: why precisely Germany?"

"I had a fellowship to study German philosophy. That's the official story. But there was something else..."

"You wanted to see what the people were really like here, after all those terrible things happened?"

"I think that was it."

"And how did your parents feel about your coming?"

"Badly, in the beginning."

"I can imagine."

I lit one cigarette after another and ordered a second beer. Questions like Herbert's were common back home, but no one had ever posed them to me in German.

"Have you experienced anything negative here?" he asked.

"Yes," I answered.

"I'd really like to hear about it," said Herbert. "Please speak from your heart."

"Well..." I paused. "Perhaps the worst thing is the silence. I'm happy that you asked me about it at all, Herr Heller. No one ever does."

I was wrong. The worst thing was not the silence but what happened when it broke. Herbert Heller was well-meaning, old-fashioned and warm. Ordering another round, he said festively: "Now call me Herbert, and this is Gitta." We clinked glasses and switched to the familiar *du*. But what was unleashed was a torrent of pleas.

"Haven't other countries done terrible things? Do they always do everything right? What about America with the Indians? And why can't the Israelis set us a good example?" Herbert stopped only to catch his breath. "We were twelve in 'thirty-three—what could we have done? We lived in a little village where nobody knew what was happening. You could see they had to wear the yellow star, but after that—"

"And we had nothing against Jews," broke in Gitta. "My father was true to the kaiser. We were the only ones who didn't hang out the swastika. Us and the dentist. My father never said 'Heil Hitler.' When I was fifteen I had to beg to be allowed to join the BDM—" You might call it the Nazi Girl Scouts.

"But not," interrupted Herbert, "because she was a—"

"I understand," I told them. "All the other girls were in BDM."

"He wouldn't even buy me a uniform. I had to run around and borrow a skirt here, a blouse there, never a real uniform like the others..."

"One has to let bygones be bygones," said Herbert. "It's just like a marriage. You have to forgive, or nothing ever works."

A marriage? I wondered. Herbert's metaphors were touchingly familial. "Some say we're still guilty. That's like berating your son for the rest of his life: remember how naughty you were as a boy?"

I felt, dimly, used. Herbert sought more than satisfied curiosity from the first Jew he'd met since the war. Was it the simple unloading of forty years' shame? Was I being enlisted in an effort to bring his child closer?

"Lotte had a phase where she was always blaming us: why didn't you do something against them? Later I think she realized how dangerous it was back then, not everyone can be a hero—"

Not everyone can be a hero, and Herbert is a nice man. About Gitta I was not quite sure.

"But there's always been anti-Semitism," she said, "and I'd like to know why."

"Out of envy," suggested Herbert. "Because they were so enterprising."

"Or did it have something to do with Jesus?" Gitta probed.

"There are good people here too, right?" prodded Herbert.

"Yes, of course."

"And bad ones everywhere, aren't there? The human race is wicked."

"Yes."

"I'll tell you one thing," said Herbert. "The Jews should come back here and fight. Everybody has to struggle sometimes—now the Jews should too."

"Unfortunately," I answered, "not everybody thinks like you here."

Lotte called the next day under a pretext. We chatted for a moment before she offered, "My parents were very ... excited about the conversation yesterday."

"So was I," I told her. "You're lucky, you know. They're very open people. Nobody here has the nerve to broach those subjects."

"I suppose," she conceded dully. "But look at what they say when they do."

* * *

Much has been said of beginning from nothing, wiping slates clean. Who could oppose it? Yet everyone everywhere was touched, if not maimed. The next generation, on both sides, was bound. Claudio called it Ger-manic depression. (We could laugh, it was easy—our parents were clean.) There were no neutral acts, no unportending gestures. Death meant too little, birth too much.

Consider the first act by which parents determine the life of a child. Shout "Jakob" on a Berlin playground and three small blond heads are quite likely to turn. For some it was anger, for others, remorse; Jewish names were almost trendier in recent years than Nazi names during the Third Reich. Nazi names? Those with the initials H.-J., for example, which stood for Hitler-Youth. Hermann-Joseph, Hans-Jürgen, Hans-Joachim. In the war generation, but for an occasional Karl-Heinz, they're the only double names which are commonly found.

But what's in a name? More important is a look at how children are raised. And in this, as in other matters, the generation whose parents came of age in the war is hell-bent on negating the lessons which they themselves learned.

* * *

*T*wo philosophers were talking of objects. The German wished to prove that they had no importance. "My father," he said, "was simply the product of a bad education."

"How's that?" asked the Israeli.

"He refused," said the German, "to use the Bible for cigarettes. After the war, during the paper shortage. Pages of the Bible made the best rolling paper, on account of being thin. But he wouldn't see that; still imprisoned by his upbringing."

"I wouldn't use the Koran for rolling cigarettes," said the Israeli. "And I wouldn't let my children do so either."

"Then you're educating them to be obedient," remonstrated his colleague.

"To be respectful," corrected the Israeli.

"Respect," said the German, "is the foundation of state order."

"Respect," said the Israeli, "is the foundation of everything."

* * *

*W*e had gathered on parents' night at the day-care center to discuss a recurrent problem. Johannes, at three and a half the oldest child in the group, was increasingly aggressive; his greatest pleasure lay in hitting smaller children.

"But it won't do to be moralistic," said Amelie's mother, Olga. "We don't want to tell him to be *good*." After watching other parents rush to agree with her, I ventured to break in.

"Aren't we *talking* about a moral problem?" I asked. "It's wrong for big children to bully smaller ones. That's something they have to learn."

Olga turned to me patiently. "Morality," she explained, "is a power trip in which weaker people are dominated by the rules of the stronger. I spent my whole childhood listening to rules. 'That isn't done.' 'You may not.' 'You shall not.' I'm not about to tyrannize a child with morality!"

"Isn't there a difference between saying 'That isn't done' and helping a child learn to care for other people's feelings?"

Olga considered. "But Johannes *wants* to hurt the other children. That's why he hits them. We can't deny him his right to aggression."

"Aggression," said the teacher, "has a positive side too. It helps you survive in this lousy society."

Another mother demurred. "We're talking about negative aggression. I don't like it when Johannes bites my son."

"You don't like it. Your son doesn't like it. But those are your *feelings*. It won't do to talk about morality."

"Do you understand now, Susan?" They looked at me, satisfied, forbearing and kind. It seemed hardly the moment to mention my Ph.D. in philosophy, or to embark on a general discussion of ethical relativism. That wasn't the point. Their parents' moral authority had proved to be fraud. They'd inherited nothing they dared to bequeath.

Still it barely made sense. Could the sins of the fathers be so great that their children had lost the very notion of sin? At home I questioned Michael, for I'd often heard the word "moral" used as a term of abuse. Despite the fact that the only heroes of the last generation—those who resisted, and continued to do so—were among the few to call themselves moralists.

"What about Helmut Gollwitzer, what about Gunther Anders? They're the only decent ones around. And if they're not afraid of morality, why are you?"

"Look," he answered. "I was born after the war. After morality was destroyed. And the moralists, even the real ones—they didn't prevent it either."

* * *

Verarbeitung, f.: manufacturing; treatment; processing; working up; working through; digestion; thorough study; elaboration; working out; working over.

Reviewing Nikolas Frank's book, the Jewish journalist Henryk Broder wrote that he could only be thankful his own parents had been on the other side of the barbed wire. Often it was tempting to feel more compassion for the children of the murderers than for those of their victims. For people like Marina tend to lie low.

"Somebody told me we have to work over Auschwitz and I left the room. First the Germans worked over the Jews—into lampshades and mattresses—and now they want to work over Auschwitz too."

She spoke with the recklessness born of pride and despair. Marina's long hair was brushed back, tinged with henna; her eyes were blue and pale. She isn't very good at drinking and that was evident the first time I saw her.

We met at Terzo Mondo, for lack of a better retreat. The kneipe looks shabby. The shade of blue on the wall recalls something Greek; a thousand old leaflets folded into paper airplanes are stuck in the ceiling. "Terzo Mondo" is Italian for "Third World." Political groups meet in the back room regularly, though Kosta, the owner, is said to be a weathercock. There was something about the place that felt like giving up and going home; anything at all could be said there.

"Is it true," asked Marina, "that Tugendhat is leaving Germany because of anti-Semitism?"

"That's what he said," answered Michael. "There was a piece in the TAZ."

"That can't be right," she insisted. "Something else is going on. Of course they're anti-Semites. What else is new? I don't see anyone anymore. I've got my taxi, I write in the morning, basta." She fumbled with a flickering lighter. Michael bent forward to light her cigarette. "You're different," she told him. "I can tell that you came from a happy family. There's a light in your eyes. You've still got a chance."

"Michael didn't come from a happy family," I said.

"*Ach*," she scorned. "What do Americans know about unhappy families?"

Touché.

Leaning on the bar Marina told us her story. Her Jewish father was murdered at Auschwitz. Her Communist mother escaped to the Soviet Union but succumbed to typhus just after the war. Before dying she had asked her oldest friend to take her small daughter.

"I know why she did it," said Marina through half-clenched teeth. "I understand, I really do." But Marina's adoptive mother had proceeded to marry a high-ranking SS officer. "He was head of operations in Köln, can you imagine, my stepfather?"

So the girl was raised by the people who slaughtered her family. The fifties were bitter with the stink of defeat. The end of the war brought the peace of the desert. There was rubble to be cleared, and the spirit which can give hope to hard times was elsewhere. The Allies filled the streets with posters showing pictures of the gas chambers and the words "You are guilty of this evil!" The conquered people sniggered at the Americans, feared Russian revenge. They looked to their feet, and counted their own dead.

"And now they want vergangenheitsverarbeitung," said Marina.

Kostas unbuttoned his shirt and stepped to the microphone. He is handsome and massive, like Agamemnon. On many a night he'll sing strong plaintive songs in a major key. Before picking up his guitar, he winked at the three of us standing at the bar.

"I can't stay," said Marina. "My taxi's outside."

* * *

I'd long before learned to take the helpless stammers, the shocked stares, the embarrassed affability; there was no way to mention you're Jewish without them. It was easy to be insolent when I was alone. But my son had just begun to walk when I saw with sudden horror that I understood all the mothers who raised their children in hiding *after* the war.

Instinctively, thoughtlessly, we'd begun to repeat it. The frightened secret subterfuge when it threatened to unfold. "You looking forward to a nice Easter?" The day-care worker's question had been harmless. The heartbeat before the answer: was it exaggerated, paranoid?

Every time we suspected our suspicions, something happened to confirm them. Fat friendly Ella's reaction exceeded my fears: "If I'd known you were Jewish, I wouldn't have taken him." Not because she really had anything against Jews, and that business with the gas chambers, she'd like to kill Hitler personally for it. But with such momentous information she'd have doubted her ability to treat Benjamin as a child like any other.

Ella was honest; that's why we'd liked her in the first place. At the next day-care center we lived double lives. The real one after-hours, with our friends, the outsiders. The tightrope politeness we put on for our son.

"This is getting absurd," we told each other as the summer wore on. "It's nineteen eighty-eight. They're all progressive."

"The worst," said Michael.

"What could happen?"

"You know it yourself."

They *were* all progressive, so it would be subtle. No remarks like Ella's, no expressions of shock. Just an excess of caution, an increase of distance. Twenty pairs of kid gloves which no child should endure.

"They'll find out sooner or later."

"How?"

"He's talking more."

"They don't listen."

"If we switched to the Jewish Kindergarten—?"

"Next year, at the earliest. Under police escort."

Forty-three years after the end of the war it strained the bounds of reason. There were moments when my heart stopped somewhere between fear and relief, sure that they were about to discover what we'd carefully concealed. For weeks leading up to the High Holidays, I couldn't enter the day-care center without a tremor. My own transformation shamed me. — You'll be a coward damned forever if you don't say it now. You're not your husband's mother, there's no reason to hide. — Surely, but surely, our fears were extreme. I cast about for a natural opening.

It came without warning.

She was a filmmaker, he was a computer specialist. Our children had brought us together; the conversation wandered in search of other common ground. Their apartment was much grander than ours, but that needn't prevent us from cursing landlords together. We commiserated easily, leaving out a few details; their landlord was trying to evict them too.

"I hate to say it," said Ulrike, "but he's a Jew—"

"And he vindicates all the prejudices against Jews," finished Bernhard with a smirk.

Michael excused himself to walk down the stairs. My thanks-for-the-dinner smile froze in midair.

It wasn't uncommon, and it wasn't mysterious. Jewish meanness was clutched like a drowning man's straw. Every instance of it might help get their country off the hook. Not entirely, of course: most felt that the gas chambers went much too far, but something had to happen, with greedy Jews running Weimar.... As the decade wore on, talk of corrupt landlords and the oppression of the Palestinians were greeted with relief. I understood the longing to vindicate their parents. It was the vindication of other parents' fears which led me to dismay.

Ulrike called to make an excruciating apology. As we'd left, she'd remembered that I was American, and I could well be ... Michael too? *Ach* so! Then that was the reason he looked so Italian. She hoped we weren't offended; it was all so very touchy. Had I seen the film *Yentl*? It was one of her favorites. Could we try, in the future, to work through the past?

Meeting afternoons in the day-care center, we smiled so hard that our muscles ached.

Talking Tacheles

Alex's daughter had chicken pox, and she sent me her invitation. "So you'll invent an American paper," she suggested.

"Use your imagination." That's how I came to attend the press conference for the opening of the Jewish Museum of Berlin.

Before the basement of the Martin-Gropius-Bau police checked visitors' identification and bags. I felt like a thief as I waved my invitation, hoping it was too dark for the others to see my very red face. The original Jewish Museum was founded by the Jewish Community, with the support of private contributions, to document Jewish history in Berlin. It opened just ten days before the Nazis came to power and was closed in 1938 with nearly every other Jewish institution in Germany. After the war the objects which hadn't been plundered were gathered in the basement of the Berlin Museum while a few interested persons urged the city to build them a home. The solution being celebrated that morning was a provisional one: the city had set aside three rooms of the Martin-Gropius-Bau to serve as a Jewish Museum until permanent quarters could be found.

Had it been worth the trip, the flustered lie? The speech given by the museum's director contained nothing I hadn't heard before. At the podium the director drawled, listing dates, describing objects, naming names. "We are fortunate to have with us today the artist who painted a series remembering the Holocaust especially for the museum," said the director. "Ms. NN, whose grandparents came from Eastern Europe but who has come to us today from New York." Two rows ahead of me I watched the back of a young woman rise and bow. There was light applause before the audience scattered upstairs to get a first glance at the museum itself.

I had so many reasons to feel ill at ease. There were lovely prints, but they were hard to reach in the press of the crowd. And the ignorant chatter fell hard on my ears. I stood behind three reporters commenting on the objects displayed in glass cases.

"What's that doing in a Berlin museum?" asked one, pointing to a seder plate. "It looks North African."

"The label says it comes from Poland."

"But it looks North African to me."

"It's all kitsch, this stuff."

"And those are what they use for circumcision," said the last, pointing to three mezuzahs which, with a certain sort of imagination, might vaguely resemble rusty pocketknives.

It was an hour for making deals and doing business, I noted, and shook my head broody, resolving to return on a quieter occasion. But I was not to be exempted this time.

"Excuse me," said a man at my side. "Are you the artist?"

"No," I answered, "I'm just another American wearing a red sweater."

He smiled, disconcerted. "Ah, yes. She was wearing a red sweater too."

I considered adding: I also have curly dark hair, and if you knew anything about these matters you would know right away that my grandparents came from Eastern Europe too. But I left it at the red sweater.

"And what are you doing here?" he asked.

Still fearing, absurdly, that someone might take exception to my unofficial presence at this gathering, I searched for something to say. Alex's daughter has chicken pox? Pointing to my notebook, the questioner came to my aid. "I see you're taking notes—are you a writer?"

Was I a writer? Two months earlier Michael had cooked a vat of bouillabaisse and invited our friends to celebrate the fact that I'd completed my doctoral dissertation. Then we cleared away the dishes and sat down to contemplate the fact that we were both unemployed. There was a commission or two from the radio, a New York agent who liked the beginning of my manuscript. Did that mean I was a writer?

"Yes," I answered, after a hurried breath.

"Do you live in West Berlin?"

I nodded.

"And you don't belong to any of the literary organizations here? VS? NGL?"

I shook my head.

"Why is that?" asked the man.

"I still write mostly in English," I answered unhappily, feeling more like a swindler every second.

"But that doesn't matter." He extended his hand. "I'm Olaf Kleingeld. President of the board of directors of the NGL. What do you write about?"

"I'm working on a book about vergangenheitsverarbeitung," I said, trying to sound convincing.

"Vergangenheitsverarbeitung!" exclaimed Olaf. "That's wonderful! The NGL is organizing a big project on the subject of vergangenheitsverarbeitung for the seven hundred fiftieth anniversary of Berlin next year. You'd be welcome to join us. Perhaps you'd like to read something from your book? We pay an honorarium, of course, for every reading."

I looked at him more closely. His waist was pudgy; his graying round head nodded and smiled unexceptionably. Was this a come-on? Could this be the way business is done in Berlin?

We stood unsteadily against flat cases holding family photos and deportation orders.

"Would you like to work with us?" Olaf repeated.

"I'd like to know more about the project," I told him. We shook hands, exchanged phone numbers and parted.

At the door to the museum a waiter was busy arranging a buffet. Among the hundred open-faced sandwiches spread with cheese or herring were three containing a slice of roast beef and a dollop of horseradish. I took one of them, walked to an unlit corner, and ate in a mood of elation and shame. Had it been mere isolation which kept my hands clean? Being viewed as a writer, making contacts and fees—the whirl of dangled prospects let me treat the opening as one like any other. A place to be seen, a time for trade. Something seemed changed forever, that day, by a case of chicken pox and two red sweaters.

On the watch for objections, with a little remorse, I went for the second of the roast-beef sandwiches.

* * *

"What's the NGL?" I asked Michael that evening.

"The New Society for Literature."

"What do they do?"

"Hold readings. Organize projects. Take money from the Senate and distribute it to writers." He wasn't feeling expansive.

"And who's Olaf Kleingeld?"

"*Ach*, Olaf. Dances at every wedding. You must have seen him somewhere. Ask Claudio."

"Who's Olaf Kleingeld?" I asked Claudio when we'd met by chance at a café the following week.

Claudio didn't answer directly. He looked at me, put down his spoon and glanced at the door.

"I can hardly help my friends if they don't inform me what they're up to," he said, vexed.

I was mystified, but Claudio often intended that.

"Olaf Kleingeld," he continued after a pause, "told me half an hour ago that a Dr. Susan Neiman is going to organize a project about vergangenheitsverarbeitung for the NGL. I was, by the way, just elected to the board of directors."

"Organize it? He told me that there *was* a project, and asked if I wanted to be involved."

"I think it's a good idea that you do."

"But what do they have in mind?"

Nothing very clear, as emerged when we met together. Berlin was about to spend millions of marks celebrating what was perhaps its 750th birthday. The Jewish Community intended to participate with its own program of cultural events. But Olaf felt it was important that this not remain the only celebration of Jewish contributions to the city; something should be forthcoming from the German side as well. Vergangenheitsverarbeitung was not a new concern for Olaf: he had once edited a monograph about left-wing anti-Semitism, and had written an essay of his own as well. He brought a photocopy of the latter "so you can know where I stand."

"But what sort of thing are you planning?"

Olaf shuffles while talking, even when he's sitting down. He hadn't planned anything, and there wasn't much of a budget. It might be enough to invite a Jewish author from Israel, and one from, say, London.

"Why in the world should we celebrate Jewish life in Berlin by inviting writers from Israel and London?"

"*Na*," considered Olaf, "perhaps we could hold readings of the great old Berlin Jewish authors. You know, Tucholsky, Benjamin, Sachs, Döblin—"

"Isaac Babel was here too, in the twenties," said Claudio. "Maybe a whole program devoted to Babel—"

"I just think it's important that we do *something*," said Olaf. "We have six thousand marks—"

"Look," I said, "if I'm going to be involved in this project, I don't want another weepy pious recitation of all the great Jewish contributions to German culture. Germans love dead Jews, and they know all their names."

"So come up with something better," said Claudio. "That's why we're here."

"Are there any Jewish writers in Berlin today?" asked Olaf.

"Edgar," I said, "will always read for an honorarium."

"And in East Berlin?"

"There's Stefan Heym. But Edgar Hilsenrath and Stefan Heym just had a joint reading at the Academy of Arts in June."

"They don't have to be famous," said Olaf. "The NGL is committed to the support of lesser-known authors. Like yourself, for example."

"I think," said Claudio, "that Susan should take over this project." And turning to me: "It would do you good...."

* * *

*T*he Jews whom I spoke with thought I'd gone mad. A lot of work, a little money, and for what? Another little program, bora of guilt, raised in shame, for an audience which hadn't a prayer of understanding it anyway? But Claudio knew that his arguments struck home. I was tired of being an observer; I wanted to learn how to work in Berlin.

The first idea failed, though not for lack of trying. It was impossible to organize a program celebrating contemporary Jewish literary culture because there was nothing to celebrate. A week of phone calls turned up an East Berliner who'd once written a fine novel about the Warsaw Ghetto but now declined to identify himself as a Jew, a feckless Russian imitator of Sholem Aleichem and four unknown Americans living in West Berlin. If I counted myself.

And if we rounded it out with a couple of other acts? I was told of a man who was trying to organize the first postwar Jewish theater in Berlin; he had been, it was said, a big director in Moscow. "Shalom!" he began every conversation. "What good news can you tell me?" Olschan made up for his uncertain command of German with a string of Yiddish jokes and a boundless quantity of chutzpah. He was full of ideas just waiting for funding, and was delighted to be approached by the NGL.

"For six thousand marks I can give you my performance of the first book of Genesis. Three actors and a speaker. He just reads the Bible. The rest is done with Hindu dance. It was too eclectic for the Community. But dance had a great religious function in India, and there are suggestions that the ancient Hebrews—"

"Olschan," I told him, "we can't spend the entire budget on one performance. And it's a literary organization, they want texts. I was thinking of a festival, some readings, a little theater, perhaps that group that does Yiddish folk music in East Berlin?"

"Total kitsch," said Olschan. "Why do you want to bother with them?"

* * *

"Give it up," said Michael. "You're wasting your time. There is no Jewish culture in Berlin nowadays, literary or otherwise. And nobody really wants it either."

I wondered if he was right when I read Olaf Kleingeld's own article. He had offered it to me as his contribution to the subject of vergangenheits-verarbeitung; the article recited the woes of his childhood. Like millions of others, his family left their native Prussia after the war, when much of the Greater German Reich fell to Poland. Growing up as an outsider wasn't easy; "for reasons of survival," wrote Olaf, he "began to play soccer with the boys in the village."

"Survival!" I fumed. "How can he use the world 'survival' in a context where—"

"Hush," said Michael, smiling. "Olaf comes from the town where the Second World War began. How else do you expect him to write?"

"But he told me this was his article about *Jewish* questions. The only word about Jews is the mention of a Jewish *cemetery*. In his village. With a picture of a gravestone."

Michael gave me a look that said: You weren't born here, you've got a lot to learn.

* * *

Perhaps I would have given up if I hadn't met Merve. It was only a few months earlier that Merve had learned, upon her mother's death, that she came from a Jewish family. Her dreams and days were taken over by the subject anyway, and she belonged to the board of directors of the NGL.

"The project has already been budgeted. Better that we take it over than someone who has less of a notion about these things than we do."

"I see the point," I told her. "But what are we going to do?"

"Write a play," said Claudio.

"Write a play?" I repeated. "But I can't write German."

"You and Merve, then. Olschan can direct it."

"But I've never written a play. And I've just met Merve. And as for this Olschan—"

"I think it's a perfect solution," said Claudio. And since nobody had a better one, Merve and I began meeting evenings in her living room.

* * *

For months, we talked. Merve was alone, secluded from tradition. Even her despair was unique. For most Germans the discovery that someone in the family tree was excluded by their very nature from being party to the crime is cause for profound, extended relief. With Merve it was different. She had always believed in another Germany, had based her life on working for it. She herself, she believed, was proof of her conviction that all Germans weren't closet Nazis. She knew she wasn't racist. On the contrary: she felt at home with Jewish authors, at ease with foreign ways, in a manner that seemed deep-seated.

"And now to discover that I'm different not because I'm different, but because my mother was Jewish—it leaves me hollow. Disappointed. I don't know what to think."

But despair was a sensation she rarely indulged in. Merve rose at five every morning to write poetry for two hours before going off to work as a printer, her hands red and swollen from the chemicals at the press. She dressed in leather, and sent funky postcards drawn in six shades of magic marker. When she berated her daughter I heard the proletarian tones of her mother's voice.

"There's plenty of toothpaste left there," she growled. "You just have to squeeze. I'm a war child, Anna. I don't throw things away."

Merve would tell me the things she remembered: fetching her brothers' shoes for the cellar every night during the bombings. Trudging through snow to the Baltic before the advancing Russian army. Her mother's premonitions, intimations, only hints. That was her childhood, so much lay forgotten: how her father organized the Aryan identity papers. Where the relatives remained. Why her mother kept silent all those years after the war.

Babel, Scholem, Hebrew grammar. Since the news about her mother she read widely, without system, and came to me for answers. Rarely could I tell her what she wanted to know. From her questions, from our stories, we began to construct.

* * *

We had written, rewritten, retyped, cut and pasted. Worked nights, smoking Camels, in Merve's jumbled room. By September there was a play, or something like one; six sketches showing lives that Jews lead in Berlin.

"How many actors?" asked Olschan.

"Four."

"How many male, how many female?"

"Two of each would be best, but that's not so essential. What's important is that three of them be Jewish."

"I've got an Italian who can play anything, and a terrific German actress who looks like a JAP if you ever saw one—"

"Looks aren't the issue, Olschan, they have to be able to get the points—"

"Not to worry," said Olschan. "Just leave it to me."

Fortunately, I didn't. I gave the Italian who'd never heard of Pesach a crash course in Jewish history. I took the JAPpy-looking German to the Jewish store she had to portray. I explained jokes, displayed gestures, showed distinctions of tone. I worked like a dog and I loved it. The actors had questions, proposals, complaints. That line didn't follow, that scene wasn't clear. We listened, argued, rewrote once again. A bottle of water stood on the floor of Olschan's apartment; rehearsals were often interrupted by long telephone conversations in Russian.

"He's Jewish," said Merve. "But is he a director?" It was too late to think of looking for another. The play was to open on November 6. At the dress rehearsal the night before, Olschan yelled without stopping, pointing a knife at my arm.

"I've got nothing against fighting, Olschan, but don't you think you could put down the knife?"

"What knife?" he shouted. "That's a letter opener!"

* * *

I didn't dare to turn around, but there it was. The first laughter. Fine, low, melancholy Jewish laughter. Not three minutes into the play and they were laughing. On the edge of my seat I felt the full room behind me. They were even laughing at lines I'd feared no one would get. Danny, the Italian, was quick enough to improvise. The applause came later, and the praise. Alex brought over a bottle of champagne the next day. But the sweetest second was the one when I heard the first laughter, and I knew we had done something right.

At the next performance there were more Germans, fewer Jews and less laughter. The audience was as solemn as the director of the Literature House, who wrote a note to Merve. He couldn't attend the premiere, but he begged for her understanding: he had nothing against Jews, he was all for vergangenheits-verarbeitung, his absence was due to purely personal circumstances. But laughter has conditions, it has to be learned. We celebrated at the back table in Terzo Mondo, far into the morning.

* * *

After *Talking Tacheles* had been performed, Claudio proposed that the NGL devote a permanent committee to the subject of Jewish life in Berlin. I demurred when asked to organize it. Much of *Talking Tacheles* had been devoted to pointing out the *fishiness* of vergangenheitsverarbeitung. The release that comes when childhood taboos are shattered, the shiver of importance that's lent to an otherwise ordinary evening. Worse: a morbid fascination with the crimes of the Nazis, masking unbroken discomfort with the existence of live Jews. I couldn't see the point of a permanent committee on the subject; I had, for the moment, said what I had to say.

"And the others?" asked Claudio. "The Senate is prepared to give money. It would be a shame to lose the opportunity."

There were a few other Jews in the literary society. None of them wanted to be involved. And there the matter might have rested but for Evelyn. She wasn't a bad poet, but she couldn't write prose: all her letters came out in the tightly twisted bureaucratic language which Goebbels had mastered. That mightn't have mattered if she hadn't been paranoid. I'm not speaking loosely, it's a clinical term, and Evelyn had spent years in Berlin's most notorious psychiatric ward.

If you were a paranoiac born in Germany in the forties, how would you best fight to prove you were sane? How could you show that your persecutions weren't delusory, but based in cold fact? If you were clever, you might naturally reason: you are being persecuted on all sides because you have Jewish blood.

Evelyn searched for proofs of her Jewish descent with the ardor that others had sought to prove they were Aryan, half a century ago. Anybody who's spent time with one suffering from paranoia knows the effort and ingenuity with which they justify their visions. — In her mother's village was a Jewish cemetery. None of her relatives lay buried in it? But that just showed how well they had managed to hide their origins. — Her father had the same name as a Jewish resistance fighter. He himself was no resistance fighter, but a Nazi soldier? But that's precisely what was needed, to conceal his own ancestry. Evelyn filled reams of paper to vindicate her claims, and she sent them all over town. I thought, with compassion, of poor Rabbi S.

In better times one person's disorder may be a private matter. Now delirium belonged to the public domain. It was a year, after all, when the newspapers advertised a contest to determine the future of the former Gestapo grounds: the winner would receive ten thousand marks and the opportunity to realize his proposal.

Before television cameras Berlin's former mayor announced that a team of experts had been imported to decide what to do with the Wannsee Villa.

(Experts on what?)

"For the Wannsee Villa no longer belongs to the Germans but to the Jews of the world...."

(As a consolation prize?)

"While it is a place of horror, it is also a place of triumph; it was, after all, *eleven* million Jews that were supposed to be murdered...."

It was a time when conferences were held to determine appropriate preparations for the Ninth of November. Ceremonies commemorating Reichskristallnacht were held every year, but the upcoming anniversary was the fiftieth, and that called for something special.

"Fireworks," I muttered, "and Karajan directing *Parsifal* at the Siegessäule..."

"You're getting cynical," said Michael, "or completely meshugge."

Newly elected to the board of directors, Evelyn insisted that the NGL too arrange a program for the anniversary of Kristallnacht. Particularly since they were planning to sponsor a reading of Arabic literature in November. Wasn't that tactless, even anti-Semitic? No one protested this treacherous equation of Arabs and Nazis. Like marionettes pulled by a master, they jumped in alarm. What would be said in the Senate? The NGL anti-Semitic? Not on your life! Heads were lowered, plans were hurried. Claudio conferred with Dr. Kleingeld: Evelyn was to head the "Jewish Life in Berlin" committee, whose first business would be to commemorate the Ninth of November. It was unimportant that nobody knew how to do it. The Senate would support it—never very generously, but surely—and that would be that.

* * *

Enter Frank, itinerant theater director. His last production had been a children's festival in the Olympia Stadium, whose climax was to enter the Guinness Book of World Records by lining up 3,401 people sitting on each other's laps in a row. Now Frank had a project just made for Kristallnacht. He wanted to produce *The*

Investigation, Peter Weiss's drama about the Auschwitz trials, on the grounds of the former Gestapo headquarters. The audience would stand on the site of the recently exposed torture chambers; the grounds would be lit by lamps resembling those which were used in the concentration camps. The whole production would cost 220,000 marks, but there was a low-budget version, should the fund-raising fail. To ensure that the performance be unimpeachably Jewish, Frank had found a producer. Balding indefatigable Kurt was undeniably Jewish. Nothing else was known about him for certain except that most of what he says couldn't possibly be true, though reliable sources suggested that he really did fight with Che Guevara in Bolivia. A Mossad agent? A Kennedy in-law? Confidant of Elie Wiesel, Willy Brandt and Albert Einstein? Once, with tears in his eyes, he gave Michael a mezuzah, to be cherished, he said, for it had been in his family for two hundred years. On the back was engraved "Made in Israel."

Kurt had seen *Talking Tacheles*, and was moved. Perhaps the NGL would care to sponsor this project as well?

* * *

Was she delighted? Was she relieved? *The Investigation* looked made-to-order. In stark lines Weiss made measured verse of the transcripts of the Auschwitz trials. One after another, unnamed witnesses recounted. How the children were murdered, how the women were tortured. One after another, the accused denied. The play had been written in 1965, shortly after Weiss himself had witnessed the Auschwitz trials. But wasn't its message timeless? Evelyn assured the promoters full support: everything would be set in motion to produce *The Investigation* on the Ninth of November, 1988. Her letters, sent three times a week to 150 prominent Berliners, now ended with a quotation from the play.

The second meeting of the committee was held on Rosh Hashanah. I called it a scandal. A group that meets on Rosh Hashanah to discuss plans for Kristallnacht has perfected a perversion. In the name of vergangenheits-verarbeitung the dates instigated by the Nazis are celebrated while the Jewish holidays, like every other element of Jewish tradition, remain obscured and forgotten. Evelyn was sorry: she hadn't known it was Rosh Hashanah. In fact, she'd never heard of Rosh Hashanah. Ignorance must be forgiven in this sad silent land. To compensate for her lack of knowledge of Jewish tradition, she could, however, prove her goodwill by showing erudition in other matters. Name a concentration camp. Any old concentration camp, even an obscure one. There was hardly a detail which Evelyn hadn't studied....

* * *

The madness that leads to a backhanded celebration of the murderers is a general one; it would never have disqualified Evelyn for leadership of the "Jewish Life in Berlin" committee. But as I mentioned before, poor Evelyn was paranoid, and her letters got weirder and weirder. There were complaints to the manager, the board of directors. Dr. Kleingeld responded by reinterpreting a bylaw that forbade Evelyn to send her missives on NGL stationery, but the complaints didn't stop. The secretary of the Jewish community protested, the Senate made inquiries. Dr. Kleingeld begged pardon: Evelyn's psychiatric history was no secret, one had thought she was cured; now it seemed perhaps mistaken to entrust her with the organization of such a, well, delicate matter. There were whispered conferences; a solution was found. Evelyn would be sacrificed to save vergangenheitsverarbeitung. A contract was drawn in which the NGL promised to promote the production of *The Investigation* as its Kristallnacht project, without the collaboration of Evelyn S.

Formal solutions are usually treacherous. Evelyn sought revenge for this act of betrayal. She made known her vow: should the others attempt to produce *The Investigation* on Kristallnacht without her at the Gestapo grounds, she would produce *The Investigation* on Kristallnacht without them at the Breitscheidplatz! The groundwork had already been laid; there was, after all, a rival literary organization in Berlin. Its antagonism to the NGL was no secret to anyone.

Who could have dreamt it? In the chill Berlin November, two outdoor productions. One at the site of Gestapo headquarters, the other overlooking the bombed-out cathedral in the center of town. The productions sponsored by Berlin's partner literary organizations, always on the watch for a chance to undermine the other. From one end of the city to the other, the loudspeakers blare, sparing no detail of the crimes which gave Auschwitz a name. Where fifty years earlier, the synagogues burned...

Surrealistic? But imagination isn't my strong point. The spectacle was prevented only because the two groups fought so long that it was too late to raise funds, find actors or rent equipment in time for the Ninth of November. Perhaps Providence is less mysterious than reputed.

Good-bye to Berlin

After years of doubt and discussion it was settled: we were bound for America. No more Bulgarian pianos repeating soft phrases, no winter nights leaning against the tall coal oven, no high bare walls, no chestnut tree. Melancholy in Berlin has an ornamental quality, each day the backdrop for a discourse on desolation; encouraging sentimentality, and spurning it. So I'd miss the dull drop of chestnuts in the courtyard, I'd be gone when the acacias sweeten the air on the corner those two weeks in May. It was time to begin to accept it, untying my heart from that window, that door.

"And if I came up with an absolutely foolproof way to kill Borchert?" Michael tumbled into the room.

"There is none."

"I have one," he insisted.

"Besides, it isn't Borchert. It's what he represents."

"Yes and no."

We wavered, in turns. Leaving wasn't easy, however many shades of gray reflected the streets of Berlin.

* * *

I paused to listen, then called Benjamin to the window. "A *Leierkastenmann!*" he beamed. We thrilled to lean from the balcony to watch the organ-grinder make his slow way down the street; nowadays they are rare. When he reached our door I wrapped a coin in paper, as I'd learned to do, and threw it to the pavement. He called up his thanks, and Benjamin waved. But where were the Berliners, who had known this since childhood? Up and down the Sesenheimerstrasse the windows stayed shut.

Benjamin wanted to follow him; we raced down the stairway. I gave up the fight against sentiment and began to teach my son the words to "Lieber Leierkastenmann" till the organ-grinder disappeared behind the playground. We kicked a ball through sand now colored by fallen leaves. "The other playground!" repeated a boy on the bench, and his mother stood up soundless, face wracked by petty defeats. Abject wind drove brown hair harmless, reconciled once again irredeemable days. Cobblestones smelled of fish where the market had been. "*Our* market," said Benjamin. Out of breath and chilly we went to Tantana for cocoa.

"You don't greet me anymore," said Murad to Benjamin, but the distance was open, he looked at us differently. Others would come in our place, and soon. Michael took less time to chat with the Turks playing backgammon by the counter. What we had left was saved for the people it hurt most to leave behind.

"Look," I said to Irena, "there are all kinds of reasons. But a Jew can't live here without going crazy. Sooner or later."

"A mensch can't live here without going crazy." She smiled when she said that, but hard. "We'd move to Zagreb tomorrow if there was enough to eat there."

"It's true," I answered. "All of our friends are trying to leave."

"Trying? Look how many are gone."

No more nights like that: parties taking place in three or four languages, poetry read, music played in a kitchen, the mixture of ease and excitement that I found nowhere else. Irena spoke of the death of European Bohemia, but I was skeptical. Not as dead as it is where I come from; I could not know what we would find.

* * *

"We're going to America," I said to Frau Kalish.

"Forever?" she asked. "Sit down."

"Probably forever. Maybe we'll come back."

"But you're giving up your apartment?"

"We had to. You remember, with the mezuzah—"

"So why did you have to put the mezuzah on the outside? You can hang it inside too. Look at mine." She pointed to the door.

"We thought we didn't have to hide it."

Frau Kalish raised her eyebrows. "America. It's a shame you're leaving, but I wish you luck. Probably better for you. The little one can go to a Jewish school there."

I nodded.

"You moving to where your parents live?"

"No. To where I've got a job."

"What kind of a job?"

"At the university."

"What'll you do at the university?"

"Teach."

"*Ach so.* Pay well?"

"Not very."

"Hmm." She shuffled to the counter. "You think your husband will like it there?"

"He thinks so. I hope so."

Frau Kalish shook her head. "It's so hot in New York. I was there once in August. Terrible climate. *Naja*."

"I wanted some matzah meal," I said.

"You making kneydlach?"

"The soup's on the stove."

"If you make kneydlach today, what'll you have tomorrow?"

I blinked guiltily; it was a Thursday afternoon. "*Na*, there'll be soup left for Shabbos, and I'll make some fish to go with it."

"Carp?"

"Freshwater fish is contaminated."

"I know plenty of people who buy carp," said Frau Kalish, and she sold me a packet of matzah meal. "Good luck to you," she said, "and my best to your husband."

"Oh but no," I said. "We'll come and say good-bye before we go."

* * *

*L*ate in November, when the moving men had come and gone, we invited a hundred people to create a gallery in our empty apartment. The film projector never started, the cat nearly died, but the walls were covered with pictures, and there were readings, a juggler and a concert with harp. Caught in the moment, people swayed on the floor singing "Tumbalalaika." Who knew when they would meet again? We fought tears, drank schnapps and caught the last-minute train.

* * *

*F*or months friends wrote to say we'd left just in time. What was left of Berlin looked bleaker every day. The neo-Nazi Republican Party had garnered enough votes to command a voice in the government. Edgar's new novel had won a major prize; swastikas were chiseled into the bookstore doorway the morning after he read from it. There were troubles in the East, but it seemed ordinary news, until the night we heard a rumor and ran out to a bar to find a working TV.

"They're dancing on the *Wall*, that's Brandenburger *Tor*!" The city of unlimited possibilities had surpassed itself. No wonder there was dancing: that unimaginable breaking of boundaries was so very Berlin.

"They come from over there," shrugged the bartender. It seemed to explain our request to switch to the news channel.

"You Germans?" asked the drunk at my side. Michael nodded impatiently.

"C'mon, c'mon," I muttered at the screen. "Enough with James Baker, get back to Berlin."

"You Nazis?" continued the drunk. "Well, gee," he murmured as Michael moved sideways, "I was only trying to start a little friendly conversation."

"The Wall's over, you're free now," said his buddy to Michael. "Think we can get back to the football game, Adolf?"

"That's not funny," I told him. "We're Jews."

"Buncha tightwads," said the drunk. "Never trust 'em."

Speechless in New Haven I got very very drunk. It was one way of maintaining a link to Berlin.

There was also the telephone: everyone speaking the same euphoric tone. The wryness and irony of seasoned Berliners gave way, for a moment, to simple wonder. This was partly due to awe. The Wall had become such a part of the landscape that its breach was as strange as if space had gained a dimension, or all the rivers started flowing backward. But there was also real hope, for the first time in years, and it wasn't for a world in which everyone has access to video. The American press showed the joys of East Germans rolling westward. But in the early days of the revolution, many West Berlin hearts faced east.

"They've been through fire. They're tougher than we were in 'sixty-eight. There's a chance, for the first time—"

"A real democratic socialism! It's what we'd always dreamed!"

"I'm looking for an apartment in Prenzlauer Berg!"

Blunt blasé Berliners hugged teary-eyed strangers, watered gray streets with champagne. After twenty-eight years an undeclared cloud had been lifted from the city.

"The war," they cried, "is finally over!"

A day or two passed before it was remembered that the Wall had been stormed on November 9. Catching the fever across four thousand miles, I began to theorize.

"For years we debated about reparations. Decent people said there couldn't be any, for that kind of crime. But what if—"

"What if—"

"On the Ninth of November—"

"The fifty-first anniversary of Kristallnacht—"

"The end of the cold war, the beginning of peace and justice—"

"For the whole world—"

"From German soil—"

"Would *be* a reparation, a real one, this time?"

I didn't bother to suppress the tears. Anything at all was possible.

* * *

"You're coming, of course?" said the friends.

"Of course," we answered. At the rates we were spending on telephone calls, airplane tickets were a bargain. By the time we arrived in Berlin in December, something like a hangover had begun to settle in. The air was choked with the stink of the Trabis, tinny East German autos built without pollution controls. Lines were longer, the city was full. Wide-eyed East Germans wandered on every street; to my great amusement, we were often addressed as if we were some of them.

The Wall was still standing, but the guards were ebullient as they waved people through. "Now don't work too hard!" one called with a grin. Having borne the weight of twenty-eight years on their shoulders, their relief was plain.

I crossed the border to ask Lilli Segal what would happen, knowing that no one could predict the future, though no Berliner talked of anything else. It was an uncertain time. The dreams of a new world which sustained sleepless nights were dissolving. The drive toward reunification, unimaginable days before, had begun. The masses who had challenged party bosses pretending to speak in their name by shouting "*We* are the people!" were now chanting "We are *one* people!" In defiance of whom?

"*Ach*, the Saxons," snorted Lilli. "That's who cheered Helmut Kohl. Most conservative state in the country. They were worse than Bavarians during the war."

The exodus of half a million over the Hungarian border had empowered the movement for democratization within. Those leaving had surrendered, but inside the GDR were the kinds of voices I knew. "We're staying here!" they had chanted, undaunted. The leaders of the bloodless revolution took the GDR's antifascist heritage seriously; some had returned from wartime exile in New York or Moscow to help build a new Germany. They were not seeking reunification, but a state which lived up to the principles on which it had been founded. Their demands sounded easy: abolish party privilege, open the media, allow unlimited travel, stop treating the people like unruly children. That's how it began. Now the world had seen the pictures of crowds on the Kudamm, weeping over the profusion of bananas and beer. On the other side of the border the opposition parties formed a group called the Coalition of Reason. Had they a chance?

"Something had to happen," said Lilli, chopping onions. Though she'd stopped counting the visitors who had crossed her doorstep in those weeks, she was still offering lunch. "Would you rather have lamb or beef?" Watching her open the tinned meat I wondered, like many West Berliners in those days. The Segals were privileged East Germans, from the upper middle class of a classless society. And still they (often) ate meat out of cans. How could we scorn the hordes swarming to seek something fresh?

Stale food could always be fixed up with a sauce. More formidable had been the outworn stance of the old guard, repeating phrases which had once roused millions but became simply the basis of a repressive bureaucracy. "The case with Mitch Cohen did it for me," said Lilli. "That's when I began to lose hope for the party."

A friend rang to alert her to the live broadcast of the opposition's attempt to create a platform. Lilli turned on her television, and called Jascha to the living room. "Democracy," he said discouraged, with just the faintest air of bemusement. Watching the proceedings was, vaguely, a citizen's duty; eighty-one and weary, he seemed anxious to return to his research. And the broadcast was disheartening: after more than an hour of discussion the only point of agreement was a motion to break for lunch.

"The SED will get thirty percent," said Lilli. Her estimate of the communist vote was higher than others. "People aren't so unreasonable," she said. "The party made mistakes, but they know how to govern. And Gysi is a good man."

"How's he received?"

Lilli spread her hands. No one denied the intelligence of the new head of the party, a lifelong Communist who had defended opposition leaders under the old regime. "But I've heard many say 'that Jew Gysi.' Even comrades."

"Comrades?"

"Comrades. Whereby only his father was Jewish, and an atheist at that. But what can I say? Racism is growing all over, these days. Have you heard what the Bulgarians are up to?"

"You may want to finish your political discussion before the next visitor arrives," said Jascha. "A nice person, but we don't know how reliable she is."

Plump scarred Gabi had sought all the glamour a Western dime store could offer. The sequined lavender sweater she wore clashed woefully with her hennaed hair, but she didn't seem to notice. Those days were good ones for people like Gabi. She had seen the writing on the Wall and left East for West Berlin two years earlier. Secure in a now-coveted apartment, she could return to the East laden with shopping bags full of goods to distribute with an air of having been right all along. "I'm only sorry I didn't do it sooner," she said of her new life in the West. Four rooms in Steglitz, a new VCR and two dogs. She worked as a dental assistant; as an East German refugee she received many bonuses through comfortable state support. The turmoil now gripping the city didn't interest her; East Germany had been a lost cause from the start.

I found her quite dull, and faintly unpleasant. Watching her chitchat as she unwrapped packaged trinkets I wondered what connection she had to our hosts. When Lilli left the room, Gabi told me. She had lived in the apartment next door. Everyone else forsook her after she took the final step of applying for a legal exit permit. "Even my family, can you imagine? Three years waiting for a visa and everyone shut the door in my face. Now the border is open, they're happy to see me. Especially when they need a new radio or a pair of jeans. Back then, though—I would have killed myself without the Segals." Gabi knew that they often supported the party, but she didn't care much about politics. What mattered was the way they'd treated her, so different from the others. "The word is 'mensch,'" I mumbled, but I knew it didn't translate.

"I'll stay on the barricades!" Lilli told me in parting. What else could an elderly heroine do?

* * *

At Mitch's place in Kreuzberg there was a doleful Hanukkah party, with hand-painted gifts and frozen potato cakes, an old Berlin specialty. "They're nothing but latkes," he said, and we tried to be gay.

"What are the Jews saying about it all?" I pressed.

"What's a Jew to say," answered Merve, "when the whole thing took place on November ninth?"

Only a year earlier, the speaker of the West German Parliament resigned amid scandal: his Kristallnacht speech wasn't pious enough. In the wave of euphoria after the borders were opened, fifty years of self-conscious commemoration hadn't stopped politicians from proposing that November 9 become the national holiday. On the western side of Brandenburger Tor popular hand had changed the street names: the Street of June 17 was painted over to read STREET OF NOVEMBER 9.

"So quickly they forget?" said the Community, but they, like the others, were taken unawares. Now they were watching, trying to still the shudders rising at the sight of masses chanting "God bless our German Fatherland!" Edgar had decided to retain his American passport.

Thousands of visitors descended on Berlin for the New Year's celebrations at the Wall, hoping to catch a replay of the intoxication which had swept the city when the border fell. But the foreigners who lived there stayed home.

"The weather is awful," said Ingrid, "and I'm not going out to celebrate reunification."

"Why should I look at Brandenburger Tor when I can't get across?" lashed Irena.

The borders were open: to German citizens. The two hundred thousand foreigners living in West Berlin were still confined to the two old crossing points, although the fees and the rigamarole had been reduced. With access to

Brandenburger Tor and twenty-one other new openings restricted by blood, they were excluded from the revels at the start.

"C'mon," I said weakly, "it's a historic occasion."

"A million drunken Germans celebrating the Fatherland?"

In the end we joined a motley group bound for a party in a cold atelier. As the clock neared eleven, most of us rose for a half-hearted trip to the Wall. It was the end of an era, and rules might be broken.

"Germans only!" said the guard checking passports at the now pointless border.

"*Ausländer raus!*" shouted Michael in rage. The firecrackers had started. Next to us stooped two Turks who had been turned away.

"Twenty years I live here," muttered the elder.

"Let's try the new entry at Prinzenstrasse," said Peter. There the guard, in a holiday mood, tried to be helpful: the foreigners among us could cross a mile further down at Checkpoint Charlie.

"But the Germans can't cross there."

"Correct."

"We wanted to go together. Some of us are families."

"Can't help you."

"Fuck it," said Michael. I shivered with fever, and the New Year's rockets which had always been alarming were now in full swing. The reeling streets seemed to menace. We left the Wall to search for a cab.

Safe inside it I began to enjoy the fireworks circling Brandenburger Tor, not far from the road we were crossing at midnight. Bells were ringing as I strained backward to get a better view.

"Twelve o'clock," said the young cabdriver, breaking the silence. "A happy new year, I wish for us all."

"I hope so," said Michael skeptically.

"Some people," said the cabdriver, "wonder whether everything will continue as peacefully as it started."

"Yes," said Michael, "and I'm worried about nationalism."

"And why are we the only people in the world who have no right to be nationalistic?" burst the driver angrily. "Forty years they've been telling us it's a shame to be German. All because of a few jerks from before I was born—"

"Let's go to Tantana," said Michael to me, and we danced, desultory, inside the darkened Turkish kneipe where Murad was giving away champagne.

* * *

The headiest idea is the hardest to recall: for a few brief months millions of people took history in their hands, convinced of the notion that nothing was impossible. With hindsight the process seems merely inevitable. East Germans shared a number of desires with their Warsaw Pact neighbors: to see the world, eat better produce, be rid of a monotonous bureaucracy. They also had a fetter to shake which was theirs alone. Many exiting refugees said it quite clearly. They were tired of being the only Germans to pay the debts of the war.

The East paid its debt in quite literal terms. While the Marshall Plan devoted millions to rebuild the shattered Western economy, the Russians dismantled what remained of East German industry as reparation for the devastation the war had wreaked on the Soviet Union. This put the two Germanies on unequal footing, leaving a lag which would be hard to overcome. As their Western relations celebrated the "Economic Miracle" of the fifties and sixties, East Germans had to be content with bitter words about justice.

But the burden they bore was not simply material. While the West just grew jaded and shinier, the East had the air of a fallen country. One might say the whole nation served decades-long sentences for the Nazis' crimes. This makes little sense as historical claim; the Allies never envisioned the permanent division of Germany. But metaphor is often more potent than fact. Critics of the drive toward reunification spoke less of current political concerns than of theological ones: had the Germans suffered enough to atone for their sins?

East Germans felt that they had. "You're guilty, guilty, guilty!" moaned a dolorous writer I knew. "As a child of the GDR, I had that shit coming out of my ears! I'm trying to free myself! I can't hear anymore!" Vergangenheitsverarbeitung was a pillar of state, imposed from above with graying edicts and soulless school plans. Erich Honecker's authority was not only backed by all the apparatus of the secret service but by the knowledge of his ten years in a Nazi concentration camp. As the image of penitent endurance grew fainter, the GDR lost its raison d'etre. An end to moral stigma *and* a piece of the Western pie—the combination proved irresistible.

***

What will be missed is not the border, nor a practice of vergangenheitsverarbeitung which could not outlive the Wall, but a way of life which belonged to another era. Now that it's waning, Berliners talk tough, naming economic reasons for the mood which gripped us all. But the cheap rents, state subsidies, the soft pace of big business weren't enough to account for it. Some people called it the island mentality. The Wall had protected Berlin from the future, guarding a metropolis rife with slow dreams. Behind the border, the promise of absolute boundlessness. Did that explain the breath of exultation behind the absence of smile?

Premises

When you hear the word "Wannsee," do you think of the water? Or the villa on the banks where the conference which decided upon the Final Solution was held? Does it go back and forth, does it change over time?

It was my sister who first cajoled me to go bathing at the hot little beach on West Berlin's largest lake. She'd come for a visit, and stayed to become a successful singer. Her friends are much younger than mine. Their parents did not fight or hide or die in the war. Perhaps the sins of the fathers only visit for a generation; their talk is of other things. She hadn't known what the Wannsee Conference was when she urged me to join her for a day at the lake.

"And I don't really care about the exact date," she returned.

"January twentieth, nineteen forty-two, I looked it up this morning." Scanning the water, I turned toward the west. A water-skier tottered and fell. "There"—I pointed—"somewhere behind the trees. Lunch was served, and champagne. Jews had been killed earlier in Russia, but that was the place where the plans became systematic. "They discussed deportation, country by country. Eichmann took the minutes. The only question that was really debated was the fate of the Mischlinge, and assimilated Jews who were married to Aryans."

"Like Michael's mother?"

"Like Michael's mother."

My sister spoke gently, full of love and of fear. You're obsessed, she told me. I know why it's hard for you, I know who your friends are, but couldn't you make it a little easier on yourself?

"No," I said.

We walked toward the lake gleaming with big ships and little ships, lazy the sun.

"It's not just a matter of who my friends are. That's what philosophers call an occasional cause." I stopped for a moment; it was that kind of day. "Did you ever hear about the Lisbon earthquake?"

I told her the story as we walked through the woods: two centuries ago it had only taken an earthquake, a few thousand people, one city destroyed, just one lousy earthquake to shake the Enlightenment, to force men to doubt there was reason in the world.

"But they could have said they just didn't know enough yet to understand the causes of earthquakes."

"Ah-hah. That's what Kant said. But he was always a merciless optimist. Voltaire wrote *Candide* after the Lisbon earthquake."

"I didn't know that."

"*Candide* was his response. Best of all possible worlds, everything has its sufficient reason. Voltaire was shattered."

"Umm-hmm," said my sister. We walked a little farther. "I'm still not quite sure what you're getting at."

"Forty years after the Wannsee Conference, don't you see that the Lisbon earthquake was a joke? I was writing about *reason.* That's what I'm supposed to be *doing.* Before I came here I could do it. Oh, I'd read plenty of history already. But somehow it's different when you live where the earthquake began."

At the level beach a hundred people lay stretched in the sand, discarded clothing under their heads. The better-looking ones were even bolder, playing Frisbee or handball, trying to look as if they didn't know they were being watched and measured by people trying to look as if they weren't watching and measuring. Was it refreshing to be out of the city, where every vacant lot may call up the bombings? Two fat boys before us began to kick sand. "Are you crazy?" shouted their mother in broad Berliner dialect. "You must be missing a wheel!"

A line of swans appeared on the water.

"Where else can you go?" asked my sister. "With the Wall all around us, there are no excursions to the country."

"I know," I answered.

"I brought some watermelon," said my sister, and we had a summer day, of a sort, before we turned to go home.

We weren't used to riding the S-Bahn; East Berlin had just sold it to the West. The stations themselves looked undecided about which side they were on. Shabbier than those of the West-owned U-Bahn, they were short on benches or objects of comfort. Only the large billboards advertising Marlboros betrayed that the property now belonged to a state which does not own the means of production. Inside the trains the light warm wood of other times was being replaced by a beige synthetic substance.

"Look," I said, turning. "Gothic script."

"What?" asked my sister.

I gestured to the sign. "It must be left over. From before the war." BERUN-WANNSEE, read the letters, "Berlin-Wannsee," called the conductor. We stepped with the others to the fresh waiting train.

* * *

I never mourned the early Enlightenment, for the world which has been given to us is everything but reasonable. At least since Lisbon it should have been clear: if there's going to be reason in the world, it is we who will have to put it there. For one whose life has been staked on this possibility, the consequences of Wannsee present a double betrayal. Never did intellect flounder so colossally. On both sides. I repeat: the highest proportion of Nazi Party members came from the educated class of Germans. And those who still believe in what the medievals called the consolations of philosophy have only to read Jean Améry to be convinced that the intellectual prisoners at Auschwitz were the most helpless of all.

Flailing, I placed a quotation from a Primo Levi character on my wall: "And bear this in mind. I believe in three things: vodka, women, and the sub-machine gun. Once I also believed in reason, but not anymore."

Still I sit at my desk and think about premises. For the problem I've been struggling to resolve is (also, inescapably) a conceptual one. Sometimes, for a moment, I believe that I've grasped it. The Germans and I were starting from different assumptions; having learned that, I spent years trying to discover what theirs were. Even now I'm uncertain that I've got them quite right. For a premise is something which may bring forth a yawn, but hardly a jolt; something that's learned, at the latest, when you learn that the whole is greater than its parts, that boys become men but not girls or lions, that crying over spilt milk is wasting your breath. But the premises I'm seeking are anything but obvious: I still cannot state them without something like shock.

Premises are things left mostly unstated; one must work to uncover them behind what is said. "We were all cold in Treblinka," said the guard in Claude Lanzmann's film *Shoah*. What's his premise? It's no different from that of the millions of viewers who refused to watch the film on German television. "I lost a husband on the Front, a mother in the bombings, why should I recall all those terrible years?" For all of them: the war was a calamity, like a nightmare, a flood. Perhaps some people (Jews) happened to suffer more than others (Germans)—but those are the breaks, when the times are hard.

Native assumptions about the course of the war are even easier to ferret from German-made films. One commemorating the fortieth anniversary of the bombing of Dresden began by declaring: "Dresden's turn was late. First came Warsaw, Rotterdam, Coventry, Nürnberg." Here the bombing of Dresden is portrayed as part of a temporal sequence, undercutting possible attempts to posit a causal relation between the destruction of Dresden and the destruction of other cities. The film gently nodded to the question of responsibility: "Hitler had devastated much, but who would dare destroy *this*? It was destroyed: the Frauenkirche suffered the same fate as Coventry Cathedral." There are still many Germans who believe that the war was begun by an entity called International Jewry, but no assumptions of that kind can be derived from these remarks. More cleverly, in avoiding the issue of guilt altogether, it managed to suggest that there was none. Rather: war is hell, and all is reputedly fair in it. Everybody suffers, and everybody sins.

The depth at which these premises are held is revealed by the fact that the Germans can't imagine anyone else thinking about the war with different ones. This wasn't made clear to me by an interview with an SS guard, or even a commentary on public television, but by a novel written by Bernt Engelmann, whose antifascist stand was proven in the war. The book's hero is a young American who comes to the Federal Republic on business, and discovers that most of the leading citizens he meets are unrepentant former Nazis. The passage purporting to describe his enlightenment struck me dumb with astonishment.

> He had always regarded the illegal or even inhumane acts which were supposed to have occurred during the Nazi period to be partly exaggerations of Allied war propaganda, and partly the arbitrary actions of isolated Gestapo bosses and SS officers. 'Such things,' as he liked to call them, can unfortunately happen everywhere and especially during wartime, even with Americans, for example, in Viet Nam. In regard to Germany, 'such things' had for Hartnell only historical significance. He had believed

> them to have as little to do with present-day Germans as the so-called 'Reign of Terror' under Robespierre had to do with the present-day French.

One could fault the book on literary grounds: a novelist's task is to describe the world from inside his character's skin. But such criticism seems picky, and not to the point. This projection of German assumptions onto American characters represents another sort of failing entirely. The gap between Engelmann's vision and the real dispositions with which present-day Americans approach German territory seems too vast to explain.

* * *

Not a few Americans view Jews who've lived in Germany as traitors to decency itself. For those who reproached me there were no shades of gray. They saw the Second World War as an epic, the ultimate showdown between evil and innocence. They'd forgotten that the Allies blocked ports to frantic refugees, refused to bomb railway lines leading to the death camps. American war propaganda publicizing Nazi crimes refrained from even mentioning Jews for fear of arousing hometown anti-Semitism. That America no more entered the war to save the Jews than Lincoln fought secession to free the slaves should have been clear long ago. But national myths are remarkably resilient, surviving the work of the best historians, and the longing for one last good fight shelters deep in our consciousness.

"Wasn't it hard meeting old people?"

One day I noticed I had passed the point of looking at every old man on a German street and wondering: where was he when. A missing leg still prompted speculation: did he lose it on the Eastern Front? Serves him right. — But a cripple is a cripple, you know there was a draft on, people had no choice about going to war. Except the really big Nazis, and concentration-camp guards, who were exempted from danger. Despite that knowledge it was hard to feel quite as sorry for the fellow as one might.... All that passed through my head in the two seconds it took to perceive a wooden leg. But seeing old people was no longer the hard part.

"So what was the hard part?"

Something Americans no longer imagine: Not being able to say one is Jewish without producing a bombshell. Not even knowing which words to use. Germans say "*Jüdische Herkunft*," or "*Jüdische Abstammung*." "Are you of Jewish extraction?" The simple word "Jew" gets stuck in their throats.

Once I met a minor diplomat at a large birthday party. We took to each other immediately, and after a time he said, "I bet you come from the southern part of the United States." I wondered how he'd guessed. He couldn't quite explain it: he'd just sensed something southern. The gestures, the intonations; he supposed it was rather like the difference between northern Europeans and Mediterranean peoples. Suddenly I smiled. "I was born in Atlanta," I told him, "but that's not what you mean. I'm an atypical southerner. What you're noticing is that I'm Jewish." The poor man was distraught. "Oh *no*," he protested, "that's not something I would *notice*. That plays no role at all for me!"

Jokes, more than most things, depend on shared premises. Some days it was laughter I missed most of all.

* * *

A quick rule of thumb: it isn't a premise if you find it worth stating. "The Jews are only human too" does not express a premise but a hard-won insight. Only human too, that is: full of human frailty, deserving of human mercy. The statement contains a note of forgiveness, the readiness to ignore sin and error in the recognition of the Other as a creature like me. I flinched every time that sentence was spoken. For it only revealed the premise which had been discarded in order to utter it: the Jews are not (might not be) human too. And it laid bare another: the Jews may have been dreadful, but German magnanimity will wipe the slate clean. I refer, for those who suspect I'm overreading, once again to Améry; a few years after his release from Auschwitz, he was assured by a Kölner businessman that the Germans bore the Jews no grudges.

I spoke of forgiveness; I know that it's hard. Germans born after 1930 or so had little opportunity for other ways of thought. It isn't merely that their chances of meeting living Jews were severely limited. Further: "Jew" became a concept with a role in their world: as enemy of the people, as accuser and victim, as anything else but a fellow like me.

It's not unsimilar to the use of the word "Nazi" in the everyday stuff of American dreams. "Nazi" just *means* the devil incarnate, the location of evil. The premise behind this offers hopeful illusion: if sin looks like that, we can rest with the righteous.

I have learned much which led me to expose and discard that assumption. If it didn't sound so strange, I would willingly say: the Nazis (well, most of them) were only human too. Berliners would look at me oddly, as if I'd asserted that water is wet. I have come to acknowledge a commonplace of thought. Does that allow us to begin from shared ground?

* * *

Sleep pierced by hurried whispers, barking dogs, bright lights and barbed wire. Nazi nightmares visit even the happiest Jewish children occasionally; before the images the war left us, one must have called it the bogeyman.

Nightmares are private, something like premises. When they emerge they are simple and raw, exposing matter which withstands the light poorly. I needed years just to grasp it: German dreamers do not put themselves in the place of the Jews. The land of *Dicker* and *Denker* has no imagination.

Of what do they dream? It isn't that they envision themselves in the place of those executioners who could write, after the war, of the relative difficulties of shooting Gypsies and Jews. (The Gypsies were noisier, pleaded and cried.) Nor do they merely see themselves as a subtler sort of prey, though something of that can be found at the threshold. Perhaps the very problem, for young Germans, is that no reflexive movement is automatic; nobody else's shoes seem to fit. They cannot stand in those of their parents; those of the victims are impossibly strange.

Those closest know just how strange they can be: recently the paper reported that a group of young German Jews made a trip to Auschwitz. Children of survivors, their dreams had been peopled by Nazis so long that the ramp left them cold. Death isn't holy when you grow in its shadow; certain sorts of thought-experiments were familiar as mother's milk. "Would you rather fuck the SS guards, or go to the gas?" called a young man. "Fuck the guards!" replied the teenage girls, sitting down to try out a barracks bunk.

All this in a land which claims Kant as its own; where one hears over coffee that fascism's roots lay in the Enlightenment. In vain I searched the streets for an echo of his simplest thought: you carry out those actions which you can imagine carrying out for everyone.

* * *

I*s* a decision to leave Berlin a conclusion? It is, of a sort, but it's also just that: a decision to leave. Here there are no conclusions, no heroes, no law. Even the enemy can be so hard to find.

"You're not the first person to lose their sense of morality after coming to Berlin," said Michael. "The trouble is, you haven't lost it completely."

Arriving in Berlin with little but Hollywood movies and philosophers' examples to sustain me, I was moved to the core by the very idea of vergangenheitsverarbeitung. Six years later, silence seemed better than the best of intentions. Faced with yet another word about the Nazis, I would counter with the wisdom of that most awful of Yiddish curses: may his name and every memory of him be blotted out forever.

Here's looking at you, kid.

With which of the natives had I come to agree? Asked for a balance, I felt the force of every claim:

- There has been no vergangenheitsverarbeitung.
- There has been one, of course.
- It's worthless, obscene.
- But it's better than nothing.
- No it's time to forget.
- The Germans have changed.
- They're still Nazis at heart.
- The Allies were no better.
- Well, not by much.
- The Turks are oppressed here; no lessons were learned.
- More babies die in Harlem than in the slums of Malaysia.
- Everything that can be said can be said simply.

Decades after the war was over, Berlin remained a monument to devastation, permanently recalling not only the deaths of 58 million, and the undoing of our imagination, but the wreck of generations to follow. Not even the rabbi nourished hope for restoring the Jewish community. And educated Germans view the prospect of renewing Central European culture without Jews to be at best a very dubious one.

It's not much to live for, keeping the dead. History imposed an impossible task. It is this, I believe, not innate Teutonic menace, which explains the periodic right-wing outbursts. Germans devoted to working through the past seem bound to succumb to blind pathos or morbid fascination. Those who, like Helmut Kohl invoking the mercy of a late birth, call for an end to vergangenheitsverarbeitung, risk becoming Nazi apologists. They are damned if they do, they are damned if they don't. They are, quite simply, damned.

I do not know what could redeem them. Just possibly the recognition that they are not alone.

About the Author

Susan Neiman was born in Atlanta, Georgia, in 1955. In 1972 she began to study philosophy at C.C.N.Y. and then Harvard, from which she graduated in 1977 and received a Ph.D. in 1986. In 1982 she received a Fulbright Fellowship to study at the Freie Universität-Berlin. She lived in Berlin until 1988, up to the collapse of the Wall, studying, teaching, translating and writing for Berlin public radio and stage. Since then, she has been a professor of philosophy at Yale University and at Tel Aviv University. In 2000 she joined the Einstein Forum in Potsdam, Germany, and became its Director. She has published *The Unity of Reason: Rereading Kant* and *Evil in Modern Thought*. Her most recent book, *Moral Clarity: A Guide for Grown-up Idealists*, was named one of the "100 Notable Books of 2008" by *The New York Times*.

www.quidprobooks.com

Made in United States
North Haven, CT
17 February 2023

32701096R10124